THE INTERNATIONAL ANNUAL ON DESIGN AND ILLUSTRATION

DAS INTERNATIONALE JAHRBUCH ÜBER DESIGN UND ILLUSTRATION

LE RÉPERTOIRE INTERNATIONAL DE DESIGN ET D'ILLUSTRATION

EDITED BY/HERAUSGEGEBEN VON/RÉALISÉ PAR

B. MARTIN PEDERSEN

PUBLISHER AND CREATIVE DIRECTOR: B. MARTIN PEDERSEN

ASSISTANT EDITORS: HEINKE JENSSEN

DESIGNER: MARTIN BYLAND

PHOTOGRAPHER: WALTER ZUBER

GRAPHIS PRESS CORP, ZURICH (SWITZERLAND)

GRAPHIS PUBLICATIONS

GRAPHIS, International bi-monthly journal of graphic art and photography

GRAPHIS DESIGN, The international annual on design and illustration

GRAPHIS PHOTO, The international annual of photography

GRAPHIS POSTER, The international annual of poster art

GRAPHIS PACKAGING, An international survey of packaging design

GRAPHIS DIAGRAM, The graphic visualization of abstract, technical and statistical facts and functions

GRAPHIS COVERS, An anthology of all GRAPHIS covers from 1944-86 with artists' short biographies
    and indexes of all GRAPHIS issues

GRAPHIS ANNUAL REPORTS, An international compilation of the best designed annual reports

GRAPHIS CORPORATE IDENTITY 1, An international compilation of the best in Corporate Identity design

POSTERS MADE POSSIBLE BY A GRANT FROM MOBIL, A collection of 250 international posters commissioned by Mobil
    and selected by the Poster Society

GRAPHIS-PUBLIKATIONEN

GRAPHIS, Die internationale Zweimonatszeitschrift für Graphik und Photographie

GRAPHIS DESIGN, Das internationale Jahrbuch über Design und Illustration

GRAPHIS PHOTO, Das internationale Jahrbuch der Photographie

GRAPHIS POSTER, Das internationale Jahrbuch der Plakatkunst

GRAPHIS PACKUNGEN, Ein internationaler Überblick der Packungsgestaltung

GRAPHIS DIAGRAM, Die graphische Darstellung abstrakter, technischer und statistischer Daten und Fakten

GRAPHIS COVERS, Eine Sammlung aller GRAPHIS-Umschläge von 1944-86 mit Informationen über die Künstler
    und Inhaltsübersichten aller Ausgaben der Zeitschrift GRAPHIS

GRAPHIS ANNUAL REPORTS, Ein internationaler Überblick über die Gestaltung von Jahresberichten

GRAPHIS CORPORATE IDENTITY 1, Eine internationale Auswahl des besten Corporate Identity Design

POSTERS MADE POSSIBLE BY A GRANT FROM MOBIL, Eine Sammlung von 250 internationalen Plakaten, von Mobil
    in Auftrag gegeben und von der Poster Society ausgewählt

PUBLICATIONS GRAPHIS

GRAPHIS, La revue bimestrielle internationale d'arts graphiques et de la photographie

GRAPHIS DESIGN, Le répertoire international de la communication visuelle

GRAPHIS PHOTO, Le répertoire international de la photographie

GRAPHIS POSTER, Le répertoire international de l'art de l'affiche

GRAPHIS EMBALLAGES, Le répertoire international des formes de l'emballage

GRAPHIS DIAGRAM, La représentation graphique de faits et données abstraits, techniques et statistiques

GRAPHIS COVERS, Recueil de toutes les couvertures de GRAPHIS de 1944-86 avec des notices biographiques
    des artistes et le sommaire de tous les numéros du magazine GRAPHIS.

GRAPHIS ANNUAL REPORTS, Panorama international du design de rapports annuels d'entreprises

GRAPHIS CORPORATE IDENTITY 1, Panorama international du meilleur design de l'identité corporate

POSTERS MADE POSSIBLE BY A GRANT FROM MOBIL, Une collection de 250 affiches internationales commandées par Mobil
    et choisies par la Poster Society

PUBLICATION No. 201 (ISBN 3-85709-190-8)

© Copyright under Universal Copyright Convention

Copyright 1990 by Graphis Press Corp., 107 Dufourstrasse, 8008 Zurich, Switzerland

No part of this book may be reproduced in any form without written permission of the publisher

Printed in Japan by Toppan

Typeset in Switzerland by Setzerei Heller, Zurich

Typefaces: Garamond ITC Light Condensed, Futura Extra Bold

I have said often enough where I draw the parallels between advertising and fine art. And that I believed there were always producers of reality who paid people to confirm this reality - and their confirmation of this now fills the museums. □ What I haven't yet mentioned, though, is another evidence of this statement that I come across more frequently these days. It's the public discourse that's always going on about advertising and design. Some twenty years ago these things were practically never talked about in public. Or if they were, then in the classic paranoid hidden-persuader tradition. But advertising and design are closing in more and more toward the hub of a generally well-meaning public interest. Moving inward from the rim, that grey zone of seduction, where they help to fulfil a consumer culture of wanting to sell people something they don't require and which doesn't satisfy any basic needs but those that the producers have only just invented. Today, trade publications as this one for instance are being read more than ever with keen interest by a public who know nothing of the profession. Not only by exponents of semiotics, structuralists, artists and kids struggling to make a living in the art of communications, but by all kinds of people interested in media. So the debates that rampage throughout the pages of books and magazines are of great general interest. □ On private television recently I saw a special program about advertising, where interviews with insiders were expertly conducted, and the latest advertising films were admired, and where the public were responding to burning questions. This new public - the children of those who vigorously damned and disclaimed advertising - queue up in front of cinemas and pay for tickets without batting an eyelid to watch and applaud advertising for hours on end. □ This all leads to a highly unusual perspective for the designer. In the future - apart from the potential consumers wooed by producers - there will be a second public, a connoisseur one. This public will critically observe the work of the designers, control their work and wag their fingers at those responsible if their craftsmanship is slipshod or their language and aesthetics are botched up. This new public will initiate debates, cook up philosophies, give sign systems a new meaning. And above all - and this is already being demonstrated - it will call the doers and authors of advertising and design by name. □ This is precisely the well-known historic situation that we had in the Renaissance, where the names of artists were torn out of anonymity and made famous - clear proof of an energetic interest in a living art. Behind this aesthetic importance the original functions of advertising for products and companies slope off into the hinterland. □ In this way the design of a stamp will replace architecture. The campaign will stand in place of the altarpiece. The product design will supersede sculpture, and so on. □ In the time of a re-naissance of the Renaissance, designers will be exposed to public interest. This will drive us forward to socially momentous high performances. And we can all look forward to that day. □

Michael Schirner, born in Chemnitz (Germany) on 5.16.1941, studied at the Academy of Visual Arts in Hamburg. From 1969 to 1984 he held various positions at large advertising agencies in Germany. He has been manager and associate of the KKG Project Agency in Dusseldorf – since 1984 and the company was renamed Michael Schirner Advertising and Project Agency in May 1987. Michael Schirner has written numerous articles in trade magazines and has had two books published: "Advertising is Art" (Werbung ist Kunst) and "Poster and Practice" (Plakat und Praxis).

Ich habe oft genug gesagt, wo ich Parallelen zwischen Werbung und bildender Kunst sehe – etwa, dass es immer schon Produzenten von Wirklichkeit gab, die sich für Geld Leute hielten, die ihnen diese Wirklichkeit bestätigen sollten und deren Wirklichkeitsbestätigungen heute die Museen füllen. □ Einen weiteren Beweis für die Behauptung, dem ich in letzter Zeit immer häufiger begegne, habe ich noch nicht erwähnt: Das ist der öffentliche Diskurs über Werbung und Design. Vor gut zwanzig Jahren wurde über diese Dinge so gut wie überhaupt nicht öffentlich nachgedacht und wenn, dann in den Kategorien der klassisch-paranoiden Geheime-Verführer-Tradition. Aus der Grauzone von Verführung und Erfüllungshilfe einer Konsumkultur, die den Menschen etwas verkaufen will, was sie gar nicht brauchen, also nicht ihre realen Bedürfnisse befriedigt, sondern solche, die erst die Produzenten erfunden haben, rücken Werbung und Design mehr und mehr ins Zentrum eines wohlwollenden öffentlichen Interesses. □ Heute werden Fachpublikationen, wie zum Beispiel die vorliegende, mehr denn je vom fachfremden Publikum mit Interesse gelesen, nicht nur von Semiotikern und Strukturalisten, Künstlern und Kids, die einen Beruf in der Kommunikations-Branche anstreben, sondern von allen möglichen Leuten, die sich für Medien interessieren, und die Debatten, die auf Buch-und Zeitschriftenseiten toben, sind von einem breiten allgemeinen Interesse. □ Neulich sah ich im Privatfernsehen wieder einmal die Spezialsendung über Werbung, wo Interviews mit Insidern fachmännisch geführt werden, neueste Werbefilme zu bewundern sind und dem Publikum offensichtlich brennende Fragen beantwortet werden. Dieses neue Publikum – die Kinder derjenigen, die Werbung heftig verdammten und ausbuhten – steht Schlange vor Kinos und bezahlt wie selbstverständlich Eintritt dafür, sich stundenlang Werbung anzuschauen und zu beklatschen. □ Dies alles führt zu einer höchst eigenartigen Perspektive für die Gestalter. In Zukunft wird es neben den potentiellen Konsumenten, die von den Herstellern umworben werden, ein zweites Publikum geben: ein kulinarisches. Dieses Publikum wird die Arbeiten der Gestalter kritisch begleiten, kontrollieren und den Verantwortlichen auf die Finger klopfen, wenn sie handwerklich, sprachlich und ästhetisch schludern und stümpern. Dieses neue Publikum wird Debatten initiieren, Philosophien auskochen, Zeichensysteme umdeuten und vor allem – was sich jetzt schon abzeichnet – es wird Täter und Autoren von Werbung und Design namhaft machen. □ Dies aber ist genau die aus der Renaissance bekannte historische Situation, wo Namen von Künstlern aus der Anonymität gerissen und bekannt gemacht wurden, was ein sicheres Indiz für ein lebendiges Interesse an einer lebendigen Kunst ist: Hinter ihrer ästhetischen Bedeutung treten die ursprünglichen Funktionen der Werbung für Produkte und Firmen zurück. □ So wird die Gestaltung einer Marke an die Stelle von Architektur treten, die Kampagne an die Stelle des Altargemäldes, das Produkt-Design an die Stelle der Skulptur etc. □ In der Zeit einer Renaissance der Renaissance wird die Arbeit der Gestalter einem öffentlichen Interesse ausgesetzt sein, das uns zu gesellschaftlich folgenreichen Höchstleistungen treiben wird. Und darauf können wir uns alle heute schon freuen. □

Michael Schirner, am 16.5.1941 in Chemnitz geboren, studierte an der Hochschule für bildende Künste in Hamburg. Zwischen 1969 und 1984 arbeitete er in verschiedenen Positionen (Copy Supervisor, Creative Director, Geschäftsführer) für grosse Werbeagenturen in Deutschland. Seit 1984 ist er Geschäftsführer und Gesellschafter der KKG Projektagentur in Düsseldorf, die seit dem 1. Mai 1987 Michael Schirner Werbe- und Projektagentur heisst. Er hat neben verschiedenen Artikeln in Fachzeitschriften zwei Bücher veröffentlicht: «Werbung ist Kunst» und «Plakat & Praxis».

J'ai souvent mentionné les parallèles que j'entrevoyais entre la publicité et les arts plastiques – en ce sens, par exemple, qu'il y a eu de tout temps des producteurs de réel qui stipendiaient des gens chargés de leur confirmer ce réel, ces confirmations du réel remplissant aujourd'hui les musées. ☐ Je n'avais pas encore fait état d'un autre phénomène qui vient à l'appui de cette affirmation et qui se banalise, à savoir le débat public sur la publicité et le design. Il y a une vingtaine d'années, la discussion publique sur ce sujet était pratiquement inexistante; là où elle s'amorçait, elle se moulait dans les catégories de la tradition paranoïde classique de la persuasion clandestine. Or, la publicité et le design émergent progressivement de la zone de clair-obscur de la persuasion et de leur contribution à la mise en place d'une société de consommation acharnée à vendre au public ce dont il n'a pas besoin, à ne pas satisfaire ses besoins réels, mais les besoins créés par les producteurs. Et tant la publicité que le design en viennent à se positionner au centre d'un champ d'intérêt public empreint de bienveillance. ☐ De nos jours, les publications spécialisées telles que la présente sont lues dans une mesure croissante par un public intéressé et non spécialisé, et non pas seulement par les sémioticiens et les structuralistes, les artistes et les jeunes espoirs visant une activité professionnelle dans les secteurs de la communication. Elles suscitent ainsi l'intérêt de toutes sortes de gens attirés par les médias, et les débats animés portés à leur connaissance par la presse et l'édition semblent fasciner le plus grand nombre. ☐ L'autre jour, j'ai regardé sur une chaîne de télévision privée une émission consacrée à la publicité, avec des interviews de qualité professionnelle et la présentation de nouveaux films publicitaires. Les téléspectateurs avaient l'occasion de poser des questions d'actualité sur la publicité, qui semblaient leur tenir à cœur. Or, ce nouveau public – les enfants de ceux qui ont décrié la publicité et l'ont vouée aux gémonies – fait la queue devant les cinémas et accepte tout naturellement de payer pour voir pendant des heures des films publicitaires et les applaudir. ☐ Tout cela mène à une perspective bien singulière pour les styliciens. C'est qu'il va y avoir à l'avenir, en plus des consommateurs potentiels courtisés par les fabricants, un second public composé de gastronomes. Ce public de connaisseurs s'évertuera à accompagner la gestation des travaux de design d'un œil critique, ils les soumettra à un contrôle et alertera les responsables lorsque les productions seront par trop indigentes au triple plan du métier, du langage et de l'esthétique. Ce nouveau public provoquera des débats, inventera des systèmes philosophiques, donnera un autre sens aux signes, mais surtout – et c'est ce qui se dessine déjà – il saura identifier les auteurs et les coupables de la publicité et du design. ☐ On s'achemine ainsi très précisément vers la situation historique que nous avons connue à la Renaissance, où les noms des artistes étaient arrachés à l'anonymat et portés à la connaissance du public, ce qui témoigne d'un intérêt vivant pour un art vivant: les fonctions primaires de la publicité en faveur de produits et d'entreprises s'effaceront derrière leur signification esthétique. ☐ C'est ainsi que la conception d'une marque prendra le relais de l'architecture, la campagne publicitaire celui du retable, le design industriel celui de la sculpture, etc. ☐ L'attention publique nous poussera à optimaliser nos performances. Nous pouvons dès aujourd'hui nous en réjouir. ☐

Michael Schirner, né le 16.5.41 à Chemnitz, fit ses études à la Hochschule für bildende Künste de Hambourg. Entre 1969 et 1984, il travailla à divers postes dans de grandes agences de publicité en Allemagne. Depuis 1984, il est responsable de la gestion et associé de l'agence KKG à Düsseldorf, qui s'appelle Michael Schirner Werbe- und Projektagentur depuis le 1er mai 1987. Il a publié de nombreux articles dans des revues professionnelles et deux livres: «La publicité, c'est de l'art» (Werbung ist Kunst) et «Affiche et pratique» (Plakat und Praxis).

Is modern design really any good? Well, it's for damn sure not as good as *we* think it is, all of us stuck here like flies buzzing against the windowpane of the present moment. But that's a mistake every era makes. Excusable. Very human. Fine. □ What will people think of this stuff, say a hundred or even two hundred years from now? Will they copy it? □ I don't think they will. Or if they do copy it, I don't think they'll realize they're doing so. To explain this, I'm going to have to wield some monstrous, inexcusable generalizations that will no doubt enrage a good number of you. Just relax for a while and imagine you're in a big pillow fight. □ The "Flavor of the Month" in design over the past 25 years could be loosely termed eclecticism. Our designers and architects and art directors graze upon thousands of years of design riffs with unprecedented ease. Never before has so much of design history been so easily accessible to so many people. Never before have so many typefaces from so many historical periods and designers been so emphatically in use at one time (due no doubt to the fact that a font is now a single disk of acetate rather than a 300-pound drawer of lead). Spectacular new building materials – foams and laminates and plastics – have enabled architects and designers to mimic classical design elements with the ease of a Lincoln Log set. We are the Design Gypsies, roaming the past, smushing a little of this with a little of that and getting, well, an annual report. □ If you find all this a bit fast and loose, compare our times with the first 25 years of this century, when the last thing anyone might do would be to simply cut a design idea out of the past whole cloth. Yipes. Corbu and Wright, Mondrian and Van Doesburg, certainly Gropius and Klee and Mies at the Bauhaus – these guys explicitly strove to make design a singular expression of their own time, a time that was different from all that had come before. They talked and wrote endlessly about capturing the spirit of the age, the *innerste Wesen* (inmost essence), the thing about their moment that would become part of the permanent in human history. □ Maybe we're somehow shallower than those guys, but I don't think so. Pioneer design gypsies like Marcel Duchamp with his readymades and the high priest of us all, Andy Warhol, showed that the idea of appropriating big hunks of existing stuff could be immensely eloquent, resonant, disorienting. □ Rather, I think the problem with design right now, the real disappointment of it, is the thought of where all this eclecticism will ulti-

mately lead us. It's starting to get a bit mechanical already, this stuff. The pattern – of abruptly joining together historically disparate symbols and styles, and then making them Siamese twin slaves to some present function – is all too apparent. It's no fun anymore. Big Bauhaus skyscraper plus Chippendale chest equals AT&T building. So what? Beer plus art deco steamship poster graphics equals award-winning poster. Whoa. A whole lot of our most successful illustrators are people like Douglas Fraser or Anthony Russo who treat modern subjects with a style exquisitely rooted in the past. Any office building worth its Roche-Bobois has a Hellenic column *somewhere* or at the very least a Japanese rock garden. And so on. In despair at all this, not just because it seems to belie some implicit fear of the future, but because – as the age of people who gruffly nail together beautiful things from the past – we will ultimately become invisible. Future generations will look through us to the originators of these icons, exposing us as handlers of culture rather than creators of it, a kind of clever but forgettable delivery service. □ What's more, even if we *do* get noticed someday, it's not impossible that a lot of the wit and sensitivity we presume to be explicit in these appropriations will be lost over time. What if people stop chuckling at our terrific jokes and conclude that we were merely out-and-out thieves (which, of course, some of us are)? □ In closing, I'd like to tell you that these practices can't go on forever (would it be fun to add the AT&T building to Viennese pastry design?), but I'm not sure that's the case. A lot of the success of eclecticism unfortunately stems from its fun and accessibility, from the fact that even relatively unsophisticated people can imagine its admixtures. Eclecticism is here for while because it can be *sold*, Jack, up and down the brand management system, to government agencies, to CEO's with throbbing building budgets, any day of the week. But that is a subject for another time. □ For now, think about all this as you thumb through one of these annuals for ideas. And be very careful. □

Jeffrey Goodby is a writer, illustrator, and principal partner at Goodby, Berlin & Silverstein in San Francisco. His illustrations have appeared in numerous publications, including Time *and* Harvard Magazine. *His advertising work has included television and print campaigns for Royal Viking Line, Heinz, Polaroid, and The Christian Brothers. GB&S was selected Agency of The Year last year by* Advertising Age.

Ist modernes Design überhaupt gut? Verdammt sicher ist, dass es nicht so gut ist, wie wir glauben. Wir sind auf die unmittelbare Gegenwart fixiert. Das ist ein Fehler, der in jeder Epoche gemacht wird. Entschuldbar, sehr menschlich. □ Was werden die Leute über dieses Zeug in hundert oder zweihundert Jahren denken? Werden sie es kopieren? □ Ich glaube nicht. Sollten sie es doch tun, glaube ich nicht, dass sie es bewusst kopieren. Um dies zu erklären, muss ich einige ungeheuerliche, unentschuldbare Verallgemeinerungen ins Feld führen, die zweifellos einige von Ihnen verärgern werden. Entspannen Sie sich und stellen Sie sich einfach vor, dies sei eine Kissenschlacht. □ Was im Design in den letzten 25 Jahren «in» war, könnte man grob mit Eklektizismus umschreiben. Unsere Designer, Architekten und Art Direktoren zehren von Tausenden von Jahren Design-Geschichte, und zwar leichten Herzens und ohne grosse Gewissensbisse. Nie zuvor war so viel Design-Geschichte so vielen Leuten so leicht zugänglich. Nie zuvor waren so viele Schriftarten aus so vielen verschiedenen Epochen und von so vielen Entwerfern gleichzeitig in Gebrauch (was natürlich darauf zurückzuführen ist, dass eine Schriftart jetzt auf einer einzigen Diskette zu haben ist und nicht in Form einer im wahrsten Sinne des Wortes bleischweren Schublade). Neue Baustoffe – Schaumstoffe, Verbundstoffe und Plastik – machten es Architekten und Designern möglich, klassische Design-Elemente mit Leichtigkeit zu imitieren. Wir sind Design-Vagabunden, ziehen durch die Vergangenheit, matschen ein bisschen von diesem und ein bisschen von jenem zusammen, und was entsteht daraus – ein Jahresbericht. □ Wenn Sie finden, all dies sei ein bisschen leichtfertig dahergesagt, vergleichen Sie unsere Zeit einmal mit den ersten 25 Jahren dieses Jahrhunderts, als niemand daran gedacht hätte, einfach Design-Ideen irgendwo aus dem Zusammenhang zu nehmen. Le Corbusier und Wright, Mondrian und Van Doesburg, Gropius, Klee und Mies van der Rohe vom Bauhaus – ihnen allen ging es darum, Design zum Ausdruck ihrer eigenen Zeit zu machen, eine Zeit, die anders war als alle Zeiten zuvor. Den Geist der Zeit einzufangen, das innerste Wesen, das Hier und Heute, das einmal Teil der Menschheitsgeschichte werden würde, das war ihr Thema, über das sie endlos sprachen und schrieben. □ Das Problem beim heutigen Design, das wirklich Enttäuschende dabei, ist der Gedanke, wohin dieser Eklektizismus schliesslich führen wird. Jetzt schon fängt das Zeug an, ein bisschen mechanisch zu wirken. Das Muster, nach dem man vorgeht – historisch ungleiche Symbole und Stile

zusammenzufügen und wie siamesische Zwillinge für irgendeine heutige Funktion einzusetzen –, ist nur zu offensichtlich. Das macht keinen Spass mehr. Eine ganze Menge unserer erfolgreichsten Illustratoren sind Leute wie Douglas Fraser oder Anthony Russo, die für moderne Themen einen Stil verwenden, der zur Vergangenheit gehört. Jedes Büro, das seiner teuren Roche-Bobois-Möbel würdig ist, hat irgendwo auch eine griechische Säule oder zumindest einen japanischen Steingarten. Und so weiter. □ Ich finde das zum Verzweifeln, nicht nur weil das Zukunftsangst bedeutet, sondern weil unsere Zeit – als Epoche der Leute, die schöne Dinge aus der Vergangenheit zusammengeschustert haben – schliesslich unsichtbar sein wird. Zukünftige Generationen werden durch uns hindurch auf die Urheber dieser Ikonen schauen, sie werden uns als Handhaber, nicht als Schöpfer von Kultur blossstellen, eine Art schlauer Lieferdienst, den man getrost vergessen kann. □ Auch falls eines Tages doch von uns Notiz genommen wird, ist nicht auszuschliessen, dass viel von dem Witz und dem Einfühlungsvermögen, das unserer Meinung nach in diesen Kombinationen von Anleihen steckt, mit der Zeit verlorengegangen ist. Was passiert, wenn die Leute über unsere grossartigen Witze nicht mehr lachen können und zu dem Schluss kommen, dass wir einfach Diebe waren (was einige von uns natürlich sind)? □ Abschliessend möchte ich Ihnen sagen, dass man so nicht ewig weitermachen kann (würde dem AT&T-Gebäude nicht ein wenig Wiener Zuckerbäcker-Stil guttun?), aber ich mache mir keine grossen Illusionen. Der Erfolg des Eklektizismus ist zum grossen Teil leider auf seinen Witz und die Verständlichkeit zurückzuführen, auf die Tatsache, dass sogar relativ anspruchslose Leute die Beigaben erkennen. Eklektizismus bleibt uns wahrscheinlich noch eine Weile erhalten, weil er sich jederzeit verkaufen lässt, an die Produkt-Manager ebenso wie an staatliche Behörden oder das Management-Kader, das immense Bau-Etats verwaltet. Das jedoch ist ein anderes Thema. □ Denken Sie an das Gesagte, wenn Sie in einem dieser Jahrbücher Ideen suchen, und seien Sie sehr, sehr vorsichtig. □

Jeffrey Goodby ist Autor, Illustrator und Partner von Goodby, Berlin & Silverstein in San Francisco. Seine Illustrationen sind in zahlreichen Publikationen erschienen, u.a. in Time *und* Harvard Magazine. *Was Werbung betrifft, hat er Presse- und TV-Kampagnen für Royal Viking Line, Heinz, Polaroid und The Christian Brothers gemacht. GB&S wurde letztes Jahr von* Advertising Age *zur Agentur des Jahres gewählt.*

Le design moderne vaut-il vraiment quelque chose? Eh bien, il n'a très certainement pas autant de valeur que *nous* lui en reconnaissons, nous autres mouches qui bourdonnons, le nez contre la vitre du quotidien. Mais c'est là une erreur commune à toutes les époques. Excusable, en somme, et très humaine. O.k. □ Qu'est-ce que les gens penseront un jour de ces réalisations, dans cent, dans deux cents ans? Auront-ils envie de les copier? □ Pour mon compte, je ne le pense pas. Et même s'ils s'avisaient de les copier, je ne pense pas qu'ils s'en rendront compte. Pour expliquer ce que je veux dire, je vais devoir proférer quelques généralisations monstrueusement abusives et parfaitement inexcusables qui vont en faire bondir plus d'un. Allez, détendez-vous un moment. Imaginez que vous êtes en train de participer à une bataille rangée avec des coussins qui volent de toutes parts. □ Ce qui caractérise le design depuis 25 ans pourrait être qualifié d'éclecticisme au sens large du terme. Nos styliciens, nos architectes et nos directeurs artistiques paissent l'herbe de pâturages vieux de milliers d'années, sans se gêner et parfaitement conscients de ce qu'ils font, – merci pour eux. A aucune autre époque, autant de tranches d'histoire du design n'ont été accessibles à autant de monde. Jamais on n'a eu recours à autant de caractères provenant d'époques et de designers variés. L'usage frénétique en a certainement été facilité par le fait que le moule à fonte de 150 kg a été remplacé par un simple disque d'acétate. De nouveaux matériaux de construction spectaculaires, des mousses, des laminés, des plastiques, ont permis aux architectes et aux designers de reproduire de manière simple comme bonjour n'importe quel type classique. Nous sommes les tsiganes du design, pillant à notre gré les trésors du passé, mâchurant un peu de ci avec un peu de ça pour fabriquer par exemple un rapport annuel. □ Si vous trouvez que j'en fais trop, et à la hussarde, comparez donc notre époque avec les 25 premières années du siècle où on se serait bien gardé de tailler une idée de design dans le tissu bigarré du passé. Aïe! Le Corbusier et Wright, Mondrian et Van Doesburg, très certainement Gropius, Klee et Mies du Bauhaus – ces gars-là ont eu à cœur de faire de leur design l'expression unique de leur époque, une époque radicalement différente de toutes celles qui l'avaient précédée. Ils discutaient et écrivaient inlassablement pour cerner l'esprit de leur époque, son «innerstes Wesen», sa quintessence, ce qui, au cœur du moment qui passe, allait s'intégrer au patrimoine de l'humanité. □ Je pense plutôt que le problème, avec le design actuel, la déception qu'il nous procure, est dû à l'avenir que

nous prépare tout cet éclecticisme. Ses techniques commencent déjà à prendre un tour mécanique. Le truc qui consiste à assembler de façon incongrue des symboles et des styles d'époques différentes, pour en faire des frères siamois au service d'une fonction moderne – ce truc-là est éventé. Ce n'est plus guère amusant. Toute une série de nos illustrateurs les plus en vue font comme Douglas Fraser et Anthony Russo: ils abordent des sujets modernes dans un style délicieusement ancré dans le passé. Tout immeuble de bureaux digne de son Roche-Bobois s'enorgueillit d'une colonne grecque placée n'importe où, ou tout au moins d'un jardin de rocaille japonais. Etc., etc. □ Tout ça me désespère, pas seulement parce que ça traduit une vague appréhension de l'avenir, mais parce qu'à force de clouer grossièrement ensemble les beautés diaphanes du passé, on finira par se rendre invisibles en tant que contemporains d'une entreprise insensée. Les générations futures braquant leur regard sur les créateurs de ces icônes nous verront en transparence et nous assigneront un simple rôle de manipulateurs d'une culture que nous n'aurons pas créée, faisant de nous les exécutants d'un service de messagerie certes ingénieux, mais voué à l'oubli. □ Il y a plus encore: même si un jour lointain quelqu'un nous remarque. Quelle perspective à vous faire frémir que d'imaginer des gens que nos blagues visuelles hilarantes ne dérideront plus et qui concluront froidement que nous étions de vils voleurs (ce que certains d'entre nous sont de toute façon)! □ Pour terminer, j'aimerais affirmer que ce genre de pratique ne saurait se poursuivre indéfiniment. Mais je ne me fais aucune illusion. Malheureusement une bonne part du succès que rencontre l'éclecticisme provient du fait que son humour est perçu par un public même peu sophistiqué. L'éclecticisme risque ainsi de durer, et cela d'autant plus que ça se vend bien, en amont et en aval du système de commercialisation des grandes marques, aux agences gouvernementales, aux P. D. G. qui ont des budgets de construction rutilants. Mais c'est un autre sujet. □ Pour l'instant, je vous invite à penser à tout ça en feuilletant l'un de ces annuels à la recherche d'idées. Ce faisant, soyez très, très prudent. □

Jeffrey Goodby est un auteur et illustrateur, le principal collaborateur de Goodby, Berlin & Silverstein à San Francisco. Ses illustrations ont paru dans de nombreuses publications, Time *et le* Harvard Magazine *entre autres. Il a en outre participé aux campagnes de presse et de TV de Royal Viking Line, Heinz, Polaroid et The Christian Brothers. L'année passée, GB&S a été nommée Agence de l'année par* Advertising Age.

ADVERTISING

ANZEIGEN

ANNONCES

Buddie's Place, S. Liberty Street–upstairs (around the corner from "Fashions for the Larger Woman Shop"), Jackson, Tennessee and George Dickel. Ain't Nothin' Better.

Lake L. Black's weekend retreat (10 miles south of highway 207, Claude, Texas), "Firearms and wives must be left outside," and George Dickel. Ain't Nothin' Better.

ART DIRECTOR:
BOB WYATT
PHOTOGRAPHER:
HARRY DEZITTER
COPYWRITER:
TOM COLEMAN
AGENCY:
LEO BURNETT, CHICAGO
CLIENT:
GEORGE A. DICKEL & CO.
■ 1-4

■ 1-4 For this campaign for *Dickel* Whiskey, the photographer travelled through the American south – taking in Claude (Texas), Blounts Creek (N. Carolina) and Jackson (Tennessee) among other locations – in order to take shots especially characteristic of this region. (USA)

■ 1-4 Für diese Kampagne für *Dickel*-Whiskey reiste der Photograph durch den amerikanischen Süden, um besonders charakteristische Bilder dieser Region zu machen. Der gemeinsame Slogan: «Was Besseres gibt's nicht.» In allen Anzeigen wird der Ort der Aufnahme angegeben. (USA)

■ 1-4 Pour cette campagne de publicité, le photographe a sillonné le sud des Etats-Unis, ce qui lui a permis de trouver des sujets particulièrement typiques de cette région. Les annonces portent toutes le même slogan: «Il n'existe rien de meilleur» et le nom du lieu où la photo a été prise. (USA)

City Barbershop, 322 S. Kearney Street. "No appointment necessary—sideburns our specialty." Clarendon, Texas
and George Dickel. Ain't Nothin' Better.

Secret fishing hole of the Little Meadows Hunt Club, Pembroke, Virginia (location cannot be divulged)
and George Dickel. Ain't Nothin' Better.

■ 5-8 Examples from a promotional campaign in the form of magazine and newspaper ads as well as posters for a Mexican beer marketed under the *Simpatico* label. (USA)

■ 5-8 Beispiele aus einer Werbekampagne in Form von Zeitschriften- und Zeitungsanzeigen sowie Plakaten für ein mexikanisches Bier mit dem Namen *Simpatico*. (USA)

■ 5-8 Exemples d'une campagne publicitaire pour une bière mexicaine appelée *Simpatico*, parue sous forme d'annonces dans des magazines et des journaux. (USA)

ART DIRECTOR:
TERRY SCHNEIDER
DESIGNER:
TERRY SCHNEIDER
PHOTOGRAPHER:
C.B. HARDING
AGENCY:
C.B. HARDING STUDIOS
CLIENT:
BRANDEVOR USA
■ 5-8

SIMPATICO
THE GOLDEN BEER
IN THE BLACK BOTTLE.
IMPORTED FROM MEXICO
BY BRANDEVOR USA,
REDMOND, WA ©1989.
PHOTO: C.B. HARDING

ART DIRECTOR:
Jacques Vauchelle
PHOTOGRAPHER:
Daniel Jouanneau
COPYWRITER:
André Lomuscio
AGENCY:
Alice
CLIENT:
Française de Brasserie
■ 9-11

13 h 56 mn.

Bien entendu, je partis tout de suite sur les fouilles. Un endroit sinistre. Du sable gris à perte de vue et une chaleur qui nous obligeait à refroidir nos outils toutes les 20 minutes. De ma vie, je n'ai autant souffert. Tels des esclaves, pendant 5 mois on a creusé. Pour rien. La fatigue et l'inanité de nos efforts instillaient en nous un violent désir de fuir. Et pourtant les cartographes ne cessaient de nous exhorter à continuer. Documents d'époque à l'appui, ils tentaient de nous convaincre qu'une ville avait dû s'élever là où nous creusions. Nous n'en pouvions plus. On boucla le camp. C'est en déplaçant l'un des treuils qu'on les trouva. Notre excitation était telle que nous ne sentions même plus la morsure des 2 soleils.

14 h 28 mn.

14 h 32 mn.

Je tins moi-même à dégager les 3 boîtes. Tu ne me croiras pas, mais elles étaient encore comme neuves. Il y avait bien une étiquette, mais totalement effacée par le temps. A l'analyse, quelques traces de contamination perduraient encore, mais sans aucun danger. On démonta les boîtes. A l'intérieur, 2 axes solidaires, reliés par un ruban recouvert d'oxydes non encore identifiés. Argaïl, le premier, fit le pontage intellectuel. Il déclara qu'il devait s'agir d'unités d'informations et qu'au musée il y avait quelque chose qui... On courut au musée. Il employa plus d'une heure à reconstituer les branchements primitifs de l'appareil. Un voyant rouge s'alluma. Il glissa l'une des boîtes à l'intérieur. Elle se fit avaler. Pétrifiés, on se regarda. Nous étions tous en eau.

14 h 46 mn.

15 h 04 mn.

Les boîtes contenaient des images animées. Elles démentaient tous les livres sur nos Pères Fondateurs. C'est incroyable. Ils ne connaissaient ni la guerre ni la violence. Rien dans leurs rapports n'indique qu'ils aient été mus par des facteurs agressifs. Ils riaient et souriaient constamment ! Autre chose : leur passion du beau. Un vrai culte. Leurs gens, leurs vêtements, leurs maisons, leurs objets semblaient dominés par l'esthétique. Plus le temps passait et plus mes yeux s'embuaient. Je sais que la semaine prochaine, tu seras parmi nous. Entre temps mon cher fils, j'ai besoin de ton aide. Avant chaque séquence il y a un mot que je ne connais pas : publicité. Pourrais-tu interroger tes machines ? Je dois te laisser. J'ai besoin de quelque repos pour faire retomber la pression.

15 h 27 mn.

■ 9-11 "1:56 p.m. to 3:27 p.m." – this is the title of the copy written in the form of a novel by André Lomuscio, the plot of which is about thirst. These double-spread ads for *Tuborg* beer show clearly what happens with the beer. The slogan is "Moderate your thirst." (FRA)

■ 12 Almost as bad as a plunging stock market? The text – and shot of a pint of *Stella Artois* beer smashing to the ground – underscores the reasoning. (GBR)

■ 9-11 «13 Uhr 56 bis 15 Uhr 27» – so der Titel dieser «Novelle» von André Lomuscio über Durst. In diesen doppelseitigen Anzeigen für *Tuborg*-Bier, in denen der Text jeweils einer Aufnahme gegenübergestellt ist, sieht man, was mit dem Bier geschieht. Der Slogan: «Mässigen Sie Ihren Durst.» (FRA)

■ 12 «Der Krach von '88» – fast ebenso schlimm wie ein Börsenkrach sei ein zerbrochener Krug mit dem kostbaren *Stella Artois*-Bier, so der Text dieser Anzeige. (GBR)

■ 9-11 «13 h 56 mn – 15 h 27 mn». Tel est le titre d'une nouvelle d'André Lomuscio dans laquelle il est question de la soif. Dans ces annonces double page pour la bière *Tuborg*, le texte est directement mis en regard de l'image. Chacune de ces photos illustre les qualités de cette boisson. (FRA)

■ 12 «Le krach de '88»: si l'on en croit le texte, une chope de bière *Stella Artois* brisée est une catastrophe presque aussi terrible qu'un krach à la Bourse. (GBR)

What's almost as bad as a plunging stock market?

A plummeting pint of Stella Artois.

While your loss may not equal that sustained on Black Monday, it will be significant nevertheless.

And far more tangible than any loss you may have suffered on paper.

If only we could lessen the damage.

But that would mean no more wonderfully fragrant. hideously expensive Saaz hops from Czechoslovakia.

No more costly treks around Europe to find the choicest barley.

And certainly no more waiting six weeks for Stella to mature in its own good time.

We'd have to hurry things along, just as other people do.

True, no longer would you have to consider breaking up your portfolio of blue-chip shares to pay for a pint.

But we suspect if the resulting brew ended up on the floor you'd be pleased, not pained.

Stella Artois. Reassuringly expensive.

The Crash of '88.

ART DIRECTOR:
ALAN FLEMING

PHOTOGRAPHER:
JOHN WALLACE

COPYWRITER:
NICK HAZZARD

AGENCY:
LOWE HOWARD-SPINK LTD.

CLIENT:
WHITBREAD & COMPANY

■ 12

■ 13 Full-page ad on behalf of *Smirnoff* Vodka with a slogan proclaiming the sovereignty of this liquor. (USA)

■ 14 Advertisements appearing during the Christmas season for *J&B* Scotch Whisky. (USA)

■ 15 Full-page advertisement for Bourbon whiskey marketed under the *Old Grand-Dad* label. (USA)

■ 16 The reference to *Absolut* Vodka in the text of this ad is reduced to a minimum – all is left to the familiarity of this label. (USA)

■ 17 Advertisement for a product by the Christian Brothers. It's all a question of maturity – which is exactly what applies to a good cognac. (USA)

■ 13 «Seit über einem Jahrhundert unübertroffen.» Ganzseitiges Inserat für *Smirnoff*-Wodka. (USA)

■ 14 «Ohne J&B sind die Festtage nicht dasselbe.» Zu Weihnachten erschienene Anzeige für *J&B*-Scotch Whisky. (USA)

■ 15 Ganzseitige Anzeige für Bourbon Whiskey der Marke «*Old Grand-Dad*» – «Ich und mein Grossvater». (USA)

■ 16 Der Hinweis auf *Absolut*-Wodka im Text dieser Anzeige ist verschwindend klein – es wird auf die Bekanntheit dieser Marke gesetzt. (USA)

■ 17 «Brüder. Speziell alt.» Hier geht es um die Frage des Reifens, wie es auch für einen Cognac notwendig ist. Anzeige für ein Produkt der Christian Brothers. (USA)

■ 13 «La vodka qui règne depuis plus d'un siècle.» Annonce pleine page pour la vodka *Smirnoff*. (USA)

■ 14 «Les jours de fête ne sont pas les mêmes sans *J&B*.» Annonce pour le whisky écossais J&B, publiée à Noël. (USA)

■ 15 Annonce pleine page pour la marque de whisky américain «Old Grand-Dad»: «Mon grand-père et moi». (USA)

■ 16 Le texte fait allusion à la vodka *Absolut*, une marque tellement connue en Amérique qu'il n'est même plus besoin de la nommer complètement. (USA)

■ 17 «Brothers (frères). Extra-vieux.» Il est ici question du vieillissement du cognac, processus indispensable si l'on veut obtenir un produit de qualité. (USA)

ART DIRECTOR:
BOB COLE
PHOTOGRAPHER:
JODY DOLE
COPYWRITER:
*GERRY SUSSMANN/
PETER FAULKNER* (USA)
AGENCY:
McCANN ERICKSON
CLIENT:
HEUBLEIN, INC.
■ 13

ART DIRECTOR:
CHRIS GRAVES
COPYWRITER:
CRAIG DEMETER
AGENCY:
GRACE & ROTSCHILD
CLIENT:
THE PADDINGTON CORP.
■ 14

WAS MACHT FREUDE?

WMF!

WAS MACHT FREUDE?

WMF!

Tafeltje Dekje

De Hollandse Keuken

Art Director:
Detlef Blume
Illustrator:
Detlef Blume
Photographer:
Hans Hansen
Copywriter:
Gerd Fehling
Agency:
Struwe & Partner
WMF Württembergische
Metallwarenfabrik AG
◄■ 18, 19

Art Director:
Jan Willem Nijsen
Desinger:
Jan Willem Nijsen
Photographer:
Tobias Reymond
Stylist:
Renée Zindler
Copywriter:
Maartje Van Niedeu
Agency:
PRAD
Client:
Nederlands Zuivelburo
■ 20, 21

■ 18, 19 Examples from a series of double-spread advertisements in magazines for WMF kitchenware under the slogan: "What gives you pleasure?". (GER)

■ 20, 21 From an ad campaign for Dutch cheese. Slogans: "The table is laid" and "Dutch cooking". (NLD)

■ 18, 19 Beispiele aus einer Kampagne mit doppelseitigen Zeitschriftanzeigen für WMF-Küchenzubehör unter dem Slogan «Was macht Freude?». (GER)

■ 20, 21 Anzeigenkampagne für holländischen Käse: «Der Tisch ist gedeckt», «Die holländische Küche». (NLD)

■ 18, 19 Annonces double page d'une campagne parue dans les magazines pour les ustensiles de cuisine WMF. Le slogan: «Ce qui fait plaisir». (GER)

■ 20, 21 Campagne d'annonces pour le fromage hollandais. «La table est mise», «La cuisine hollandaise.» (NLD)

Are your Health Plan costs getting harder and harder to swallow?

The BIG problem with most employee health plans isn't the cost of initial enrollment.

It's the cost of annual renewal.

That's why you need a plan that not only gives your employees the coverage they want, but also provides the yearly cost controls you need.

Like the Direct Choice® plan from NWNL, an innovative combination health plan with all the benefits of an HMO, plus the freedoms of an indemnity plan.

You see, within the Direct Choice plan, we've developed the kind of diagnostic tools that help you spot problems and keep rates down—year after year.

For instance, we employ cost management reports to identify where your costs have increased and then help you select options to control them.

Our Utilization Review helps prevent over-utilization and minimize expenditures, while assuring quality and appropriate care.

What's more, for larger companies, we base your rates on your own company's experience, not a general community rating.

And Direct Choice encourages employees to seek care through primary HMO physicians.

So if your health plan costs look like they're going to be a bitter pill to swallow again this year, call us at 372-5322 and ask for more information.

We'll help you get rid of those growing pains.

DIRECT CHOICE®
The health plan that keeps your business healthy.

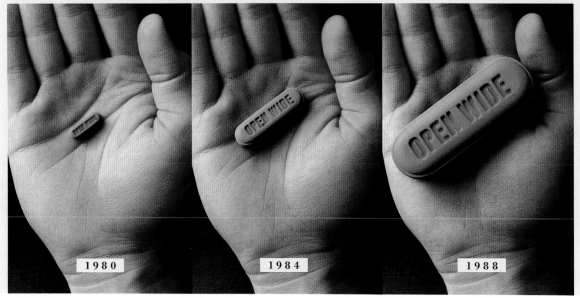

1980   1984   1988

ART DIRECTOR:
JAC COVERDALE
DESIGNER:
JAC COVERDALE
PHOTOGRAPHER:
TOM CONNORS
COPYWRITER:
JOE ALEXANDER
AGENCY:
CLARITY COVERDALE RUEFF
CLIENT:
TWIN CITIES DIRECT CHOICE
■ 22

■ 22 Magazine advertisement for a health insurance plan - referring to the burden of increased costs for the members of some health plans. (USA)

■ 23-25 Advertisement campaign issued on behalf of *Heineken* beer. One of the headlines ("Message in a Bottle") also happens to be the title of a hit number by the English group "The Police". (CAN)

■ 22 «Sind die Kosten Ihrer Krankenversicherung immer schwerer zu schlucken?» Magazin-Inserat für eine Krankenversicherung. (USA)

■ 23-25 Anzeigenkampagne für *Heineken*-Bier: «Der grüne Standard (Evergreen)»; «Womit hast du das verdient?»; «Botschaft in einer Flasche» (diese Headline ist auch der Titel eines Hits der englischen Gruppe «The Police»). (CAN)

■ 22 «Le coût de votre assurance maladie est-il de plus en plus difficile à avaler?» Annonce pour une assurance maladie parue dans des magazines. (USA)

■ 23-25 Campagne d'annonces de la bière Heineken: «Le vert standard (Evergreen)»; «Qu'as-tu fait pour mériter cela?»; «Message dans une bouteille» (ce headline est aussi le titre d'un succès du groupe anglais «The Police»). (CAN)

THE · GREEN · STANDARD

AFTER ALL, THERE'S HEINEKEN

WHAT · HAVE · YOU · DONE
· TO · DESERVE · THIS?

AFTER ALL, THERE'S HEINEKEN

ART DIRECTOR:
Carl W. Jones

PHOTOGRAPHER:
Tim Saunders

COPYWRITER:
Paul Joyce

AGENCY:
Vickers & Benson

CLIENT:
Heineken

■ 23-25

MESSAGE · IN · A · BOTTLE

AFTER ALL, THERE'S HEINEKEN

ART DIRECTOR:
GAVINO SANNA
PHOTOGRAPHER:
ALDO BALLO
COPYWRITER:
GASPARE GIUA
AGENCY:
YOUNG & RUBICAM
CLIENT:
ARTEMIDE
■ 26, 27

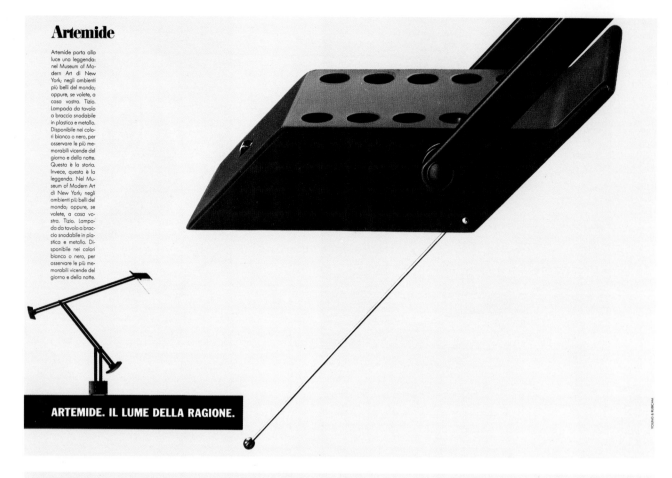

Artemide

Artemide porta alla luce una leggenda: nel Museum of Modern Art di New York; negli ambienti più belli del mondo; oppure, se volete, a casa vostra. Tizio. Lampada da tavolo a braccio snodabile in plastica e metallo. Disponibile nei colori bianco o nero, per osservare le più memorabili vicende del giorno e della notte. Questa è la storia. Invece, questa è la leggenda. Nel Museum of Modern Art di New York; negli ambienti più belli del mondo; oppure, se volete, a casa vostra. Tizio. Lampada da tavolo a braccio snodabile in plastica e metallo. Disponibile nei colori bianco o nero, per osservare le più memorabili vicende del giorno e della notte.

ARTEMIDE. IL LUME DELLA RAGIONE.

■ 26, 27 Examples from a series of newspaper ads for modern lighting produced by Artemide. (ITA)

■ 26, 27 Beispiele aus einer Serie von Zeitungsanzeigen für Beleuchtungskörper von Artemide. (ITA)

■ 26, 27 Deux exemples d'une série d'annonces de journaux pour les luminaires d'Artemide. (ITA)

Artemide

Zen. Lampada da terra. Il design di Ernesto Gismondi indica una filosofia per le diverse necessità dello spirito, da interpretare attraverso due chiavi di lettura: un diffusore superiore, orientabile, illumina l'ambiente; un diffusore inferiore scopre una luce circoscritta, da meditazione. Base e stelo in metallo verniciato nero. Diffusori in alluminio anodizzato. Questa è la storia. Invece, questa è la leggenda. Zen. Lampada da terra. Il design di Ernesto Gismondi indica una filosofia per le diverse necessità dello spirito, da interpretare attraverso due chiavi di lettura: un diffusore superiore, orientabile, illumina l'ambiente; un diffusore inferiore scopre una luce circoscritta, da meditazione. Base e stelo in metallo verniciato nero. Diffusori in alluminio anodizzato.

ARTEMIDE. IL LUME DELLA RAGIONE.

ART DIRECTOR:
Peter Maisey
DESIGNER:
Peter Maisey
PHOTOGRAPHER:
Leon
COPYWRITER:
Mark Leigh
AGENCY:
*First City/BBDO
Advertising Ltd.*
CLIENT:
Henderson
■ 28, 29

■ 28, 29 From an advertisement campaign for garage doors made by Henderson. The idea behind the campaign is to associate Henderson with the best of the best – hence *Bentley*, and *Cadillac*, for instance. (GBR)

■ 28, 29 Aus einer Anzeigenkampagne für Garagentüren von Henderson: «Klassisches Design, hervorragende Technik, dauerhaft – und das ist nur die Tür.» Nach dem Motto «nur das Beste» hier ein *Bentley* und ein *Cadillac*. (GBR)

■ 28, 29 Annonces pour les portes de garage Henderson: «Un design classique, une technique remarquable, du solide – et ce n'est que la porte.» Rien n'est trop beau pour de tels garages, une *Bentley* ou une *Cadillac* par ex. (GBR)

Spring Ahead! Spring Downtown!

Heat Rises. Head Downtown!

You Are About To Go On A Fantastic Adventure. Downtown!

ART DIRECTOR:
STEPHEN DOYLE
DESIGNER:
STEPHEN DOYLE
PHOTOGRAPHER:
GEORGE HEIN
AGENCY:
DRENTTEL DOYLE PARTNERS
CLIENT:
OLYMPIA & YORK/
THE WORLD FINANCIAL CENTER
■ 30-33

April Showers Bring People Indoors!

ART DIRECTOR:
JEFF BARNES
DESINGER:
JEFF BARNES
PHOTOGRAPHER:
CHRISTOPHER HAWKER
COPYWRITER:
JEFF BARNES
AGENCY:
BARNES DESIGN OFFICE
CLIENT:
JOHNSON INDUSTRIES
►■ 34

■ 30-33 Examples from a series of ads for the many stores and restaurants in New York's World Financial Center. The headlines refer to the seasons. (USA)

■ 34 Full-page ad for individually designed dining tables for corporation offices, made by Johnson Industries. (USA)

■ 30-33 Aus einer Serie von Anzeigen für die vielen Läden und Restaurants in New Yorks World Financial Center. Die Headlines beziehen sich auf die Jahreszeiten. (USA)

■ 34 «Ein Konferenztisch von 12.00 bis 13.00 Uhr.» Ganzseitige Anzeige für Büro-Esstische. (USA)

■ 30-33 Annonces en faveur des nombreux magasins et restaurants du World Financial Center à New York. Le titre et les sujets choisis renvoient aux différentes saisons. (USA)

■ 34 «Une table de conférence de midi à 1 h.» Annonce pleine page pour les tables de bureau Johnson. (USA)

A Conference Table for Noon to 1:00

Individually-designed

dining tables for

the corporation

in blueberry, lemon,

cherry and other

tasteful colors.

Johnson Industries, Inc.

1424 Davis Road

Elgin, Illinois 60123

312-695-1242

800-346-5555

Johnson

ART DIRECTOR:
JEFF BARNES
DESIGNER:
JEFF BARNES
PHOTOGRAPHER:
GINA UHLMAN
STYLIST:
DONNA FORST
COPYWRITER:
JEFF BARNES
AGENCY:
BARNES DESIGN OFFICE
CLIENT:
JOHNSON INDUSTRIES
■ 35-38

 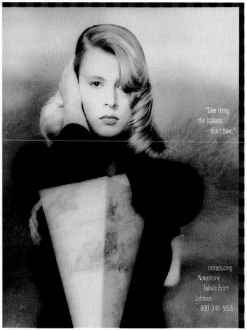 

■ 35-38 Examples of full-page advertisements from a campaign to promote *Novastone* tables that look just like marble. (USA)

■ 35-38 Beispiele der ganzseitigen Anzeigen aus einer Kampagne für die Einführung von *Novastone*-Tischen, die wie Marmor aussehen. (USA)

■ 35-38 Exemples d'annonces pleine page tirées de la campagne de lancement des tables *Novastone*. Ces modèles sont des imitations de tables en marbre. (USA)

"This marble table isn't even cold."

"It isn't even marble."

Introducing Novastone Tables From Johnson
800-346-5555

33

Mackintosh passend zum Lichtschalter.

Zwanziger Jahre passend zum Lichtschalter.

ART DIRECTOR:
Hans Günter Schmitz/
Dirk Longjaloux
DESIGNER:
Elisabeth Pangels/
Lutz Menze
PHOTOGRAPHER:
R. Petrin/U. Kowalski
COPYWRITER:
Christine Hesse
AGENCY:
Büro Hans Günter Schmitz
CLIENT:
Gira, Giersiepen GmbH & Co.
■ 39, 40

ART DIRECTOR:
Rick Biedel
DESIGNER:
Rick Biedel
PHOTOGRAPHER:
Don Penny
AGENCY:
Bonnell Design Assoc.
CLIENT:
Designtex
▼■ 41

Fabric: Grande Nouveau

DESIGNTEX

Why we offer the same sofa in 67 sizes.

Unfortunately, while most sofas come in standard sizes, many spaces don't.
So at Century Furniture we make a full line of Custom Designer
Seating to solve exactly that problem.
Available in a range of styles, each one is lavishly hand-crafted, carefully
finished, and custom made in any length from 54 to 120 inches.
Why not call 1-800-852-5552 for more information,
or for the name of a store selling Century Furniture near you?
After all, even if you're considering a new slant in decorating,
we don't suppose you mean the kind up there.

Century Furniture

Den finns i Nationalmusei samlingar, och i dess salar att vila i.
STOLEN "VAXHOLMAREN" FRÅN GÄRSNÄS.

ART DIRECTOR:
Roy Grace
DESIGNER:
Roy Grace
PHOTOGRAPHER:
Elizabeth Heyert
COPYWRITER:
Diane Rothschild
AGENCY:
Grace & Rothschild
CLIENT:
Century Furniture Company
■ 42

ART DIRECTOR:
Torbjörn Lenskog
DESIGNER:
Ake Axelsson
PHOTOGRAPHER:
Jan Bengtsson
COPYWRITER:
Jan-Axel Nymann
AGENCY:
Arbman & Lenskog
CLIENT:
Gärsnäs AB
■ 43

■ 39, 40 Double-spread advertisements from a campaign running in architectural magazines to promote *Gira* light switches and plugs. (USA)

■ 41 The name of the fabric that's being promoted here is "Grande Nouveau". Double-spread ad from a series. (USA)

■ 42 Magazine advertisement issued for Century furniture - proudly stating that the sofa comes in many sizes. (USA)

■ 43 "You'll find this in the collection at the National Gallery" - ad for the "Vaxholmaren" chair. (SWE)

■ 39, 40 Doppelseitige Anzeigen aus einer Werbekampagne in Architektur-Zeitschriften für *Gira*-Schalter und -Steckdosen. (GER)

■ 41 «Grande Nouveau» ist der Name des Stoffes, der hier beworben wird. Doppelseitige Anzeige aus einer Serie. (USA)

■ 42 «Wir können das gleiche Sofa in 87 Grössen anbieten.» Zeitschriftenanzeige für *Century*-Möbel. (USA)

■ 43 «Das finden Sie in der Sammlung der Nationalgalerie» - Anzeige für den Stuhl «Vaxholmaren». (SWE)

■ 39, 40 Annonces double page d'une campagne pour les commutateurs et prises *Gira*, parue dans des revues d'architecture. Ces modèles vont avec tous les styles. (GER)

■ 41 «Grande Nouveau» est le nom d'une étoffe. Annonce tirée d'une série conçue pour un fabricant de tissus. (USA)

■ 42 «Nous vous proposons le même sofa en 67 tailles différentes.» Annonce pour les meubles *Century*. (USA)

■ 43 «Vous la trouverez dans la collection du Musée national». Annonce pour la chaise «Vaxholmaren». (SWE)

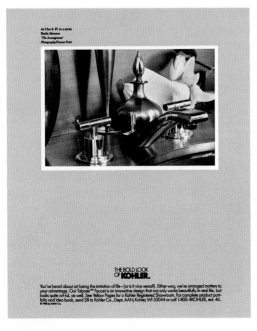

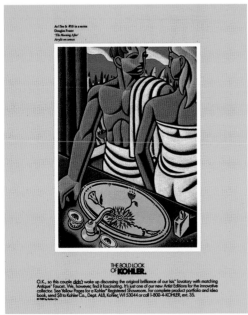

ART DIRECTOR:
KURT HAIMAN

DESIGNER:
KURT HAIMAN

ILLUSTRATOR/PHOTOGRAPHER:
SHEILA METZNER 44

DAVID JONASON/
RYSZARD HOROWITZ 45

ANTHONY RUSSO 46

DOUGLAS FRASER 47

RYSZARD HOROWITZ/
ANDRZEJ DUDZINSKI 48

JOYCE TENNESON 49

COPYWRITER:
JUDY FRISCH

AGENCY:
GREY ADV.

CLIENT:
KOHLER CO.

■ 44-49

CREATIVE DIRECTOR:
JOHN CONNELLY/MIKE FOUNTAIN

ART DIRECTOR:
MIKE FOUNTAIN

DESIGNER:
MIKE FOUNTAIN

PHOTOGRAPHER:
AARON JONES

COPYWRITER:
MIKE FOUNTAIN

AGENCY:
ICE COMMUNICATIONS

CLIENT:
BAUSCH & LOMB

►■ 50

■ 44-49 Art appears in a series of ads to promote bathroom fittings. The titles and artists of the pictures are: Sheila Metzner, "The Arrangement" – photo, Fresson print *(44)*; David Jonason, Ryszard Horowitz, "Shaping the Flow" – airbrush/photo *(45)*; Anthony Russo, "RSVP" – scraperboard *(46)*; Douglas Fraser, "The Morning After" – acryllic on canvas *(47)*; Ryszard Horowitz, Andrzej Dudzinski "The Faucet and the Frog" – mixed media, photo and illustration *(48)*; Joyce Tenneson, "Renaissance Redux" – Polaroid 20x24 Polacolor photo *(49)*. (USA)

■ 50 "The best part of disposable lenses is all the things you dispose of" – from a series. (USA)

■ 44-49 «Der kühne Look von Kohler» – Kunst in einer Serie für Badezimmer-Armaturen. Die Titel und Künstler der Bilder: Sheila Metzner, «The Arrangement» – Photo, Fresson-Druck (44); David Jonason, Ryszard Horowitz, «Shaping the Flow» – Air Brush/Photo (45); Anthony Russo, «RSVP» – Schabkarton (46); Douglas Fraser, «The Morning After» – Akryl auf Leinwand (47); Ryszard Horowitz, Andrzej Dudzinski, «The Faucet and the Frog» – Mixed Media, Photo/Illustration (48); Joyce Tenneson, «Renaissance Redux» – Polaroid 20x24 Polacolor Photo (49). (USA)

■ 50 «Das Beste an Wegwerf-Kontaktlinsen sind all die Dinge, die man wegwerfen kann». (USA)

■ 44-49 «Le look audacieux de Kohler» – l'art dans une série d'annonces pour des robinets de salle de bains. Titres et artistes: Sheila Metzner, «The Arrangement» – photo, impr. Fresson (44); David Jonason, Ryszard Horowitz, «Shaping the Flow» – aérographe/photo (45); Anthony Russo, «RSVP» – carton à racler (46); Douglas Fraser, «The Morning After» – acryl sur toile (47); Ryszard Horowitz, Andrzej Dudzinski, «The Faucet and the Frog» – technique mixte, photo et illustration (48); Joyce Tenneson, «Renaissance Redux» – polaroïd 20x24 photo Polacolor (49). (USA)

■ 50 «La meilleure chose avec les verres de contact jetables, c'est tout ce qu'on peut supprimer.» (USA)

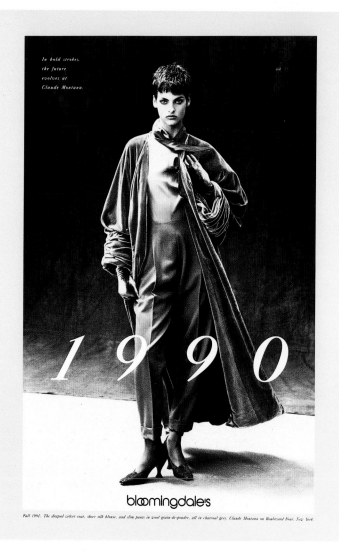

Approaching 1990, and ever more modern. Here, from the Fall collection, sleeveless unitard in navy wool crepe jersey, and notch collar fitted bodysuit in white silk crepe. The Shop For Donna Karan on Boulevard Four, New York. And in all our stores. At Your Service is our personal shopping service for women. Call June Selig, (212) 705-3135 to make an appointment.

Fall 1990. The draped velvet coat, sheer silk blouse, and slim pants in wool grain-de-poudre, all in charcoal grey. Claude Montana on Boulevard Four, New York.

ART DIRECTOR:
JOHN C. JAY
DESIGNER:
JOHN C. JAY
PHOTOGRAPHER:
STEVEN MEISEL
STYLIST:
JILL GLOVER
COPYWRITER:
CYNTHIA RITTENHOUSE
AGENCY:
BLOOMINGDALE'S
CLIENT:
BLOOMINGDALE'S
■ 51, 52

ART DIRECTOR:
H. ROSS FELTUS
DESIGNER:
H. ROSS FELTUS
ILLUSTRATOR:
MARGRET GNOTH
PHOTOGRAPHER:
H. ROSS FELTUS
STUDIO:
H. ROSS FELTUS PHOTOGRAPHY
CLIENT:
TROTINETTE
■ 53

■ 51, 52 Designer fashion for fall 1990 at Bloomingdale's is the focal point of this advertisement campaign in black and white appearing in newspapers. (USA)

■ 53 From an advertising campaign for *Trottinette* children's clothing. (GER)

■ 51, 52 Designer-Mode für Herbst 1990 bei Bloomingdales steht im Mittelpunkt dieser Anzeigenkampagne in Schwarzweiss, die in Zeitungen erschien. (USA)

■ 53 Aus einer Werbekampagne für *Trottinette*-Kinderkleidung. (GER)

■ 51, 52 La mode automne 1990 des grands couturiers constitue le sujet de la campagne d'annonces en noir et blanc de Bloomingdales, publiée dans les journaux. (USA)

■ 53 Annonce d'une campagne pour la promotion des vêtements pour enfants *Trottinette*. (GER)

■ 54-56 Examples from an ad campaign for Barney's – the New York fashion house. These full-page and double-spread ads contributed to creating a new image of this former discount company. (USA)

■ 57-59 From a series of ads with shots by famous photographers, for fashion made by the textile firm of Gap. (USA)

■ 54-56 Beispiele aus einer Werbekampagne für das New Yorker Bekleidungshaus Barney's. Diese ganz- und doppelseitigen Anzeigen, trugen dazu bei, dem ehemaligen Discount-Geschäft ein ganz neues Image zu geben. (USA)

■ 57-59 Anzeigenkampagne mit Aufnahmen berühmter Photographen für Mode des Textilhauses Gap. (USA)

■ 54-56 D'une campagne de publicité pour Barney's. Ces annonces pleine page et double page contribuèrent à donner une nouvelle image de cette maison de confection new-yorkaise qui fut autrefois un magasin discount. (USA)

■ 57-59 Des photographes célèbres ont réalisé les photos de ces annonces pour le magasin de vêtements Gap. (USA)

CREATIVE DIRECTOR:
NEIL KRAFT
ART DIRECTOR:
DOUGLAS LLOYD
DESIGNER:
DOUGLAS LLOYD
PHOTOGRAPHER:
TIMOTHY GREENFIELD-SANDERS
COPYWRITER:
GLENN O'BRIEN
AGENCY:
BNY ADVERTISING
CLIENT:
BARNEYS
■ 54-56

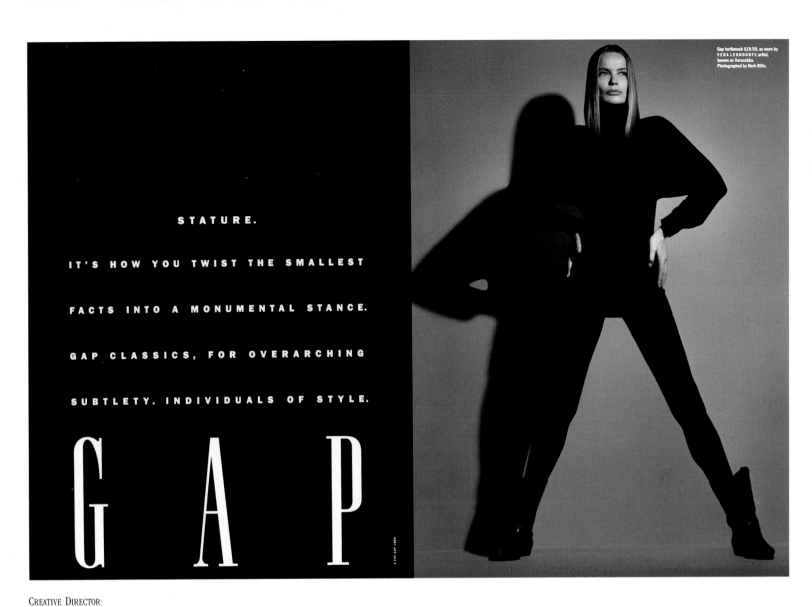

Gap turtleneck $19.50, as worn by VERA LEHNDORFF, artist, known as Veruschka. Photographed by Herb Ritts.

STATURE.

IT'S HOW YOU TWIST THE SMALLEST

FACTS INTO A MONUMENTAL STANCE.

GAP CLASSICS, FOR OVERARCHING

SUBTLETY. INDIVIDUALS OF STYLE.

GAP

CREATIVE DIRECTOR:
Maggie Gross

ART DIRECTOR:
Jim Nevins

PHOTOGRAPHER:
Herb Ritts 57, 58
Annie Leibovitz/
Herb Ritts 59

STYLIST:
Sharon Simonaire 57, 58

COPYWRITER:
Timothy Cohrs

AGENCY:
The Gap/In-House

CLIENT:
The Gap, Inc.
■ 57-59

Gap long sleeved pocket-t $18, as customized by JODY WATLEY, singer/songwriter. Photographed by Herb Ritts.

STELLAR.

IT'S WHEN YOUR ENERGY,
YOUR LOOK, YOUR GLOW,
ARE A SEAMLESS CHAIN
REACTION. GAP CLASSICS.
INDIVIDUALS OF STYLE.

GAP

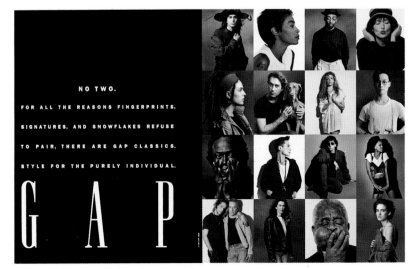

NO TWO.

FOR ALL THE REASONS FINGERPRINTS,
SIGNATURES, AND SNOWFLAKES REFUSE
TO PAIR, THERE ARE GAP CLASSICS.
STYLE FOR THE PURELY INDIVIDUAL.

GAP

PHOTOGRAPHER:
DOMINIQUE ISSERMANN
AGENCY:
EDIFRANCE
CLIENT:
NINA RICCI
■ 60, 61

■ 60, 61 From an advertising campaign for fashion by Nina Ricci, appearing in *Vogue* of Paris. (FRA)

■ 60, 61 Aus einer in *Vogue Paris* erschienenen Werbekampagne für Mode von Nina Ricci. (FRA)

■ 60, 61 Deux exemples de la campagne de publicité de Nina Ricci parus dans *Vogue Paris*. (FRA)

ART DIRECTOR:
JEFF GOODBY
DESIGNER:
JEFF GOODBY
COPYWRITER:
ANDY BERLIN/ED CRAYTON
AGENCY:
GOODBY, BERLIN & SILVERSTEIN
CLIENT:
CLARKS OF ENGLAND
■ 62

■ 62 On the occasion of a shoe trade fair - an advertisement for the British shoe manufacturers *Clarks of England* with portraits and quotations of its founders Cyrus and James Clark. (USA)

■ 62 «Wir möchten Ihnen unsere neuen Schuhe für Damen und Herren gern persönlich vorstellen.» «Aber wir sind tot». Anlässlich einer Schuhmesse erschienenes Inserat für *Clarks of England*. (USA)

■ 62 «Nous aimerions vous présenter personnellement nos nouvelles chaussures pour hommes et femmes.» «Mais nous sommes morts.» Annonce pour *Clarks of England* publiée à l'occasion d'une foire de la chaussure. (USA)

PHOTOGRAPHER:
OLIVIERO TOSCANI
AGENCE:
EL DORADO
CLIENT:
BENETTON SPA
■ 63, 64

■ 63, 64 From an advertising campaign for the Italian fashionwear firm of Benetton. These ads led to protests in the United States. (NLD)

■ 63, 64 Aus einer Werbekampagne für den italienischen Textilhersteller Benetton. Diese Anzeigen führten in den USA zu Protesten. (NLD)

■ 63, 64 Campagne de publicité pour le fabricant de vêtements Benetton. Ces annonces ont provoqué quelque remous aux Etats-Unis. (NLD)

ART DIRECTOR:
MARTIN SPILLMANN
DESIGNER:
JÖRG BIRKER
PHOTOGRAPHER:
ANDREAS HEUMANN
COPYWRITER:
GABY GIRSBERGER
AGENCY:
ADVICO YOUNG & RUBICAM
CLIENT:
SIBER HEGNER DIST. SA
■ 65-67

CHROM CHRON. THE COLOUR-TIME-WATCH.

Everybody has a watch. But nobody has time. Because time runs away in seconds. It is time for another watch: The Colour-Time-Watch. The day has 12 colours. According to the light from morning until evening. Each colour is an hour. Each colour part is part of an hour. Suddenly the moment matters. All at once it is 10 to turquoise and no longer 10 to eight.

MONDAY-MORNING, 10 TO TURQUOISE.

CHROM CHRON. DIE FARB-ZEIT-UHR.

Jeder hat eine Uhr. Aber keiner hat Zeit. Weil die Zeit in Sekunden davonrennt. Es ist Zeit für eine andere Uhr: die Farb-Zeit-Uhr. Der Tag hat 12 Farben. Je nach Licht vom Morgen bis zum Abend. Jede Farbe ist eine Stunde. Jeder Farbteil, ein Stundenteil. Plötzlich zählt der Augenblick. Auf einmal ist es Viertel nach Rosa. Und nicht mehr Viertel nach zwei. Chromachron. Im guten Uhrenfachgeschäft.

IRGENDWO, VIERTEL NACH ROSA.

RESERVIERT FÜR ZWEI, PUNKT GELB.

Jeder hat eine Uhr. Aber keiner hat Zeit. Weil die Zeit in Sekunden davonrennt. Es ist Zeit für eine andere Uhr: die Farb-Zeit-Uhr. Der Tag hat 12 Farben. Je nach Licht vom Morgen bis zum Abend. Jede Farbe ist eine Stunde. Jeder Farbteil, ein Stundenteil. Plötzlich zählt der Augenblick. Auf einmal ist es punkt Gelb. Und nicht mehr zwölf Uhr. Chromachron. Im guten Uhrenfachgeschäft.

CHROM CHRON. DIE FARB-ZEIT-UHR.

ART DIRECTOR:
BENOIT DEVARIEUX
PHOTOGRAPHER:
MARTINE DEVARIEUX
AGENCY:
DUPUY SAATCHI
CLIENT:
ALAIN MIKLI LUNETTES
■ 68

ART DIRECTOR:
MISCHA GOOD/
THOMAS SCHLAPBACH
ILLUSTRATOR:
MISCHA GOOD
AGENCY:
ATELIER ICERIPPER
CLIENT:
SWATCH AG
■ 69

■ 65-67 From an advertising campaign for the new Color-Time-Watch *Chrom Chron*: The day has 12 colors. According to the light from morning to the evening. Each color is an hour. Each color part is part of an hour. "Suddenly the moment matters." (SWI)

■ 68 Full-page advertisement for fashionable eyeglasses marketed under the *Alain Mikli* label. (USA)

■ 69 "Beautiful Handplants" – full-page advertisement for a "Pop" model of the *Swatch*. (SWI)

■ 65-67 Aus einer Werbekampagne für die neue Farbzeituhr *Chrom Chron:* «Der Tag hat zwölf Farben. Je nach Licht vom Morgen bis zum Abend. Jede Farbe hat eine Stunde. Jeder Farbteil ein Stundenteil. Plötzlich zählt der Augenblick.» (SWI)

■ 68 «Verstecken Sie sich hinter etwas Sehenswertem» Anzeige für Brillen der Marke *Alain Mikli*. (USA)

■ 69 Ganzseitiges Inserat für ein Pop-Modell der *Swatch-Uhr.* (SWI)

■ 65-67 Exemples de la campagne de lancement de la nouvelle montre en couleurs Chrom Chron: «Le jour a 12 couleurs. Suivant la lumière, du matin jusqu'au soir. Chaque couleur a une heure. Chaque ton correspond a une division de l'heure. Et soudain, c'est l'instant qui compte.» (SWI)

■ 68 Cachez-vous derrière quelque chose qui vaut le coup d'être vu—annonce pour les lunettes Alain Mikli. (USA)

■ 69 Annonce pleine page pour le lancement d'un nouveau modèle de la montre *Swatch*. (SWI)

LA PASSIONE VIVE

FENDI UOMO
PARFUMS FENDI

FENDI ROMA

WE STOLE THEIR LAND, THEIR BUFFALO AND THEIR WOMEN. THEN WE WENT BACK FOR THEIR SHOES.

The Red Indians were an ungrateful lot. Far from thanking the whiteman for bringing them civilisation (guns, whisky, disease, that kind of thing), they spent years making very bad medicine.

Naturally, during the course of their disputes, the whiteman found it necessary to relieve the Red Indians of certain items.

Thousands of square miles of land, for instance, which they didn't seem to be using.

The odd buffalo, which provided some interesting culinary experiences for the folks heading West.

And of course the squaws, who were often invited along to soothe the fevered brows of conscience-stricken gun-runners and bounty hunters.

But perhaps the most lasting testament to this cultural exchange programme is the humble moccasin.

A shoe of quite ingenious construction. And remarkably comfortable to boot.

Even now, nearly two centuries after the first whiteman tried a pair on, they have yet to be bettered.

Which is why at Timberland, all of our loafers, boat shoes and walking shoes are based on the original Red Indian design.

How is this possible? Surely a shoemaker of our standing is capable of showing a clean pair of heels to a few pesky injuns?

Not really.

Although over the years, we have managed to make some modest improvements.

Rather than use any old buffalo hide, we always insist on premium full-grain leathers. And when we find a tannery that can supply them, we buy its entire output.

We then dye the leathers all the way through so you can't scuff the colour off and impregnate them with silicone oils to prevent the leather going dry.

It is at this point that we employ the wraparound construction of the moccasin to create the classic Timberland shoe.

Using a single piece of softened leather, our craftsmen mould and stretch the upper

around a specially-developed geometric last. This has the effect of breaking the shoes in before you've even set foot in them.

It also extends the life of the shoe for many, many moons.

Our hand sewn shoes also hark back to the days before the whiteman came.

No machines. No mass production. No deadlines.

Just a pair of nimble hands making shoes in the time-honoured way.

With just a little help from the twentieth century.

Like the high-strength nylon thread, double-knotted and pearl stitched to prevent it coming undone even if it's cut or in the unlikely event that it breaks.

The two coats of latex sealant, added to stop even tiny droplets of water sneaking in through the needle holes.

And the patented process which permanently bonds the uppers to the soles.

(If the Indians had only known how to cobble soles onto their moccasins, we probably wouldn't be in business today.)

As you would expect, the result of all our

labours is a shoe which comes with a heap big price tag.

For which we make absolutely no excuses.

After all, who else uses solid brass eyelets? Or self-oiling rawhide laces? Or glove leather linings?

Come to that, what other shoemaker shows such concern for your feet when big rains come?

For example, as well as utilising all our traditional methods, our new Ultra Light range uses new technology to keep your feet dry.

They're lined with Gore-Tex to make them completely waterproof while allowing your feet to breathe. (Gore-Tex has 9 billion holes per square inch. We didn't believe it either but it works, so now we believe it.)

The soles are made from an incredibly lightweight and highly resistant, dual-density polyurethane.

And, in an uncharacteristic concession to fashion, some models even sport tightly woven waxed cotton cloth.

A far cry from the Red Indian moccasin? We certainly hope not.

Because if we ever forget our origins, or change our old-fashioned way of making boots and shoes, one thing's for sure.

A lot of people are going to be on the warpath.

Timberland Shoes and Boots, 23 Pembridge Square, London W2 4DR. Telephone 01:727 2519.

Timberland ◉

CREATIVE DIRECTOR:
PAULETTE DUFAULT

PHOTOGRAPHER:
SHEILA METZNER

AGENCY:
ELIZABETH ARDEN NEW YORK

CLIENT:
FENDI ROMA

■ 70

ART DIRECTOR:
STEVE DUNN

PHOTOGRAPHER:
EDWARD S CURTIS

COPYWRITER:
TIM DELANEY

AGENCY:
LEAGAS DELANEY LIMITED

CLIENT:
TIMBERLAND

■ 71

ART DIRECTOR:
JOHN DOYLE

DESIGNER:
JOHN DOYLE

PHOTOGRAPHER:
ERIC MEOLA

COPYWRITER:
PAUL SILVERMAN

AGENCY:
MULLEN ADV.

CLIENT:
TIMBERLAND

►■ 72, 73

■ 70 "Passion lives" – full-page advertisement for a man's fragrance created by Fendi. (GER)

■ 71 From a campaign for *Timberland* shoes. This ad relates to the fact that the shoes advertised are based on the original Native American moccasin design. (GBR)

■ 72, 73 From an ad campaign for *Timberland* shoes. Whether a storm howls through a ravine, a blizzard blows in the tundra, or a commuter has to wait on a frozen avenue in Chicago, these shoes are right for the job. (USA)

■ 70 «Die Leidenschaft lebt» - ganzseitiges Inserat für ein Herrenparfum von Fendi. (GER)

■ 71 «Wir stahlen ihr Land, ihre Büffel, ihre Frauen. Danach wollten wir auch noch ihre Schuhe.» Aus einer Kampagne für *Timberland*-Schuhe. (GBR)

■ 72, 73 Aus einer Werbekampagne für *Timberland*-Schuhe in den USA: «Für alle, die im tiefsten Winter zur Arbeit müssen.» «Man begegnet ihnen auch in den Schluchten der Wall Street.» (USA)

■ 70 «La passion vit.» Annonce pleine page d'un parfum pour hommes de Fendi. (GER)

■ 71 «Nous leur avons volé leurs terres, leurs buffles, leurs femmes. Et après cela, nous voulons encore leurs chaussures.» Campagne pour les chaussures *Timberland*. (GBR)

■ 72, 73 D'une campagne de publicité pour les chaussures *Timberland*: «Pour tous ceux qui doivent aller au travail en plein hiver.» «On les rencontre aussi dans les canyons de Wall Street.» (USA)

For all those who commute to work in the dead of winter.

Many companies have testing labs in their factories, but Timberland's is too large to fit indoors. You see, we test our boots and clothing on a stretch of Alaskan tundra 1,049 miles long.

Once a year this blizzard-whipped trail becomes the arena for the Iditarod, a race in which huskies get hot meals every sixty miles and humans snack on dried moose meat.

Although the Iditarod has been called the Last Great Race on Earth, we view it as merely the world's longest commute. For the mushers are only performing, in panoramic scale, a ritual familiar to us all.

They are facing wind, water, earth and sky to get from one place to another in an appointed time. To do this, they steel themselves in mukluks, wolverine collars and Timberland Pac Boots.

This assures them polar bear warmth in arctic environments – but you can get equally good results on a frozen shore in Chicago or a bitter avenue in New York. Whether you're commuting to the office or the trading post, look to Timberland. For extreme comfort under all extremes.

Timberland

Boots, shoes, clothing, wind, water, earth and sky.

They're also found in the canyons of Wall Street.

What could a canyon dweller have in common with a condo dweller? As far as the weather goes, probably more than you think.

For who would say that a Northeast gale howling down the corridors of Wall Street is any easier to endure than a Southwest windstorm thundering through a ravine?

Since both of these explosions of wind, water, earth and sky play a role in shaping the American landscape, it is our view that both should play a role in the design of clothing for the American landscape.

Which is why you will see your canyon dweller hit the trail in Timberland Ultralight chukkas, mountain shorts, denim shirt and windproof field coat. While three thousand miles to the east at sea level, your condo dweller hits the streets in our dress casuals and weatherbucks – classic city footwear whose tough tap sole construction and waterproofing give them longevity unheard of in the annals of urban fashion. So if you think Timberland only means the rugged outdoors, think again. Because the rugged outdoors is right outside your window.

Timberland

Boots, shoes, clothing, wind, water, earth and sky.

ART DIRECTOR:
Silvio Galbucci
DESIGNER:
Isabella Keiser
COPYWRITER:
Daniel Matter
AGENCY:
Wirz Werbeberatung AG
CLIENT:
Robert Krause
GmbH & Co KG
■ 74-76

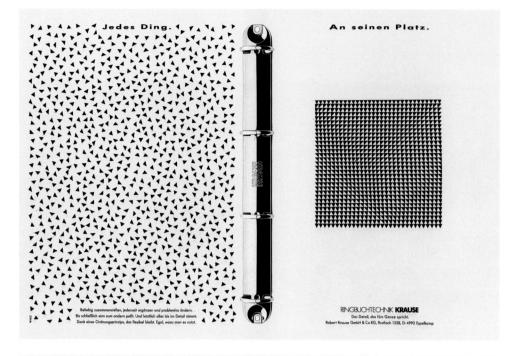

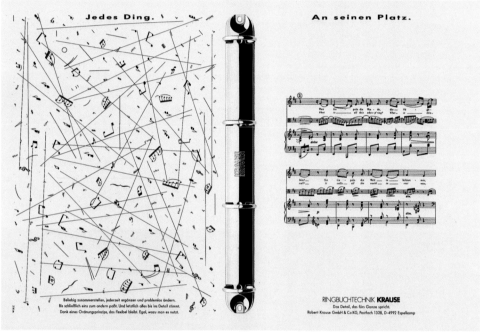

■ 74-76 Three of nine newspaper ads for spiral binders made by Krause. "Everything in its place." (GER)

■ 77 "What gives pleasure?" Ad from a campaign for WMF (Wurttemberg Metal Factory) that backs up the firm's new corporate identity. (GER)

■ 74-76 Drei von neun Zeitungsinseraten für Ringbücher von Krause. (GER)

■ 77 Anzeige aus einer Werbekampagne für WMF (Württembergische Metallwarenfabrik), die das neue Firmenerscheinungsbild unterstützt. (GER)

■ 74-76 «Chaque chose à sa place.» Trois des neuf annonces pour les classeurs à anneaux *Krause*. (GER)

■ 77 «Qu'est-ce qui fait plaisir? WMF!» Annonce pour WMF, un fabricant de métaux du Wurtemberg. Elle illustre le nouveau programme d'identité globale de la firme. (GER)

ART DIRECTOR:
DETLEF BLUME
PHOTOGRAPHER:
HANS HANSEN
COPYWRITER:
GERD FEHLING
AGENCY:
STRUWE & PARTNER
CLIENT:
WMF WÜRTTEMBERGISCHE METALLWARENFABRIK AG
■ 77

WAS MACHT FREUDE?
W M F !

Espressi, per favore? WMF macht es möglich – mit der neuen Espresso-Maschine der Edition King. Das kleine Wunder erfreut nicht nur den Liebhaber italienischen Gaumenkitzels, auch der Kenner italienischen Designs hat daran seine Freude. Denn wie so oft haben auch hier die verschiedenen Seiten des guten Geschmacks einen gemeinsamen Nenner: Matteo Thun, Prophet für Top-Design. Wenn Sie also demnächst Espresso trinken wollen, fragen Sie Ihren Fachhändler. Er serviert Ihnen das Rezept: In Cromargan®, für 4 Tassen DM 149,–* und für 6 Tassen DM 169,–*.
*Unverbindliche Preisempfehlung

Indestructible from tip to butt. Built like a rhino, this rod is tougher than Ugly Stik,™ meaner than Power Pole,™ and more affordable than both. The new Rhino rod. ZEBCO®

CREATIVE DIRECTOR:
JACK SUPPLE
ART DIRECTOR:
JUD SMITH
PHOTOGRAPHER:
JIM ARNDT
COPYWRITER:
KERRY CASEY
AGENCY:
CARMICHAEL LYNCH
CLIENT:
ZEBCO
■ 78

ART DIRECTOR:
MARK ASHLEY
PHOTOGRAPHER:
PARISH KOHANIM
COPYWRITER:
KEN LEWIS
AGENCY:
COLE HENDERSON DRAKE
CLIENT:
DUNLOP TENNIS
►■ 79, 80

■ 78 Ad for fishing rods made from rhino graphite – "The toughest of the tough and still affordable." (USA)

■ 79, 80 Tennis balls come over the net like live bullets. These advertisements are for new special tennis racquets made by Dunlop, offering "powerful wide-bodies with great control." (USA)

■ 78 «Von vorn bis hinten unverwüstlich» – Anzeige für Zebco-Angelruten. (USA)

■ 79, 80 Tennisbälle kommen wie scharfe Munition über das Netz, und man kann den Gegner in Grund und Boden spielen – so diese Anzeigen für neue spezielle Tennisschläger der Marke Dunlop. (USA)

■ 78 «Inusable d'un bout à l'autre»: annonce pour les cannes à pêche Zebco. (USA)

■ 79, 80 Des raquettes qui permettent de contrôler l'impact de la balle et d'envoyer l'adversaire au tapis - tels sont les atouts de cette nouvelle gamme de raquettes de la marque Dunlop. (USA)

THE BASIC IDEA BEHIND THE NEW MAX IMPACT WIDE-BODIES.

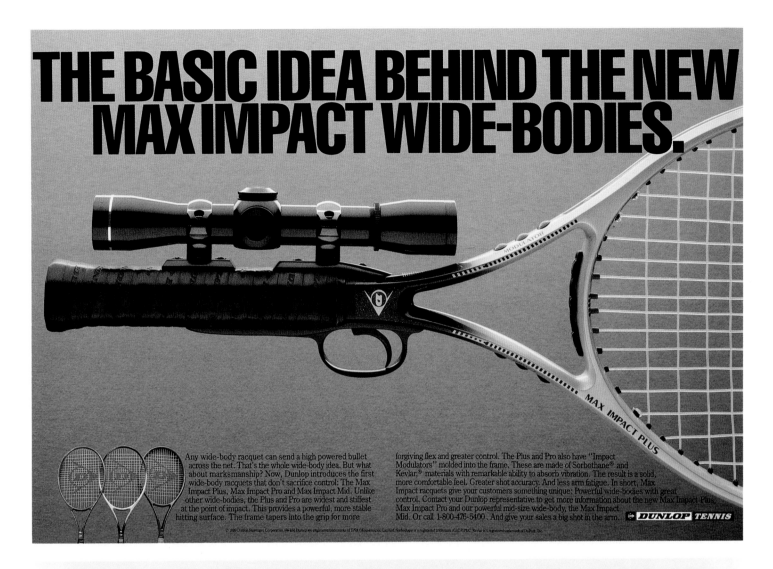

Any wide-body racquet can send a high powered bullet across the net. That's the whole wide-body idea. But what about marksmanship? Now, Dunlop introduces the first wide-body racquets that don't sacrifice control: The Max Impact Plus, Max Impact Pro and Max Impact Mid. Unlike other wide-bodies, the Plus and Pro are widest and stiffest at the point of impact. This provides a powerful, more stable hitting surface. The frame tapers into the grip for more

forgiving flex and greater control. The Plus and Pro also have "Impact Modulators" molded into the frame. These are made of Sorbothane® and Kevlar,® materials with remarkable ability to absorb vibration. The result is a solid, more comfortable feel. Greater shot accuracy. And less arm fatigue. In short, Max Impact racquets give your customers something unique: Powerful wide-bodies with great control. Contact your Dunlop representative to get more information about the new Max Impact Plus, Max Impact Pro and our powerful mid-size wide-body, the Max Impact Mid. Or call 1-800-476-5400. And give your sales a big shot in the arm. **DUNLOP TENNIS**

OUR NEW MAX IMPACT RACQUETS ALSO GIVE YOU THE POWER TO BURY YOUR OPPONENTS.

Dunlop just escalated the arms race. With three new graphite wide-bodies: the Max Impact Plus, Max Impact Pro and Max Impact Mid. The first racquets that give you wide-body power without sacrificing control.

Unlike other wide-bodies, the Plus and Pro are widest and stiffest at the point of impact for power and stability. The frame tapers into the grip for more forgiving flex and greater control. The Plus and Pro also feature an "Impact Modulator" system made of Kevlar® and Sorbothane®. Two materials with remarkable ability to absorb vibration. The result is a solid, more comfortable feel. Less arm fatigue. And greater shot accuracy.

Get the new Max Impact Plus, Max Impact Pro or our powerful mid-size wide-body, the Max Impact Mid. And beat your opponents into the ground.

DUNLOP TENNIS

■ 81-83 "Johnny Cash guitar, Lionel Hampton vibraphone, Chuck Mangione horn" – they all find the perfect version of their instrument in the new keyboard by Technics, according to these ads. (USA)

■ 84 Double-spread advertisement for a new synthesizer for guitars which promises to make the best out of any tone. (USA)

■ 85 On three consecutive half-page spreads this ad for a wireless guitar unit demonstrates that the musician need not return to the effect pedal but can control it from a considerable distance. (USA)

■ 81-83 »Johnny Cash, Gitarre, Lionel Hampton, Vibraphon, Chuck Mangione, Horn« – sie alle finden gemäss diesen Inseraten die perfekte Version ihres Instrumentes im neuen Keyboard von Technics. (USA)

■ 84 Doppelseitiges Inserat für einen neuen Synthesizer für Gitarren: »Er wird etwas aus einer Note machen, das Sie sich nie träumen liessen.« (USA)

■ 85 Auf drei aufeinanderfolgenden Seiten erschienene, dreiteilige Anzeige für ein drahtloses Fusspedal für Gitarren, das der Spieler problemlos und bei voller Bewegungsfreiheit kontrollieren kann. (USA)

■ 81-83 »Johnny Cash à la guitare, Lionel Hampton au vibraphone, Chuck Mangione au cor«: selon ces annonces, vous trouverez l'instrument approprié grâce aux nouvelles possibilités du synthétiseur de Technics. (USA)

■ 84 Annonce double page pour un nouveau synthétiseur de guitare. «Il fera faire à une seule note des choses dont vous n'avez aucune idée.» (USA)

■ 85 Pour la promotion d'un nouveau modèle de pédale pour la guitare; l'absence de câble permet de contrôler le son, tout en conservant une totale liberté de mouvement. Les trois pages de cette annonce se déplient. (USA)

AGENCY:
LEVINE, HUNTLEY SCHMIDT
CLIENT:
TECHNICS
■ 81-83

It'll make a note do things it never dreamed of.

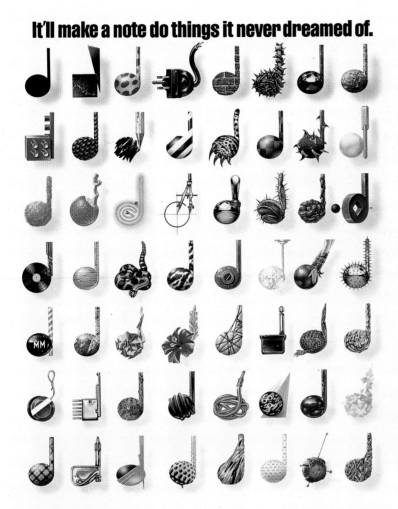

This is probably going to sound like one of those advertisements encouraging people to discover their true potential. In a sense, it is.

Because with the new Roland GS-6 Digital Guitar Sound System, you suddenly have the ability to do things with sounds you couldn't have otherwise. And the reason you can do so is simply this: Since the GS-6 is a sophisticated guitar pre-amp, you're able to simulate an incredible array of amplifier sounds.

And since its signal processing is based on Pro-Audio DSP technology, you're also able to create an incredible array of fresh new sounds.

You can choose from eight reverb modes, two of which are actually digital simulations of "spring" reverbs. (Remember that wonderful sound the old Fender Twin amp made that nothing else could? Now something else can.)

You can choose from four different chorus modes with a feedback control for creating flanging effects, as well as panning delay with up to 999 milliseconds of delay.

You can also choose from eight different distortion modes, including Special 1 and Special 2 settings. And even better, you can tailor those distortion modes simply by using its programmable pre drive and post drive controls, as well as its three-bank EQ with mid-range frequency.

Of course, while digital processing gives you a far greater range of sounds, it also

If you're considering the GS-6, here's something else to consider: the FC-100 MK II Foot Controller.

gives you far greater flexibility and control. When you want sounds that are big and broad and seem to sustain themselves forever, that's exactly what you'll get. And when you want sounds that are more subtle, the Roland GS-6 will deliver them without degrading sound quality.

Speaking of which, the sound quality in a GS-6 is nothing short of remarkable. Among other things, we've equipped it with both digital noise suppression as well as hum cancellation. That way, you have the ability to create ear-splitting distortion sounds while still maintaining studio-quality noise specifications.

Which brings us to our final point. Hopefully, you've noticed that we call the GS-6 a "Sound System." Unlike modular set-ups, ours is fully integrated with all of the processing contained in one rack-mounted unit.

And because it's programmable, you can store up to 64 patches in the memory and then call up those patches simply by pushing a button. All of which makes the new Roland GS-6 ideal for both studio and live applications.

As we see it, in order to create truly amazing guitar sounds you really need two things: the equipment and the imagination. The first one we've provided. The second one is up to you.

Roland®

RolandCorp US, 7200 Dominion Circle, Los Angeles, CA 90040-3647
213 685-5141

The new WS-100 Wireless System from BOSS.

Every Revolution Starts In The Streets.

Introducing the world's first fully automatic Quattro® drive. The new Audi V8. For a closer look, call 1-800-FOR-AUDI.

The Alternate Route.

ART DIRECTOR:
Gary Alfredson

DESIGNER:
Gary Alfredson

PHOTOGRAPHER:
Rick Rusing

COPYWRITER:
Tom Scharre

AGENCY:
DDB Needham

CLIENT:
Audi of America, Inc.

■ 86

■ 86 From an ad campaign for Audi of America introducing the new Audi V8. (USA)

■ 87 Ad for Volkswagen – the footsteps in the snow underscore the text, "...Getting you to where you're going. ...You, and whom ever you happen to be giving a lift to." (GBR)

■ 88 Showing all the "precious" things you'll find in the *Citroën 2CV*. From an advertising campaign. GBR)

■ 86 «Jede Revolution beginnt auf der Strasse.» Aus einer Werbekampagne für *Audi* «Quattro». (USA)

■ 87 «Man muss nicht einen *Volkswagen* besitzen, um sich auf ihn zu verlassen.» Die Fussspuren in dieser Anzeige sprechen Bände. (GBR)

■ 88 «Was schenken Sie ihr zu Weihnachten?» Aus einer Werbekampagne für den *Citroën 2CV.* (GBR)

■ 86 «Chaque révolution commence dans la rue.» Annonce d'une campagne de publicité pour la *Audi* «Quattro». (USA)

■ 87 «Il n'est pas nécessaire de posséder une *Volkswagen* pour lui faire confiance.» Les traces de pas dans la neige en disent long... (GBR)

■ 88 «Qu'allez-vous lui offrir pour Noël?» Annonce tirée d'une campagne pour la *2CV Citroën.* (GBR)

ART DIRECTOR:
MIKE ORR
PHOTOGRAPHER:
JACK BANKHEAD
COPYWRITER:
DAVID DENTON
AGENCY:
DDB NEEDHAM WORLDWIDE
CLIENT:
VAG (UK) LIMITED
■ 87

ART DIRECTOR:
PAUL BRIGINSHAW
ILLUSTRATOR:
MIKE BROWNFIELD
COPYWRITER:
MALCOLM DUFFY
AGENCY:
COLMAN RSCG & PARTNERS
CLIENT:
CITROËN (UK) LTD.
■ 88

You don't have to own a Volkswagen to rely on a Volkswagen.

WHAT ARE YOU BUYING HER FOR CHRISTMAS?

Some precious metal?

Some designer furniture?

A vanity mirror, perhaps?

Dare we suggest, some rubber wear?

Why not buy her the whole lot?

NOW WITH 0% FINANCE. THE CITROËN 2CV FROM £3,695.
(Including Battery.)

ART DIRECTOR:
DAVID PAGE
PHOTOGRAPHER:
DENNIS MANARCHY
AGENCY:
CARMICHAEL-LYNCH INC.
CLIENT:
HARLEY-DAVIDSON INC.
■ 89-92

It Is Not A Rational Decision.

We grow up, we leave home, and suddenly we're held accountable for every single decision we make. We're constantly reminded that we're expected to always do "The Right Thing." So, in the pursuit of not making a mistake, we base most of our decisions on cold, calculated rationale.

On the other hand, some decisions don't have to be made. They make themselves. Like the decision to own a Harley-Davidson. A lot of people would be hard pressed to give you a rational argument for owning a Harley. The reasons go beyond logic. It just feels right. You either get it, or you don't.

The Heritage Softail Classic is a perfect example. It's forced more than a few people to quit asking "Why?" and start saying "Why not?" Maybe it's the style. It is pure American emotion, expressed in two-tone paint, fringed leather bags, fishtail mufflers, and brilliant chrome. Maybe it's the relaxed beat of its V² Evolution engine. It gets right inside you.

Once you come to the decision that you can't do without a Harley, you'll probably have to answer a few questions from those who just don't get it. But you don't explain a motorcycle like the Heritage Softail Classic. If you were able to, it wouldn't be as good. No, it's not a rational decision. Which is exactly why it makes perfect sense.

Things Are Different On A Harley

When Was The Last Time You Felt This Strongly About Anything?

Wake up in the morning, and life picks up where it left off. You do what has to be done. Use what it takes to get there. And what once seemed exciting has now become part of the numbing routine. It all begins to feel the same.

Except when you've got a Harley-Davidson. Something strikes a nerve. The heartfelt thunder rises up, refusing to become part of the background. Suddenly, things are different. Clearer. More real. As they should have been all along.

The feeling is personal. It affects everyone a little differently. For some, owning a Harley® is a statement of individuality. For others, owning one means being a part of a home-grown legacy that was born in a tiny Milwaukee shed in 1903. Regardless of the reason, more people are getting to know the feeling. Harley-Davidson has reemerged as the number one selling brand of super heavyweight motorcycles in the U.S.A.

To the uninitiated, a Harley-Davidson motorcycle is often associated with a certain look, a certain sound. Anyone who owns one will tell you it's much more than that. Riding a Harley changes you from within.

The effect is permanent. Maybe it's time you started feeling this strongly.

Things Are Different On A Harley

Count Your Blessing.

You're hauling precious cargo. One very important shipment. You're picking up a Harley, your Harley, and you spare no effort. There's no such thing as going too far or being too careful, and there's no hiding your pride. It's held up for all the world to see. This is your day. All the scrimping, saving, hoping, and sweating has paid off. What was once a dream is now, finally, real steel. At long last, it's yours. Fortune has smiled.

Owning a Harley-Davidson makes things different. It's a feeling most people are unable to describe, and not being able to put a finger on it only adds to the experience. From your first ride, things are never the same again. A Harley can fill a hole in your life you never knew you had. It assumes its own place. It goes on a pedestal.

You are changed. You've become part of something bigger. Harley-Davidson is not just a motorcycle. It's 85 years of heritage. It's diesel mechanics rubbing elbows with doctors. It's 72-year-old guys coming up and talking to you about your bike. Or ever. It's being just a little bit of style next year. Or ever. It's being just a little bit fanatical, and feeling good about it.

You can't help but be affected. Let people talk. You've worked hard for it, and you deserve it. You've got your Harley. The rest is details.

Things Are Different On A Harley

■ 89-92 From a series of ads for *Harley Davidson*. The slogan common to each is, "Things are different on an Harley", and this is underscored by the texts which point out all the differences on this well-known motorcycle. (USA)

■ 89-92 Aus einer Anzeigenserie für Harley Davidson: «Eine rationale Entscheidung ist es nicht», «Wie lange ist es her, dass Ihnen eine Sache so wichtig war?», «Sie sind ein Glückskind», «Das Leben sollte so einfach sein». (USA)

■ 89-92 D'une série d'annonces pour Harley Davidson: «Ce n'est pas une décision rationnelle», «Il y a combien de temps qu'une chose a eu autant d'importance pour vous?», «La vie devrait être aussi simple que cela». (USA)

Life Should Be So Simple.

There was a time in nearly everyone's life when the most important things were the essentials—food, shelter and clothing. Things a person can't do without. For more than a few motorcycle riders, the list was one item longer. A Harley-Davidson' was an absolute necessity.
Everyone had all kinds of reasons for why their Harley'

was so important. The sound. The made-in-Milwaukee style. And of course, the feeling of owning the road. Today, one Harley in particular brings it all together. The Heritage Softail' Classic.
It evokes a time when all a rider needed was a Hydra Glide™ and a road. The styling is pure Harley

classic, with two-tone paint, leather bags, and brilliant chrome. The V² Evolution' engine is a treat for the eyes. And the ears. The sound is honest, powerful, and about as straightforward as it gets.
There might be some point in your life when you just can't do without a Harley-Davidson. Don't be surprised.

It may come soon, spurred on by the thought of a roof over your head, a full 'fridge, and the Heritage Softail Classic.
It should be so simple.

Things Are Different On A Harley

We support the AMA and recommend you wear a helmet and protective gear while riding.

ART DIRECTOR:
LINDA BERG
PHOTOGRAPHER:
JIM BRANDENBURG 93
ERIC MEOLA 94
COPYWRITER:
ANN HAYDEN
AGENCY:
RUMRILL-HOYT, INC.
CLIENT:
EASTMAN KODAK COMPANY
■ 93, 94

■ 93, 94 In view of growing competition, Kodak had the idea of putting famous photographers in the limelight with these "best shots in the world" – which were all taken with *Kodachrome* film. (USA)

■ 93, 94 Angesichts der wachsenden Konkurrenz wollte Kodak mit diesen Aufnahmen berühmter Photographen hervorheben, dass die besten Photos der Welt mit ihrem *Kodachrome*-Film gemacht werden. (USA)

■ 93, 94 Face à une concurrence toujours plus grande, Kodak a voulu, au moyen de ces images de photographes célèbres, démontrer que les meilleures photos du monde ont été prises avec des pellicules *Kodachrome*. (USA)

Jim Brandenburg

He could have used something else.
He chose Kodachrome professional film.

Eric Meola

He could have used something else.
He chose Kodachrome professional film.

ART DIRECTOR:
STEPHEN HALL
PHOTOGRAPHER:
GREGORY HEISLER 95
JOHN RUNNING 96
COPYWRITER:
KENNETH JACOBS
AGENCY:
RUMRILL-HOYT, INC.
CLIENT:
EASTMAN KODAK COMPANY
■ 95, 96

■ 95, 96 From a black-and-white campaign with shots by prominent photographers, to promote Kodak black-and-white film material. (USA)

■ 95, 96 Aus einer Schwarzweiss-Kampagne mit Aufnahmen berühmter Photographen für Kodaks Schwarzweiss-Filmmaterial. (USA)

■ 95, 96 Des photographes de renommée internationale ont réalisé les photos de cette campagne visant à promouvoir le matériel photographique en noir et blanc de Kodak. (USA)

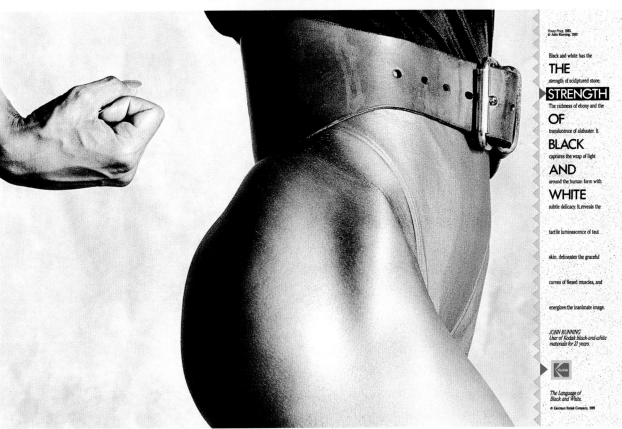

ART DIRECTOR:
LEE ERNST
DESIGNER:
LEE ERNST
PHOTOGRAPHER:
MIKE REGNIER
COPYWRITER:
DAVID MARKS/JOHN KRUEGER
AGENCY:
MULLER + COMPANY
CLIENT:
DES MOINES REGISTER
■ 100-103

■ 97-99 "Advertisements make newspapers more analytical, more factual, more critical" – examples from an advertising campaign in newspapers for newspaper-ad agents, Publicitas. (SWI)

■ 100-103 Examples taken from a series of small newspaper advertisements designed to sell space to non-commercial advertisers in the Des Moines Register Classifieds. Small ads that run in this paper, so the text says, will sell anything for you. (USA)

■ 104 "This year we'll eliminate Ireland" – from a campaign for the WWF calling for support for the rescue of the rain forests. Every year an area of forest the size of a whole country is destroyed. (ITA)

■ 97-99 Aus einer Anzeigenkampagne der Werbegesellschaft Publicitas in Zeitungen. Hier wird auf die Service-Leistungen des Unternehmens und die Bedeutung von Inseraten hingewiesen. (SWI)

■ 100-103 Aus einer Serie von kleinformatigen Zeitungsanzeigen, in denen die Vorzüge klassifizierter Annoncen dargelegt werden: «Sagen Sie Ihrem (Staub)sauger, Ihrem Schatz (gemeint sind ausgediente Musikinstrumente), Ihrer Ziege Lebewohl.» (USA)

■ 104 Dieses Jahr eliminieren wir Irland« – aus einer Kampagne für den WWF, in der um Unterstützung für die Rettung des Regenwaldes gebeten wird, von dem jedes Jahr ein Stück in der Grösse einer Nation vernichtet wird. (ITA)

■ 97-99 Annonces réalisées pour une campagne de Publicitas parue dans les journaux. L'accent est mis sur le rôle des annonces, qui permettent une vision plus analytique, plus critique, plus objective de l'information. (SWI)

■ 100-103 Dans cette série d'annonces de petit format publiées dans les journaux, on présente les avantages d'une bonne classification des annonces: «Dites adieu à votre aspirateur, à votre bien-aimé (ici, il s'agit d'un instrument de musique usagé), à votre chèvre». (USA)

■ 104 Le texte de cette annonce du WWF rappelle que chaque année, une surface de forêt tropicale grande comme un pays (ici, l'Irlande) disparaît. Le WWF cherche à rassembler des fonds pour tenter d'éviter ce désastre. (ITA)

ART DIRECTOR:
MARTIN SPILLMANN
DESIGNER:
JÖRG BIRKER
PHOTOGRAPHER:
CHRISTIAN KÜENZI
COPYWRITER:
ANDRÉ BENKER
AGENCY:
ADVICO YOUNG & RUBICAM
CLIENT:
PUBLICITAS SA
◀■ 97-99

ART DIRECTOR:
PIETRO CORDELLI
ILLUSTRATOR:
PIETRO CORDELLI
COPYWRITER:
ROBERTO PANELLI
AGENCY:
CONQUEST EUROPE
CLIENT:
WWF ITALIA
■ 104

The one that coats
is the only one you need.

If you plan to drink on New Year's Eve, Hertz would like to recommend another rent-a-car.

You don't just rent a car.
You rent a company.™

ART DIRECTOR:
JEFF GREGG
PHOTOGRAPHER:
BRUCE GREGG
COPYWRITER:
BOB WELKE
AGENCY:
LEO BURNETT CO.
CLIENT:
PROCTER & GAMBLE
■ 105

CREATIVE DIRECTOR:
SAM SCALI
ART DIRECTOR:
STEVE MONTGOMERY
PHOTOGRAPHER:
TERRY NIEFIELD
COPYWRITER:
EARL CARTER
AGENCY:
SCALI, McCABE, SLOVES
CLIENT:
HERTZ RENT-A-CAR
■ 106

■ 105 Advertising for Pepto-Bismol, to quiet your stomach indigestion after you've seen your Income tax bill. (USA)

■ 106 Full-page newspaper advertisement for Hertz-Rent-a-Car presenting itself as a responsible company by suggesting a taxi as the best choice on certain occasions. (USA)

■ 107 Newspaper ad for a recreational resort in the mountains. The text relates to the various antiques that are to be found in the region (Vermont). (USA)

■ 105 Werbung für ein Beruhigungsmittel - das sei alles, was man für die Steuererklärung braucht. (USA)

■ 106 «Wenn Sie vorhaben, Silvester zu trinken, empfiehlt Hertz Ihnen, zu einem anderen Autovermieter zu gehen.» Hertz stellt sich als seriöse Firma dar. (USA)

■ 107 Zeitungsinserat für einen Erholungsort in den Bergen. Hier wird speziell von den Antiquitäten gesprochen, die sich in der Gegend (Vermont) finden lassen. (USA)

■ 105 Publicité pour un sédatif, «la seule chose dont vous ayez besoin pour remplir votre déclaration d'impôts.» (USA)

■ 106 «Si vous comptez boire au Nouvel An, Hertz vous recommandera une autre location de voitures.» Cette annonce souligne le sérieux de cette compagnie. (USA)

■ 107 Annonce de journal pour la promotion d'un lieu de villégiature situé dans les montagnes du Vermont. On y trouve notamment des antiquités intéressantes. (USA)

ART DIRECTOR:
Jamie Mambro
DESIGNER:
Karen Marchilonis
PHOTOGRAPHER:
Phil Porcella
COPYWRITER:
Peter Seronick
AGENCY:
Rossin Greenberg Sornick & Hill
CLIENT:
Ascutney Mountain Resort
■ 107

"WE JUST GOT BACK FROM A DAY OF ANTIQUING. VERMONT IS THE PERFECT PLACE FOR ANTIQUES. THEY FEEL LIKE THEY BELONG HERE. VERMONTERS MUST HARVEST A NEW CROP EVERY MONTH. VERMONT ITSELF IS LIKE A WELL-PRESERVED, WELL-POLISHED ANTIQUE. IT SHOULDN'T BE CALLED 'THE GREEN MOUNTAIN STATE'. I'D CALL IT THE 'MOUNTAINS OF ANTIQUES STATE'. EVERYWHERE YOU TURN, DOWN EVERY DIRT ROAD, YOU'LL SEE A SIGN THAT SAYS ANTIQUES FOR SALE. WE MUST HAVE GONE TO 15 PLACES TODAY. EACH ONE WAS MORE INTERESTING THAN THE LAST. IT'S AMAZING. WALKING INTO THESE SHOPS IS LIKE WALKING BACK IN TIME. EACH ANTIQUE LETS YOUR IMAGINATION WANDER. YOU BEGIN TO IMAGINE HOW MANY PEOPLE HAVE OWNED SOMETHING. HOW MANY DIFFERENT HOMES A PIECE OF FURNITURE HAS LIVED IN. HOW MANY DIFFERENT MEALS HAVE BEEN SERVED OFF AN OLD PLATE. AND LET ME TELL YOU, DON'T THINK FOR A MINUTE THE ANTIQUE DEALERS UP HERE JUST FELL OFF THE TURNIP TRUCK. SURE THEY'LL NEGOTIATE. AND YOU CAN HAGGLE WITH THEM TOO. BUT IF YOU THINK YOU'RE GOING TO BUY A PIECE THAT'S WORTH $5,000 IN THE CITY FOR $5 UP HERE, FORGET IT. WE ALSO DISCOVERED THE FINISHING TOUCH TO A DAY OF RUMMAGING THROUGH SHOP AFTER SHOP OF OLD STUFF, WAS TO TAKE OUR CIRCA 1940 BODIES FOR A NICE SWIM IN THE POOL." FRESH AIR. WILD FLOWERS. MOUNTAIN WATER. SUMMER BREEZES. THAT'S VERMONT. AND VERMONT INSPIRED THE EXPRESSION 'THE GREAT OUTDOORS'. ASCUTNEY MOUNTAIN RESORT IN BROWNSVILLE, VERMONT WILL INSPIRE YOU. ASCUTNEY MOUNTAIN RESORT IS THE PERFECT BLEND OF OLD VERMONT AND NEW AMENITIES. THERE'S STILL TIME TO TAKE ADVANTAGE OF OUR PLAY IN VERMONT PACKAGES. PRICES INCLUDE LODGING, TAXES AND GRATUITIES, AND USE OF OUR SPORTS FACILITY, TENNIS, RACQUETBALL, INDOOR AND OUTDOOR POOLS, AEROBICS, WEIGHTROOM, SAUNA, WHIRLPOOL, TANNING BED AND MORE. THERE ARE ALSO FUN RUNS, BIKE TOURS, FISHING (EQUIPMENT NOT INCLUDED), CANOEING, MOVIES, KITE MAKING, SHOPPING, ANTIQUING, AND HISTORICAL TOURS. DAY-CARE OR DAY CAMP FOR CHILDREN 5–10 IS INCLUDED. FOR WEEKEND PACKAGES, TWO NIGHTS ARE $103 PER PERSON, DOUBLE OCCUPANCY. FOR WEEK LONG PACKAGES (7 NIGHTS), A TWO BEDROOM SUITE THAT SLEEPS 4 IS $236 PER PERSON. LIMITED ROOMS AVAILABLE. SOME RESTRICTIONS APPLY. GOLF AND HORSEBACK RIDING REQUIRE SURCHARGE. FOR MORE INFORMATION. FOR RESERVATIONS. FOR THE PEACE OF VERMONT YOU'VE BEEN LOOKING FOR. CALL TOLL-FREE 800-243-0011.

ASCUTNEY MOUNTAIN—A FAMILY RESORT AND COMMUNITY.

Wählen Sie wenigstens die richtige Agentur.   ⊗ CAA

CREATIVE DIRECTOR:
Joe Ofenböck
ART DIRECTOR:
Toni Waltinger
PHOTOGRAPHER:
Götz Schrage
COPYWRITER:
Peter Hulan
AGENCY:
CAA
CLIENT:
CAA
■ 108

ART DIRECTOR:
Charles S. Anderson/
Dan Olson
DESIGNER:
Charles S. Anderson/
Dan Olson
ILLUSTRATOR:
Charles S. Anderson/
Dan Olson/Randy Dahlk
COPYWRITER:
Charles S. Anderson
AGENCY:
Charles S. Anderson Design
CLIENT:
French Paper Company
■ 109

■ 108 From a campaign for the CAA ad agency: "At least choose the right agency" - Waldheim is depicted. (AUT)

■ 109 Ad in the style of the 40's for a new recycled paper made by the French Paper Company. (USA)

■ 110 Trade journal advertisement for an electricity plant showing computer information managers some of the hazards that poor power quality might wreak. (USA)

■ 111 From a campaign for Aerolineas Argentinas. The translation: "It does not take much to remember, to be back there, where they played the Tango." (GER)

■ 108 Aus einer Eigenwerbungskampagne der Werbeagentur CAA aus Österreich. (AUT)

■ 109 Inserat im Stil der 40er Jahre für ein neues Umweltpapier der French Paper Company. (USA)

■ 110 «Jeden Moment könnte ein Stromausfall diese Anzeige vernichten» – Fachzeitschrifteninserat für ein Elektrizitätswerk. (USA)

■ 111 Anzeige aus einer Kampagne für Aerolineas Argentinas. Sie sagt, dass man nicht viel braucht, um sich zu erinnern, um wieder dort zu sein. (GER)

■ 108 «Choisissez au moins la bonne agence.» Autopromotion de l'agence de publicité autrichienne CAA. (AUT)

■ 109 Cette annonce dans le style des années 40 a été conçue pour un nouveau fabricant de papier recyclé. (USA)

■ 110 «A tout moment, une panne de courant pourrait détruire cette pub»: annonce pour une usine électrique parue dans une revue professionnelle. (USA)

■ 111 Annonce pour une campagne de la compagnie aérienne Aerolineas Argentinas. Il suffit d'écouter undisque de tango pour se rappeler ce pays. (GER)

ART DIRECTOR:
TIM PARKER
DESIGNER:
TIM PARKER/JOEL NENDEL
PHOTOGRAPHER:
MICHAEL JONES
COPYWRITER:
ERIC GRUNBAUM
AGENCY:
BORDERS PERRIN & NORRANDER
CLIENT:
PORTLAND GENERAL ELECTRIC
■ 110

ART DIRECTOR:
KONRAD WENZEL
PHOTOGRAPHER:
BERND MAYER
COPYWRTIER:
MANFRED MARTIN
AGENCY:
TBWA FRANKFURT
CLIENT:
AEROLINEAS ARGENTINAS
■ 111

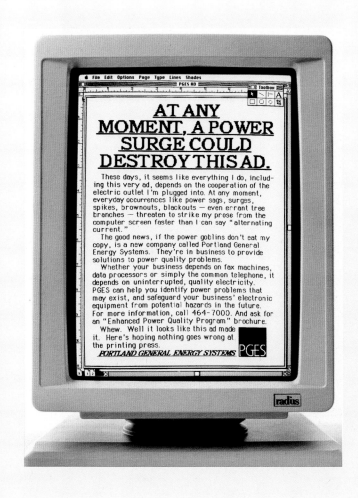

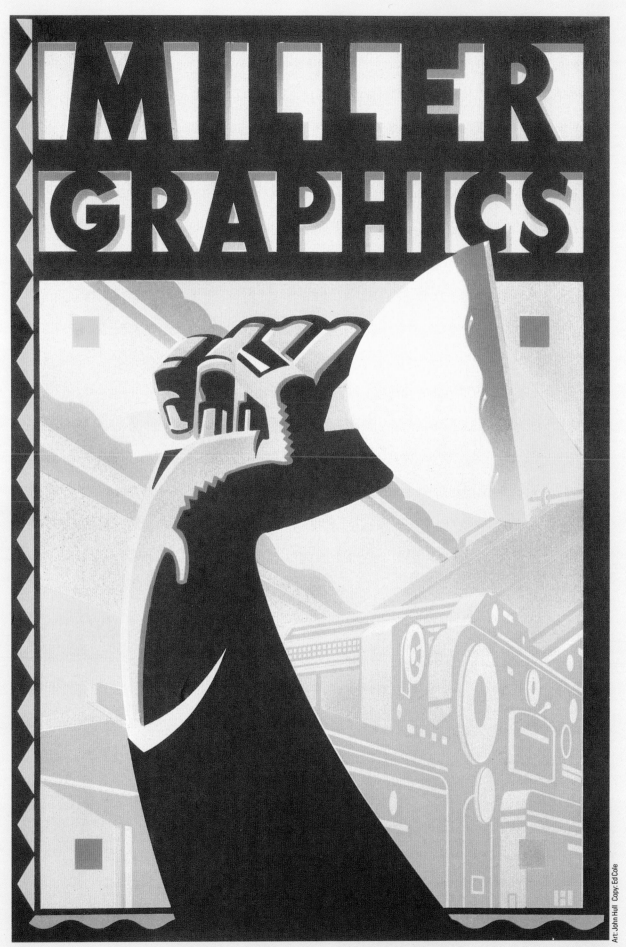

Art: John Hull Copy: Ed Cole

COMMUNICATION ARTS

COMMUNICATION ARTS

ART DIRECTOR:
DAVID WILLARDSON
DESIGNER:
DAVID WILLARDSON/JOHN HULL
ILLUSTRATOR:
JOHN HULL
COPYWRITER:
ED COLE
AGENCY:
WILLARDSON ASSOCIATES
CLIENT:
MILLER GRAPHICS, INC
◀■ 112

COMMUNICATION ARTS

ART DIRECTOR:
RICH SILVERSTEIN
DESIGNER:
RICH SILVERSTEIN
PHOTOGRAPHER:
MARC HAUSER
COPYWRITER:
DAVID FOWLER
AGENCY:
GOODBY, BERLIN & SILVERSTEIN
CLIENT:
COMMUNICATION ARTS
■ 113-115

■ 112 Advertisement for Miller Graphics Inc. who also offer printing services. (USA)

■ 113-115 From an advertising campaign appearing in trade journals on behalf of *Communication Arts* magazine showing prominent people from the American design and advertising scene: Lee Clow of Chiat Day, Paula Scher of Koppel & Scher and Jayme Odgers. (USA)

■ 112 «Der rechte Arm des Designers» – Werbung für eine Druckerei. (USA)

■ 113-115 Aus einer Inseratenkampagne in Fachzeitschriften für die Zeitschrift *Communication Arts* mit bekannten Leuten aus der amerikanischen Design- und Werbeszene: Lee Clow von Chiat Day, Paula Scher von Koppel & Scher und Jayme Odgers. (USA)

■ 112 «Le bras droit du designer» – Publicité pour une imprimerie. (USA)

■ 113-115 Cette campagne d'annonces pour le magazine *Communication Arts* est parue dans des revues spécialisées. On y présente des personnalités célèbres du monde du design et de la publicité en Amérique: Lee Clow de Chiat Day, Paula Scher de Koppel & Scher et Jayme Odgers. (USA)

ART DIRECTOR:
LEE ERNST
DESIGNER:
LEE ERNST
COPYWRITER:
JOHN KRUEGER/DAVID MARKS
AGENCY:
MULLER + COMPANY
CLIENT:
DIX & ASSOCIATES
■ 116, 117

ART DIRECTOR:
STEVE STONE
DESIGNER:
STEVE STONE
PHOTOGRAPHER:
JAY MAISEL/DAN ESCOBAR/
PETER HENDRIE
COPYWRITER:
DAVID FOWLER
AGENCY:
GOODBY, BERLIN & SILVERSTEIN
CLIENT:
ROYAL VIKING LINE
►■ 118-120

WHAT DO YOU CALL A PLACE IN THE CARIBBEAN
THAT COMES WITH 33 CHEFS, SCANDINAVIAN STEWARDESSES,
17,000 BOTTLES OF WINE AND A BUTLER?

FROM OCTOBER UNTIL APRIL, THE ROYAL VIKING STAR OFFERS FIVE TO ELEVEN-DAY CRUISES TO BARBADOS, WITH CALLS AT ST. LUCIA, MARTINIQUE AND OTHER CARIBBEAN OASES.

PARADISE.

ANNOUNCING FIVE TO ELEVEN-DAY VACATIONS
TO THE ULTIMATE DESTINATION.

BEGINNING IN OCTOBER, FIVE TO ELEVEN-DAY CRUISES TO BARBADOS, WITH CALLS THROUGHOUT THE SOUTHERN CARIBBEAN, ABOARD THE ROYAL VIKING STAR.

HEAVEN.

WHAT MAKES THE ONE ON THE LEFT
BETTER THAN THE ONE ON THE RIGHT?

FROM OCTOBER UNTIL APRIL, THE ROYAL VIKING STAR WILL OFFER FIVE TO ELEVEN-DAY CRUISES TO BARBADOS, WITH CALLS THROUGHOUT THE SUNSWEPT SOUTHERN CARIBBEAN.

THIS.

COULD YOU TURN THE OTHER CHEEK?

COOL CUSTOMER, are you? Okay, let's see how far you can get before you blow your stack.

You are walking down a street. Some youths start jeering at you: "'Ello, 'ello, 'ello." Smile. You've heard it all before, every name a copper can be called: rozzer, old bill, pig, fuzz, peeler, flatfoot, the filth. And some less complimentary. Shrug it off.

You're out in the patrol car when you see a car without lights weaving through the traffic. You flash your headlights at him to stop. Instead, he accelerates away.

Siren on. Ahead your target, still without lights, narrowly misses a woman on a pedestrian crossing and then goes the wrong way round a roundabout, while a youth leaning out of the passenger window showers you with empty beer cans and two-finger salutes.

"You can't go on the attack, whatever the provocation."

The car skids round another corner and slides into a brick wall, but the youths inside are out and running. You chase, abandoning your car with its engine still on and door left wide open. As you grab the driver, he mouths obscenities at you.

Still in control of your temper? Okay, try this.

A demonstration is turning into a riot. You're bussed in, nervous and not sure what to expect. It's frightening. The crowd, in ugly mood, surges against the frail police line.

Suddenly a lone voice calls your number. "EF203, EF203." The others take it up. "EF203, EF203." They're all staring at you, trying to psyche you out. Why you?

It gets worse. Bottles are down and burst in showers of flame. Stones and half bricks drop out of the air and threaten to brain you. You cannot leave the line.

At last the crowd starts drifting away. As the tension ebbs, you see a man step forward and deliberately stub out his cigarette on the flank of a police horse.

This all sounds a bit melodramatic, but we've made none of it up. Each of the details we've described really happened.

How would you have reacted?

Strangely, people often find that in a real emergency they stay icily calm. But stress builds up in the body like static

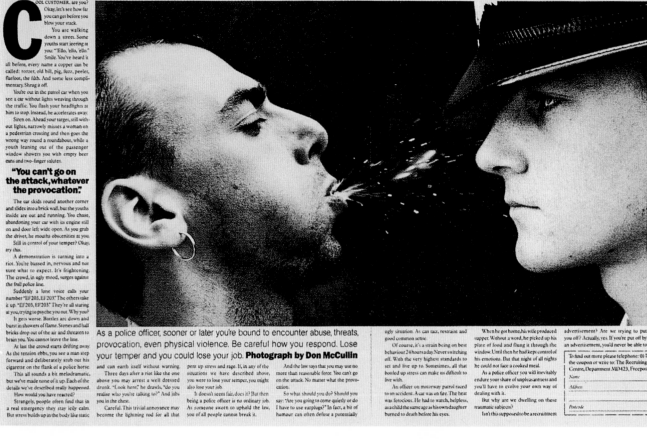

As a police officer, sooner or later you're bound to encounter abuse, threats, provocation, even physical violence. Be careful how you respond. Lose your temper and you could lose your job. **Photograph by Don McCullin**

and can earth itself without warning.

Three days after a riot like the one above you may arrest a well dressed drunk. "Look here," he drawls, "do you realise who you're talking to?" And jabs you in the chest.

Careful. This trivial annoyance may become the lightning rod for all that pent up stress and rage. If, in any of the situations we have described above, you were to lose your temper, you might also lose your job.

And the law says that you may use no more than reasonable force. You can't go on the attack. No matter what the provocation.

It doesn't seem fair, does it? But then being a police officer is no ordinary job. As someone sworn to uphold the law, you of all people cannot break it.

So what should you do? Should you say: "Are you going to come quietly or do I have to use earplugs?" In fact, a bit of humour can often defuse a potentially

ugly situation. As can tact, restraint and good common sense.

Of course, it's a strain being on best behaviour 24 hours a day. Never switching off. With the very highest standards to set and live up to. Sometimes, all that bottled up stress can make us difficult to live with.

An officer on motorway patrol raced to an accident. A car was on fire. The heat was ferocious. He had to watch, helpless, as a child the same age as his own daughter burned to death before his eyes.

When he got home, his wife produced supper. Without a word, he picked up his plate of food and flung it through the window. Until then he had kept control of his emotions. But that night of all nights he could not face a cooked meal.

As a police officer you will inevitably endure your share of unpleasantness and you'll have to evolve your own way of dealing with it.

But why are we dwelling on these traumatic subjects?

Isn't this supposed to be a recruitment

advertisement? Are we trying to put you off? Actually, yes. If you're put off by an advertisement, you'd never be able to

cope with the reality. And we need people who can cope. People who are tough, tender, sensitive, strong and disciplined, all at the same time.

People like this aren't easy to find. At present we take only one in five applicants. We'd rather look at fewer, better candidates.

Seeing you've got this far, we'll now admit that a career in the Met isn't all grief. Few jobs are as rewarding.

Ask the much loved Streatham home beat officer who, helmet under arm,

"It gets worse. Bottles arc down and burst in showers of flame."

cigar stuck firmly in mouth in flagrant disregard of regulations, can tell you the name of every child in his manor.

Ask the constable who, while patiently unravelling the intricacies of gang warfare in, of all unlikely places, Southall, has been invited to six Indian weddings in the last year.

Ask the sergeant who now runs what is virtually a Bengali advice centre in Whitechapel.

We can offer 28,000 more examples. If you don't believe us, stop any police officer in the street and ask.

When you've learned what they get out of the job, ask how they got in.

They'll tell you about our twenty week basic training course at Hendon. And life on the beat at one of London's 187 police stations where, under the tutelage of a sergeant, you will learn the art of handling people. And yourself.

Right now, your next step is to fill in and post the coupon below.

We're looking for mature, fit people aged between 18½ and 45, especially from the ethnic minorities. You should be at least 172cms tall if you're a man, 162cms if you're a woman.

Ideally, you'll have some 'O' level passes or their equivalents, but we value your personal qualities more.

To find out more please telephone: 01-725 4492 (Ansaphone: 01-725 4375) or fill in the coupon or write to: The Recruiting Officer, The Metropolitan Police Selection Centre, Department MD423, Freepost, London W2 1BR.

Name

Address

Postcode   Age

HE'S A FRIEND. DO YOU TURN YOUR BACK OR TURN HIM IN?

YOU'RE off-duty at a great party. A few people start smoking marijuana. Worse still, one's a mate of yours.

You don't want to lose a friend. You don't want to break up a party. You don't want your face smashed in. On the other hand you've sworn to uphold the law. Thousands of decent, honest Londoners depend on you doing just that. On and off-duty.

If you turn a blind eye you'll be letting them and yourself and your mates down. You could be laying yourself open to blackmail. You could terribly be hyed.

Take a deep breath and not too near the offending substance, you'll need your wits about you. Ask yourself: is it definitely cannabis? Are you absolutely sure? Are they spreading it around? Are they selling it? Or are they just quietly smoking among themselves?

Now observe the first law of diplomacy. 'engage brain before opening mouth'. In other words, consider the options.

What can you do that will most effectively halt the situation? If you simply walk out, as you may well be tempted to, you are avoiding the issue.

If you rush over and

This is one of those hot potatoes we toss to our recruits. If they handle it with good sense and good humour, they might make good coppers. If they juggle with it rashly, they can get their fingers badly charred. How would you cope? Let's study the evidence a little more closely. **Photographs by Don McCullin**

try to arrest them all, there's very little chance you'll succeed and, even if you do, that you'll make the charge stick in court.

Your social life will also be in ruins, a real blow to any young man or woman especially one with a difficult job like yours. Here are three of the options that would most impress us if you were trying to join the Metropolitan Police.

1. Have a quiet word with the host, explain your predicament and his liability, then ask him to put a stop to it.

2. Pop out to the nearest police station and report the incident.

3. Stay at the party for a while, identify the offenders and tackle the situation later, having consulted your superiors.

Do you begin to see how much responsibility you'll have? And can you see how little exercises like the one above could quickly become real conundrums?

Imagine a neighbour who refuses to tax his car while driving it from time to time. The sister of a colleague who tries to conceal permanently dilated pupils with dark glasses even on the dingiest of winter days. A well-heeled friend plagued by permanent sniffles.

1. Know, the enemy from left to right: Indian (less pakistani) cannabis, prepared opium and chart rocks.

2. The hard stuff: Morphine ampoules, chinese heroin, Dexophed capsules (stimulants) and LSD in gelatine squares. All potentially lethal.

Bad sinuses or a cocaine habit?

The local tobacconist, a friend of your dad, who tries to slip you a packet of twenty for overlooking the kids to whom he sells fags.

Your life won't be full of such tricky problems but there'll be enough of them, and it's better to face the fact now rather than later: a copper's life is not everyone's cup of tea.

To balance up this rather sombre side of the job, remember you never walk alone.

A call on your personal radio and you have all the resources of the Met at your side: colleagues, cars, helicopters, dog handlers, the river police. (In any of which you may opt to specialise, incidentally, when you've got a bit of experience behind you.)

Right now we have just 27,500 police officers looking after 10 million people

in London. In the next few months we want to build this figure up substantially.

We're looking for men and women over 18½ and mature with it. We actively welcome people from all sections of the community. If you would like to know more about the job please fill in the coupon and post it to us today.

We ask that you be physically fit or capable of getting there and stand at least 172 cms if you're a man, 162 cms for a woman. We also like to see around 5 'O' levels, though as we hope we've convinced you in this advertisement, your human qualities are just as important.

To find out more please telephone: 01-725-4492 (Ansaphone: 01-725 4375) or fill in the coupon or write to: The Recruiting Officer, The Metropolitan Police Selection Department MD 206, Freepost, London W2 1BR.

Name

Address

Postcode   Age

ART DIRECTOR:
NEIL GODFREY
PHOTOGRAPHER:
DON McCULLIN
COPYWRITER:
INDRA SINHA
AGENCY:
*COLLETT DICKENSON
PEARCE & PARTNERS*
CLIENT:
METROPOLITAN POLICE
◄■ 121

■ 121, 122 Advertisements from a press campaign to recruit new candidates to the force who according to the copy should be able to cope with difficult circumstances. Issued on behalf of the London Metropolitan Police. (GBR)

■ 121, 122 «Könnten Sie die andere Wange hinhalten?» «Er ist ein Freund. Schauen Sie nicht hin oder zeigen Sie ihn an?» Aus einer Presse-kampagne der Metropolitan Police, die Bewerber für den Polizeidienst ansprechen will. (GBR)

■ 121, 122 «Pourriez-vous tendre l'autre joue?» «C'est un ami. Allez-vous fermer les yeux ou le dénoncer?» Par cette campagne de presse, la Metropolitan Police cherche à recruter de nouveaux postulants. (GBR)

ART DIRECTOR:
JAC COVERDALE
DESIGNER:
JAC COVERDALE
PHOTOGRAPHER:
JIM ARNDT
COPYWRITER:
JERRY FURY
AGENCY:
CLARITY COVERDALE RUEFF
CLIENT:
UNITED RECOVERY CENTER
■ 123, 124

■ 123, 124 In these advertisements the United Recovery Center of Grand Forks (consultancy for relatives of alcoholics) makes direct appeals to relatives of alcoholics to come to the center for assistance and counselling. (USA)

■ 123, 124 «Nicht jeder unter Alkoholeinfluss trinkt.» «Wenn Sie mit einem Alkoholiker zusammenleben, ist das Problem, dass Sie den Kater ausbaden müssen.» – für eine Beratungsstelle für Angehörige von Alkoholikern. (USA)

■ 123, 124 Les slogans de ces annonces rappellent que les proches d'un alcoolique sont eux aussi des victimes de l'alcoolisme. Deux annonces pour un service de consultation réservé aux membres de familles d'alcooliques. (USA)

ART DIRECTOR:
GRAHAM FINK
PHOTOGRAPHER:
DON McCULLIN
COPYWRITER:
JOHN SALMON/JEREMY CLARKE
AGENCY:
*COLLETT DICKENSON PEARCE &
PARTNERS*
CLIENT:
METROPOLITAN POLICE
◄■ 122

HOW DOES IT FEEL TO TAKE THE LIFE OF AN 8 YEAR OLD?

In 1985, Morris Odell Mason was put to death by the State of Virginia despite an IQ of 66, a mental age of 8, and a diagnosis of schizophrenia. Mason apparently had no understanding of the finality of what awaited him; before his execution he asked what he should wear to his funeral.

At least 12 percent of prisoners currently on death row have been diagnosed as being mentally retarded or of borderline intelligence.

The death penalty. It's not a punishment. It's a crime.

AMNESTY INTERNATIONAL USA   322 8th Avenue • New York, New York 10001 • 212-807-8400

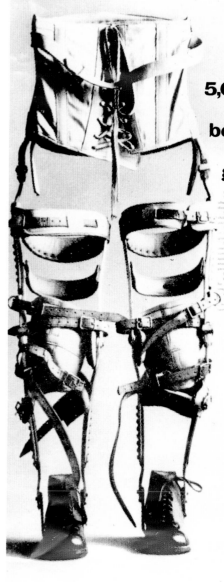

Last year, 5,000 women failed job interviews because they didn't have a good pair of legs.

Mainstream

ART DIRECTOR:
DENNIS WALSTON
DESIGNER:
JIM GRAY
PHOTOGRAPHER:
DAN GLASS
AGENCY:
THE KAMBER GROUP
CLIENT:
AMNESTY INTERNATIONAL
■ 125

ART DIRECTOR
STEVE DUNN
PHOTOGRAPHER:
PHIL MARCO
COPYWRITER:
TIM DELANEY
AGENCY:
LEAGAS DELANEY LIMITED
CLIENT:
MAINSTREAM
■ 126

■ 125 Campaign for Amnesty International to bring to public attention the inhuman nature of the death penalty and to mobilize public opinion in opposition. (USA)

■ 126 Advertisement from a campaign for Mainstream – a charity set up to help integrate people with disabilities into society. "We want people to be judged by their abilities not their disabilities." (GBR)

■ 125 «Wie fühlt man sich, wenn man einem 8jährigen das Leben nimmt?» – Aus einer Kampagne von Amnesty International gegen die Todesstrafe. (USA)

■ 126 «Letztes Jahr fanden 5000 Frauen keine Arbeit, weil sie keine guten Beine hatten.» Anzeige aus einer Pressekampagne einer Organisation zur Unterstützung behinderter Menschen. (GBR)

■ 125 «Qu'est-ce qu'on éprouve quand on exécute quelqu'un qui a 8 ans?» – Annonce tirée d'une campagne d'Amnesty International contre la peine de mort. (USA)

■ 126 «L'année dernière, 5000 femmes n'ont pas trouvé de travail parce qu'elles n'avaient pas de bonnes jambes.» Annonce d'une campagne de presse pour l'assistance aux personnes handicapées. (GBR)

BROCHURES

BROSCHÜREN

ART DIRECTOR:
Hans Peter Hötzmanseder
PHOTOGRAPHER:
Horst Stasny
STYLIST:
Silvia Zollydauer
AGENCY:
Haslinger & Keck
CLIENT:
Hagan Skifabrik GmbH
■ 127-130

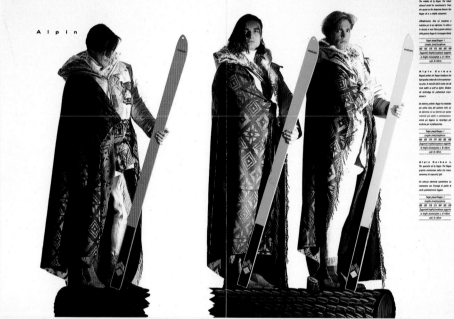

■ 127-130 Skiing presented in a new fashion. Cover and double spreads taken from a large-format brochure showing the latest *Hagan* ski collection. Color and painted elements accentuate the items shown. (AUT)

■ 131-133 Cover and double spreads taken from an advertising brochure for Proknit Corp., sports fashion manufacturer. Shown is the new athetic clothing collection "Ironworks". (USA)

■ 127-130 «Ski auf ganz neue Art.» Umschlag und Doppelseiten aus einer grossformatigen Broschüre, in der die neue *Hagan*-Ski-Kollektion gezeigt wird. Farbe und gemalte Elemente auf den Seiten setzen Akzente. (AUT)

■ 131-133 Umschlag und Doppelseiten einer Werbebroschüre für Proknit Corp., Hersteller von Sportbekleidung. Hier wird die neue Linie «Ironworks» fürs Fitness-Training vorgestellt. (USA)

■ 127-130 «Le nouvel esprit du ski». Page de couverture et trois pages intérieures d'une brochure grand format présentant la nouvelle collection de skis Hagan. Des éléments de décor peints sont intégrés à l'image. (AUT)

■ 131-133 Couverture et doubles pages d'une brochure publicitaire pour Proknit Corp., un fabricant de vêtements de sports. On y présente la nouvelle ligne pour le training, «Ironworks». (USA)

ART DIRECTOR:
ART LOFGREEN
DESIGNER:
ART LOFGREEN
PHOTOGRAPHER:
SUE BENNETT
STYLIST:
WENDY CRACCHIOLO SHEEDY
COPYWRITER:
LESLIE JOHNSON
AGENCY:
ART LOFGREEN DESIGN
CLIENT:
PROKNIT CORPORATION
■ 131-133

ART DIRECTOR:
Amy Quinlivan
DESIGNER:
Amy Quinlivan
PHOTOGRAPHER:
Sante D'Orazio
STYLIST:
Mary Bergtold
COPYWRITER:
Vicky Rossi
AGENCY:
Dayton Hudson / In House
CLIENT:
Dayton Hudson Dept. Store
■ 134-136

Issey Miyake

Matsuda

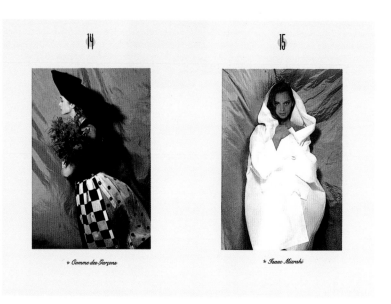
Comme des Garçons

Isaac Mizrahi

■ 134-136 Presented above are two covers from a Dayton/ Hudson catalog, below the catalog with envelope. (USA)

■ 137 Small-format catalog with casing for Bloomingdale's department store. Black-and-white photos show models from famous couturiers. The binding with thread and the manner of folding evoke a Chinese book. (USA)

■ 134-136 Oben zwei Doppelseiten aus einem Katalog für Dayton/Hudson; darunter der Katalog mit Umschlag. (USA)

■ 137 Kleinformatiger Katalog des Kaufhauses Bloomingdale's mit Kassette. Schwarzweiss-Aufnahmen zeigen Modelle bekannter Couturiers. Die Fadenheftung und Art des Faltens erinnern an ein chinesisches Buch. (USA)

■ 134-136 Ci-dessus, doubles pages du catalogue de Dayton/Hudson; en bas, le catalogue et son enveloppe. (USA)

■ 137 Catalogue du magasin de modes Bloomingsdale's, comportant des photos en noir et blanc de modèles de grands couturiers, et son emboîtage. De format réduit, il est plié et broché à la manière d'un livre chinois. (USA)

Art Director:
John C. Jay
Designer:
John C. Jay
Photographer:
Steven Meisel
Stylist:
Jill Glover
Copywriter:
Brian Leitch
Agency:
Bloomingdale's
Client:
Bloomingdale's
■ 137

PHOTOGRAPHER:
JAVIER VALLHONRAT
STUDIO:
GATTI
CLIENT:
SYBILLA
■ 138-142

■ 138-142 Cover and double spreads taken from a hard-cover catalog for Spanish designer Sybilla's fall/winter collection. The flaps of the jacket have been decoratively cut out. (SPA)

■ 143, 144 Cover and first double spread from a large-format brochure for "Aqua-Dress" sports fashion. (DEN)

■ 138-142 Umschlag und Doppelseiten eines Katalogs in Buchform für die Herbst-/Winterkollektion der spanischen Designerin Sybilla. Die Klappen des Schutzumschlags sind ausgestanzt und schmücken das Vorsatzpapier. (SPA)

■ 143, 144 Umschlag und erste Doppelseite einer grossformatigen Broschüre für «Aqua-Dress»-Sportmode. (DEN)

■ 138-142 Couverture et pages intérieures du catalogue relié présentant la collection automne/hiver 88/89 de Sybilla. Il est orné d'une jaquette dont les extrémités, découpées, décorent les pages de garde. (SPA)

■ 143, 144 Couverture et double page d'une brochure de grand format pour la mode «AquaDress». (DEN)

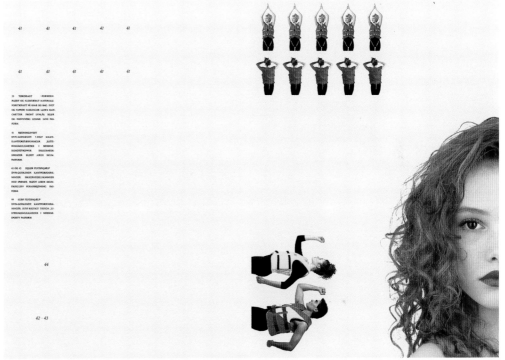

ART DIRECTOR:
FINN NYGAARD
DESIGNER:
FINN NYGAARD
PHOTOGRAPHER:
ERIK ZAPPON
AGENCY:
FINN NYGAARD
CLIENT:
AQUA-DRESS
■ 143, 144

■ 145-148 "di Bari": Catalog for Spring/Summer '90 collection from Ursula Neuhäuser. *145, 148:* Both cover illustrations. Beginning in the middle of the catalog, the pages are turned upside down. *146, 147:* Two double spreads from the catalog. (GER)

■ 149, 150 Leporello-type fashion catalog for Issey Miyake International. A transparent, printed sheet is added to the catalog. (JPN)

■ 145-148 «di Bari»: Katalog für die Frühjahrs-/Sommerkollektion 90 von Ursula Neuhäuser. *145, 148:* die beiden Umschlagillustrationen. Ab Mitte des Katalogs stehen die Seiten (einschl. des Umschlags) quasi auf dem Kopf. *146, 147:* zwei Doppelseiten aus dem Innern des Katalogs. (GER)

■ 149, 150 Leporello-Katalog für Issey Miyake International. Er ist mit einem transparenten, bedruckten Deckblatt versehen. (JPN)

■ 145-148 «di Bari»: catalogue de la collection printemps/été 90 de Ursula Neuhäuser. *145, 148:* recto et verso de la couverture. *146, 147:* deux doubles pages intérieures. Ce catalogue comporte deux pages de couverture, les images s'inversant à la moitié du fascicule. (GER)

■ 149-150 Dépliant publicitaire en accordéon conçu pour Issey Miyake International. Il est accompagné d'un feuillet imprimé transparent. (JPN)

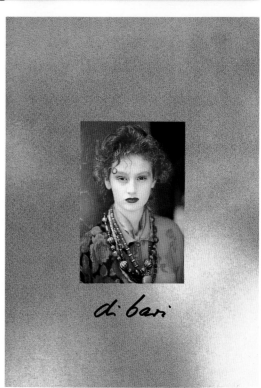

PAN 230

新しいブランドPAN230をお届けいたします。〝すべて〟を意味するギリシャ語のPANと、デザイナー秋山二実男の名前を〝ツースリーオー〟と読ませて組み合わせています。ビジネスをはじめ広義にとらえて社会的な場に出る機会を多くもつ女性たちのベーシックウエア―仕事着です。テイラードジャケットを基本とした〝ジャケット＋シャツ＋ボトム〟のコーディネイト。セットアップの提案から、色、素材違いのアイテムで自由な組み替えが可能に、カラートーンをそろえた展開をしています。本格的なメンズ仕立てをしながら、女性の体になじむよう芯の厚さの工夫、メンズ素材をソフトに仕上げるなど、着ごこちを重視し、細部に神経を行き届かせた〝あたたかな服づくり〟をしていきたいと考えています。

プレス担当 大森晶子
(Telephone:265-0651)

ART DIRECTOR:
CONNY J. WINTER
DESIGNER:
CONNY J. WINTER
PHOTOGRAPHER:
CONNY J. WINTER
CLIENT:
DI BARI / NEUHÄUSER
◂▪ 145-148

ART DIRECTOR:
MASAAKI HIROMURA
DESIGNER:
*MASAAKI HIROMURA /
TOSHIYUKI KOJIMA*
PHOTOGRAPHER:
RYUICHI OKANO
COPYWRITER:
SANAE YOSHIDA
AGENCY:
IKKS INC.
CLIENT:
ISSEY MIYAKE INTERNATIONAL
▪ 149, 150

■ 151, 152 The Spring '89 women's shoe collection from Cole-Haan with pictures pertaining to a cruise. Shown is the catalog's cover and first double spread. (USA)

■ 153 Cover from a spiral-bound catalog for the men's shoe collection 1989 from Cole-Haan. The train journey theme makes it possible to present the entire shoe collection (sports and elegant wear). (USA)

■ 154-157 Cover and examples of the double spreads from a catalog for *Gotcha* sportswear from California. All pages are collages of extremely colorful illustrations and photography. (USA)

■ 151, 152 Die Damenschuh-Kollektion von Cole-Haan für Frühjahr 89 wird mit Bildern einer Kreuzfahrt assoziiert. Hier der Umschlag und die erste Doppelseite des Katalogs. (USA)

■ 153 Umschlag eines spiralgebundenen Katalogs für die Herrenschuh-Kollektion 1989 von Cole-Haan. Das Zugreise-Thema ermöglicht die Präsentation des gesamten Sortiments von Sportschuhen bis zu eleganten Modellen. (USA)

■ 154-157 Umschlag und Beispiele der Seiten aus einem Katalog für Sportmode (*Gotcha* Sportswear) aus Kalifornien. Die aus Photos und Malerei bestehenden Collagen sind ungewöhnlich farbig. (USA)

■ 151, 152 La nouvelle collection des chaussures pour femmes Cole-Haan est associée à une croisière. Ici, la couverture et la première double page du catalogue. (USA)

■ 153 Couverture du catalogue à reliure spirale présentant la collection de chaussures pour hommes 1989 de Cole-Haan. Le thème du voyage en train permet de montrer une gamme de modèles qui va du sportif à l'habillé. (USA)

■ 154-157 Couverture et quelques pages d'un catalogue de *Gotcha* Sportswear, un fabricant de vêtements de sports. Ces images faites de collages de photos et de peintures sont extrêmement bariolées. (USA)

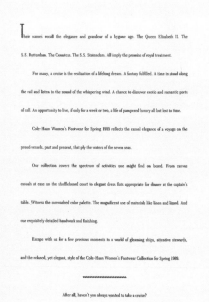

ART DIRECTOR:
ROSEMARY CONROY
DESIGNER:
ROSEMARY CONROY
ILLUSTRATOR:
CHERYL ROBERTS 151
PHOTOGRAPHER:
HOLLAND
AMERICA LINES 152
STYLIST:
MARY QUIRK
COPYWRITER:
BRIAN FLOOD
AGENCY:
CIPRIANI KREMER INC.
CLIENT:
COLE-HAAN
■ 151-153

ART DIRECTOR:
MIKE SALISBURY
DESIGNER:
STAFF OF SALISBURY COMM.
AGENCY:
SALISBURY COMM.
CLIENT:
GOTCHA SPORTSWEAR
■ 154-157

■ 158 Bloomingdale's invites its customers to discover the latest in fashion and accessories influenced by Gauguin's exotic South-Sea islands, "Where the dream of a more natural life becomes a reality for today's modern woman." All pictures shown in the catalog were reproduced by a *Canon* color laser copier. Shown is the catalog with cover. (USA)

■ 159-162 Cover and three double spreads taken from a Robbe & Berking customer brochure illustrating the pottery line in silver. Shown are lustrous silverplated items. The pages' glossiness, together with the actual pictures, demonstrate the product's high quality. (GER)

■ 158 «Lassen Sie Träume Wirklichkeit werden.» Bloomingdale's lädt seine Kundinnen ein, die neuen Kleider und Accessoires zu entdecken, aufgenommen in der exotischen Umgebung der «Gauguin-Inseln». Alle Abbildungen des Katalogs wurden mit einem Laserphotokopiergerät von Canon reproduziert. Hier der Katalog mit Umschlag. (USA)

■ 159-162 Umschlag und Doppelseiten aus einem Verbraucherprospekt für Robbe & Berking, in dem das *Alta*-Tafelgeräte-Programm in Silberlegierung bzw. Hartglanzversilberung vorgestellt wird. Die Hochglanzseiten und die Aufnahmen unterstreichen die Qualität der Verarbeitung. (GER)

■ 158 «Faites que le rêve devienne réalité». Bloomingdale's invite ses clientes à découvrir sa nouvelle ligne de vêtements et accessoires, photographiés dans le cadre exotique des îles chères à Gauguin. Les images du catalogue ont toutes été réalisées au moyen du photocopieur Laser *Canon*. Ici, le catalogue et son enveloppe. (USA)

■ 159-162 Couverture et trois doubles pages du prospectus de Robbe & Berking, présentant la célèbre ligne de couverts *Alta*, en métal argenté de qualité supérieure. Le brillant du papier glacé et la netteté de l'image soulignent la perfection de la fabrication. (GER)

ROBBE & BERKING
SILBER

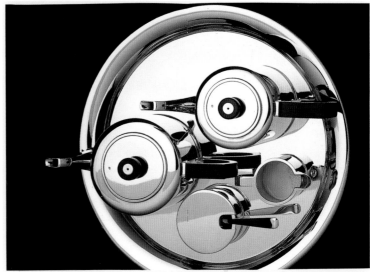

Das berühmte Besteck „Alta" von Robbe & Berking ist heute weltweit zum Leitbild für zeitgenössisches Tafelsilber geworden. Ausgezeichnet mit begehrten Design-Preisen und schon jetzt Ausstellungsobjekt in acht bedeutenden Museen. Dieses avantgardistische Besteck hat jetzt eine ebenso avantgardistische Ergänzung gefunden. Tafelgeräte – von richtungweisendem Design und zeitloser Schönheit. Wieder stammt der Entwurf von dem Hamburger Silberschmied Wilfried Moll, Träger der Hamburger und Münchener Staatspreise. Der Exklusivität des Entwurfes entspricht die Perfektion des Materials und der handwerklichen Verarbeitung. Die Alta-Tafelgeräte werden alternativ in 925/Sterling Silber – der wertvollsten international anerkannten Silberlegierung – oder in SDg-Hartglanzversilberung hergestellt. Diese Versilberungsqualität findet sonst nur bei den sehr viel stärker beanspruchten Bestecken Verwendung. Sie garantiert eine ungewöhnlich lange Lebensdauer. Ihre Silberauflage ist um ein Mehrfaches stärker als die der üblichen, ungestempelten oder mit „plated" bezeichneten Hohlwaren. Die Qualität der handwerklichen Verarbeitung zeigt sich in vielen Details, so sind zum Beispiel alle Versteifungen, Ränder und Dekore massiv und nicht hohl geprägt. Robbe & Berking hat dieses ungewöhnliche Tafelsilber für Menschen geschaffen, die mit den formalen und qualitativen Höchstleistungen ihrer Zeit leben wollen.

DIE NEUE
AVANTGARDE
IM BEREICH
EXCLUSIVEN
SILBERS

ART DIRECTOR:
JOHN C. JAY
DESIGNER:
JOHN C. JAY
PHOTOGRAPHER:
LANCE STAEDLER
STYLIST:
JILL GLOVER
COPYWRITER:
BRIAN LEITCH
AGENCY:
BLOOMINGDALE'S
CLIENT:
BLOOMINGDALE'S
◄■ 158

ART DIRECTOR:
WERNER WÜRDINGER
DESIGNER:
HEIDI WINKLER
PHOTOGRAPHER:
UWE ZISS
COPYWRITER:
WERNER WÜRDINGER
AGENCY:
WÜRDINGER & ·PARTNER
CLIENT:
ROBBE & BERKING
■ 159-162

ART DIRECTOR:
*JAMES SEBASTIAN /
JOHN PLUNKETT*

DESIGNER:
*JOHN PLUNKETT /
THOMAS SCHNEIDER*

PHOTOGRAPHER:
NEIL SELKIRK

AGENCY:
DESIGNFRAME INC.

CLIENT:
THE L.S COLLECTION

■ 163-166

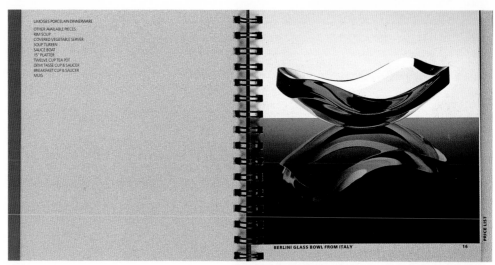

■ 163-170 Covers and double spreads taken from two small-format spiral-bound retail catalogs for gift ideas by L.S. The catalog is part of an overall identity, marketing and packaging program. Photography, structure and binding were planned as a flexible system that can be updated and reorganized periodically. (USA)

■ 163-170 Umschläge und Doppelseiten aus zwei kleinformatigen Verkaufskatalogen mit Spiralbindung für Geschenkartikel von L.S. Sie sind Teil des Firmenerscheinungsbildes. Photographie, Aufbau und Bindung der Kataloge ermöglichen jeweils eine periodische Anpassung des Inhalts an den neusten Stand. (USA)

■ 163-170 Couvertures et pages intérieures de deux catalogues de détail à reliure spirale, de petit format, pour le magasin d'articles-cadeaux L.S. Ils contribuent à l'identité globale de marque de cette maison. La photographie, la structure et la reliure spirale permettent de réactualiser périodiquement le contenu. (USA)

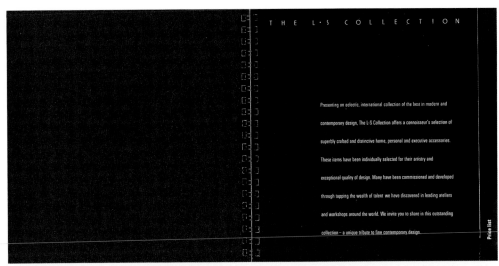

ART DIRECTOR:
*JAMES SEBASTIAN /
JOHN PLUNKETT*
DESIGNER:
DAVID REISS / JUN MAYUMI
PHOTOGRAPHER:
JODY DOLE
AGENCY:
DESIGNFRAME INC.
CLIENT:
THE L.S COLLECTION
■ 167-170

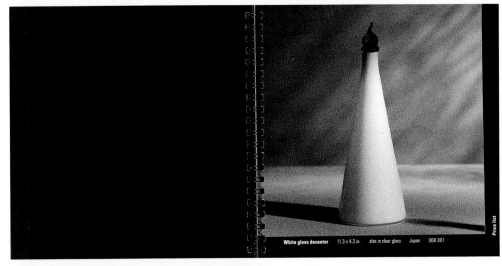

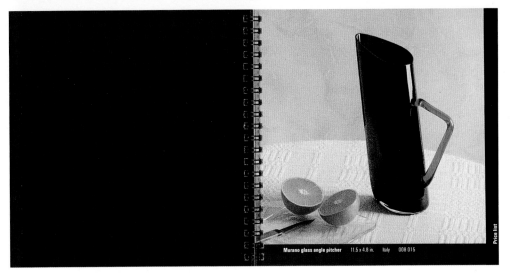

■ 171 Covers from three brochures showing armchairs designed by Michael Vanderbyl and Brian Kane for furniture manufacturer Bernhardt. Presented are two creations by Brian Kane. The "Elisabeth" design can be seen from both the front and side. (USA)

■ 172-176 Cover and double spread taken from a trapezoid brochure for the "Opus-2" collection from the Bernhardt company. *176*: The design "Radcliffe" by Michael Vanderbyl. *177*: "Orvieto" by Michael Manwaring. (USA)

■ 171 Umschläge von drei Broschüren mit Sesseln, die von Michael Vanderbyl und Brian Kane für den Möbelhersteller Bernhardt entworfen wurden. Auf der Doppelseite zwei Kreationen von Brian Kane, wobei das Modell «Elisabeth» von vorn und von der Seite gezeigt wird. (USA)

■ 172-176 Umschlag und Doppelseiten aus einer trapezförmigen Broschüre für die «Opus-2» Kollektion der Firma Bernhardt. *176*: das Modell «Radcliffe» von Michael Vanderbyl; *177*: «Orvieto» von Michael Manwaring. (USA)

■ 171 Couvertures de trois brochures présentant des fauteuils dessinés par Michael Vanderbyl et Brian Kane pour le fabricant de meubles Bernhardt. Sur la double page, deux créations de Kane, le modèle «Elisabeth» étant présenté de face et de profil. (USA)

■ 172-176 Couverture et pages intérieures d'une brochure de format trapézoïdal pour les fauteuils «Radcliffe» de Michael Vanderbyl et «Orvieto» de Michael Manwaring pour les meubles Bernhardt. (USA)

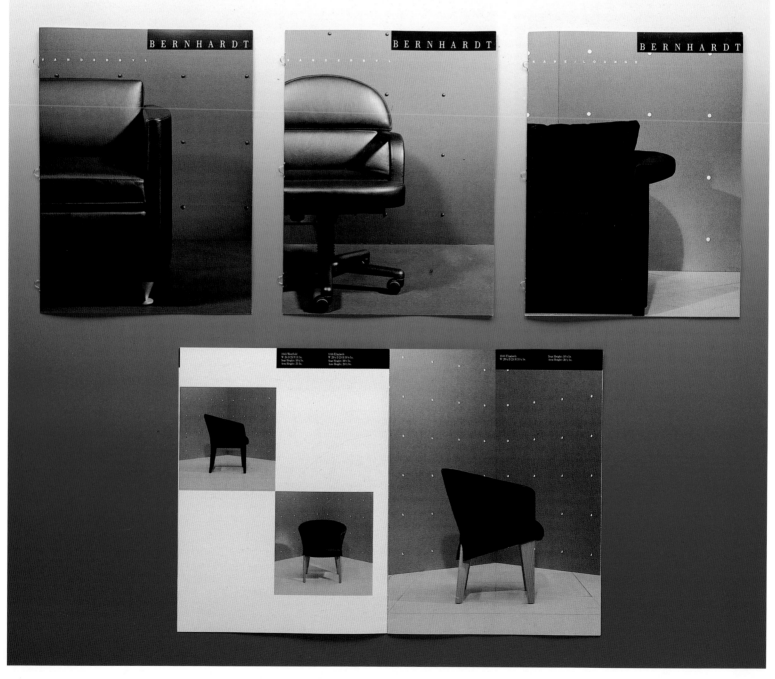

ART DIRECTOR:
Michael Vanderbyl
DESIGNER:
Michael Vanderbyl
AGENCY:
Vanderbyl Design
CLIENT:
Bernhardt Furniture
▶■ 172–176

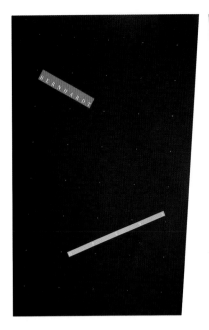

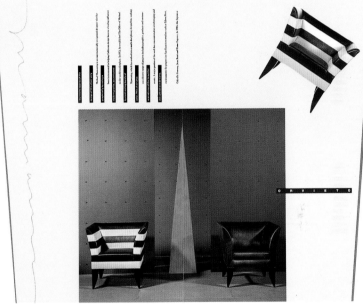

ART DIRECTOR:
Michael Vanderbyl
DESIGNER:
Michael Vanderbyl
PHOTOGRAPHER:
Omega Studios
AGENCY:
Vanderbyl Design
CLIENT:
Bernhardt Furniture
◀■ 171

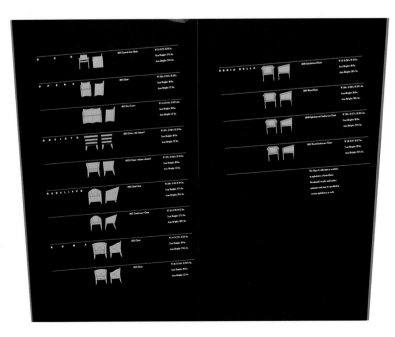

■ 177-180 Cover and double spreads taken from a catalog with designs by Ruudt Peters. Transparent paper in a variety of colors separates the pages. The basic form of the objects shown is a double bowl. (NLD)

■ 181-184 Cover and double spreads taken from a large-format catalog for the new furniture collection by Maxalto. The furniture's "surface" is made from briarwood lacquers and layers. The "surface" is then transformed by means of craftsmenship and tradition. The photography depicts the perfection of the details. (ITA)

■ 177-180 «Dedicated to» – Umschlag und Doppelseiten eines Katalogs mit Kreationen von Ruudt Peters, deren Ausgangsform eine doppelte Schale ist. Transparentes Papier in verschiedenen Farben trennt die Seiten. (NLD)

■ 181-184 Umschlag und Doppelseiten aus einem dicken Katalog für die neue Möbelkollektion von Maxalto. Die «Oberhaut» dieser Möbel besteht aus Wurzelholz und verschiedenen Lackierschichten, und dieses Material wurde nach alter Handwerkertradition verarbeitet. Die Photos konzentrieren sich auf die Perfektion des Details. (ITA)

■ 177-180 Couverture et pages intérieures du catalogue consacré aux créations de Ruudt Peters, intitulé «Dédicacé à». Des pages de papier de diverses couleurs sont insérées entre les pages du catalogue. (NLD)

■ 181-184 Couverture et doubles pages d'un épais catalogue présentant la nouvelle collection de meubles Maxalto. Ce fabricant est spécialisé dans le travail du bois; cuir, stratifié, laque ou loupe, les matériaux sont travaillés selon des procédés artisanaux. Les photos mettent en évidence la perfection de la ligne et du détail. (ITA)

ART DIRECTOR:
HENRIK BARENDS
DESIGNER:
HENRIK BARENDS
PHOTOGRAPHER:
HOGERS / VERSLUYS
CLIENT:
RUUDT PETERS
■ 177-180

MAXALTO

ART DIRECTOR:
LUCIANO SVEGLIADO
DESIGNER:
LUCIANO SVEGLIADO
STUDIO:
IKONOS
CLIENT:
MAXALTO S.P.A.
■ 181-184

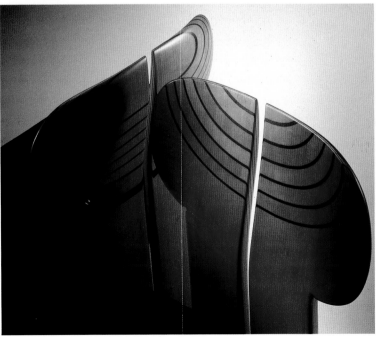

ART DIRECTOR:
RICK VAUGHN

DESIGNER:
RICK VAUGHN

PHOTOGRAPHER:
ROBERT RECK

COPYWRITER:
RICHARD KUHN

AGENCY:
VAUGHN WEDEEN / CREATIVE

CLIENT:
TAOS FURNITURE

►■ 189, 190

ART DIRECTOR:
MICHAEL VANDERBYL

DESIGNER:
MICHAEL VANDERBYL

AGENCY:
VANDERBYL DESIGN

CLIENT:
HICKORY BUSINESS FURNITURE

■ 185-188

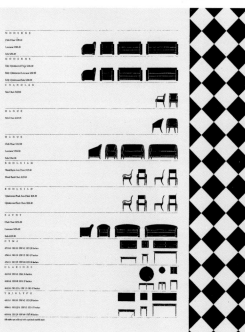

MAXALTO

"Lo splendore estetico e la fatica della mano dell'artigiano non sono semplicemente un'affermazione di un'idea del mondo, ma il riflesso della vita avita. Fin che essi tengono viti alla decadenza nei contengono una speranza" (T. Adorno). È questo speranza che rassume completamente la filosofia sottesa alla produzione Maxalto. Il nome "Maxalto" deriva dal veneto "massa alto" che significa "il più alto"; già nel nome è evidente la direzione verso cui Afra e Tobia Scarpa (gli ispiratori e progettisti esclusivi di questa azienda nata nel 1975 "da una costola" di B&B Italia) hanno inteso muovere questa realtà: la produzione di mobili di altissima qualità estetica è di manufattura.

Per Afra e Tobia Scarpa, da sempre impegnati nella ricerca ai confini tra nuove tecniche e materiali tradizionali, e soprattutto il legno il materiale da privilegiare fra tutti, poiché saturo dei valori rassicuranti di cui l'uomo contemporaneo sente la necessità. Le sfumature cromatiche denunciano la sua origine naturale, il suo calore rende l'ambiente più accogliente, la sua nobiltà si presta a interpretare forme raffinate ed essenziali.

È proprio questo antico fascino del legno, maneggiato secondo le lavorazioni tradizionali ma con le conoscenze tecnologiche proprie di un'industria moderna, che ha ispirato le esperienze, i progetti, la produzione (magistralmente diretta da Enrico Cassina) per Maxalto. Erede di una tradizione culturale del mobile come pezzo unico, come risultato prezioso delle tecniche collaudate da maestri ebanisti e antiquari, Maxalto ha ripreso questa esperienza che, chiuso il ciclo del grande artigiano non poteva morire, per maestria su una produzione industriale in cui il mobile in legno mantiene intatto il fascino del passato grazie alla scelta dei materiali, alle arti della lavorazione.

Dalla fusione di questi due mondi nasce così un metodo di lavoro in apparenza paradossale. In Maxalto, al contrario di sempre, l'artigiano è comandato dalla materia (dal suo divenire "sotto le mani" di chi la lavora), teso al risultato finale, come uno scultore, per dare vita a pezzi ogni volta irripetibili; eppure i pezzi Maxalto non hanno scarti dal progetto, non possono avere errori perché sono il prodotto di un'artigianalità non tradizionale, un'attitudine a una precisione meccanica che richiede tecnica e amore in egual misura.

La complessità e l'intelligenza di tecniche e materiali che intervengono nelle collezioni Maxalto (ad oggi no che di più di 100 pezzi), testimoniano come non si e smaterni il loro senso originario e, dunque, non si sono resi inutili, riducendoli a ricette, sconteneuti di sapienza che l'artigianato e l'arte portano con se, come eredità della storia dell'uomo.

Così, per paradosso, questi oggetti sono preziosi a dispetto della loro pericolosità, nel senso che al loro contenuto di esperienza sopravanza il pur apprezzabile discorso sui materiali e sul design. Sulla stessa unicità che le radice, le lacche, la mano, il tempo conferiscono.

Un contenuto di esperienza che, di fatto, appare oggi come una seria e propria reinterpretazione della "materia" a partire da quella più viva e nobile che è il legno.

"The aesthetic splendour and the work of the craftsman's hands are not simply the affirmation of an idea of the world but the reflection of unswerving life: as long as these oppose decadence, they contain a hope" (T. Adorno). This is the hope which completely synthesises the philosophy on the part of Maxalto production.

The name "Maxalto" derives from the Venetian "massa alto" which means highest; the name is already evident in the direction towards which Afra and Tobia Scarpa, (the inspirers and exclusive planners of this firm which was created in 1975 "out of a rib" of B&B Italia), have thought this reality should move: the production of very high aesthetic and manufactured quality.

For Afra and Tobia Scarpa, who have always been committed to research on the borderlines between new techniques and traditional materials, wood is, above all others, the material to favour as it is saturated with the reassuring values for which contemporary man feels a need. The chromatic nuances state its natural origin, its warmth renders the environment more welcoming, its substance lends itself to interpreting refined and essential forms.

It is precisely the ancient charm of wood, handled according to traditional workmanship but with the archi-technological knowledge of a modern industry, which has inspired the projects and production (impressively managed by Enrico Cassina) for Maxalto.

Heir to a cultural tradition of a unique piece of furniture, (the precious result of the techniques tested by master cabinet makers and valuers), Maxalto has resumed this craft which could be allowed to die but once the cycle of great craftsmanship ended. And had amalgamated it within an industrial production where each piece of wooden furniture wholly maintains the charm of the past thanks to the choice of materials and the workmanship arts.

The amalgamation of these two worlds creates an apparently paradoxical working method. At Maxalto, the craftsman is, strangely enough, led by the material (from its future, "at the hands" of the craftsman himself), towards a final result, like a sculptor, giving life to pieces which are unrepeatable; however the Maxalto pieces never fall below the projected standard and cannot have defects because they are the product of a non traditional craftsmanship, an attitude towards mechanical precision which requires an equal measure of technique and love. The complexity and the intelligence of techniques and materials which intervene in the Maxalto collections (which no less than 100 pieces today), testify how their original meaning has not been lost and therefore the knowledge which craftsmanship and art contain in themselves as legacy of man's history, have not become ridiculous of reduced to mere prescriptions.

In this way, paradoxically, these objects are precious despite their value, in the sense that the content of know-how surpasses the nonetheless admirable question regarding materials and design. The very uniqueness which the heartwoods, lacquers, workmanship and time confer.

A content of know-how which, in fact, today appears to be a real and proper reinterpretation of "matter", Starting off from wood the most alive and noble of all.

"La splendeur esthétique et la fatigue de l'artisan ne sont pas simplement une affirmation d'une idée du monde, mais le reflet de la vie qui à jamais contient de défiants: tant qu'ils tiennent tête à la décadence ils contiennent une espérance" (T. Adorno). C'est cet espoir que résume tout à fait la philosophie sous-jacente à la production Maxalto.

Le nom "Maxalto" dérive du vénitien "massa alto" qui signifie "le plus haut"; déjà le nom on peut comprendre la direction dans laquelle Afra et Tobia Scarpa (les aspirateurs et designers exclusifs de cette société crée en 1975 "d'une côte" de B&B Italia) ont choisi d'entraîner cette réalité: la production de meubles hauts de gamme de par leur esthétique et leur manufacture.

Pour Afra et Tobia Scarpa, engagés depuis toujours dans l'étude à la limite entre nouvelles techniques et matériaux traditionnels, c'est avant tout le bois le matériau préféré, parce qu'il est chargé des valeurs rassurantes dont l'homme moderne a besoin. Les nuances chromatiques dénoncent son origine naturelle, sa chaleur rend le cadre plus accueillant, sa noblesse se prête aux formes raffinées et essentielles.

C'est justement le charme antique du bois, travaillé selon la tradition mais avec les connaissances technologiques typiques d'une industrie moderne, qui a inspiré les expériences, les projets, la production (magistralement dirigée par Enrico Cassina) pour Maxalto.

Riche d'une tradition culturelle du meuble conçu comme pièce unique, comme le résultat sans prix des techniques des maîtres en ébénisterie et marquéterie, Maxalto a repris cette expérience qui ne pouvait se perdre une fois clos le cycle de l'artisanat, pour la préfér sur une production industrielle où le meuble en bois garde tout le charme du passé grâce au choix des matériaux et à l'art du travail.

De la fusion de ces deux mondes naît ainsi une méthode de travail paradoxale en apparence. Chez Maxalto, contrairement à tout ce qui s'est toujours fait, l'artisanat est commandé par la matière (par son soit "sous les mains" de celui qui la travaille) dirigé vers le résultat final, comme un sculpteur, pour donner la vie à des pièces que ne pourront être répétées; et pourtant les pièces Maxalto ne s'écartent pas du projet, ne peuvent être une erreur parce qu'elles sont le fruit d'un artisanat non traditionnel, une application à une précision mécanique qui exige autant de technique que d'amour. La complexité et l'intelligence des techniques et des matériaux utilisés dans les collections Maxalto (elles comptent plus de 100 pièces actuellement) sont la preuve que rien n'a été perdu de leur sens originel et que par conséquent la sagesse que l'artisanat l'art portent en eux, l'héritage de l'histoire de l'homme, ne s'est pas perdue en recettes ridicules.

Ainsi, paradoxalement ces objets sont précieux en dépit de leur richesse, en ce sens que leur contenu d'expérience dépasse le discours plus que valable sur les matériaux et le design, sur le caractère unique que la longue, les laques, la main-d'œuvre, le temps lui confèrent.

Un contenu d'expérience qui apparaît un fait aujourd'hui comme une véritable réinterprétation de la "matière" à partir de la manière la plus vivante et la plus noble qu'est le bois.

ART DIRECTOR:
LUCIANO SVEGLIADO
DESIGNER:
LUCIANO SVEGLIADO
STUDIO:
IKONOS
CLIENT:
MAXALTO S.P.A.
■ 181-184

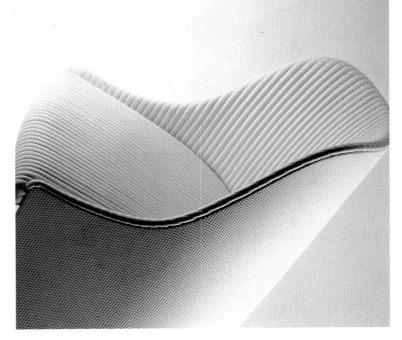

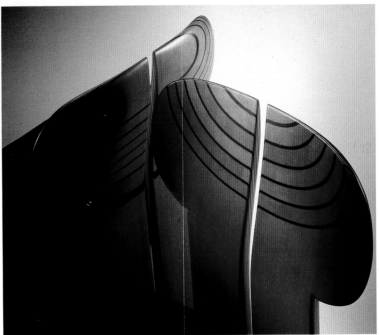

ART DIRECTOR:
Rick Vaughn
DESIGNER:
Rick Vaughn
PHOTOGRAPHER:
Robert Reck
COPYWRITER:
Richard Kuhn
AGENCY:
Vaughn Wedeen / Creative
CLIENT:
Taos Furniture
►■ 189, 190

ART DIRECTOR:
Michael Vanderbyl
DESIGNER:
Michael Vanderbyl
AGENCY:
Vanderbyl Design
CLIENT:
Hickory Business Furniture
■ 185-188

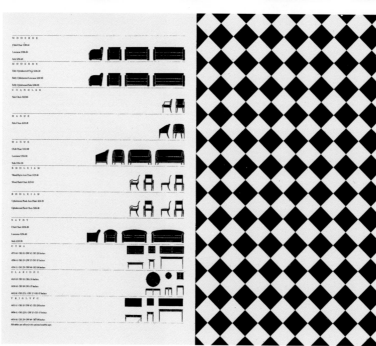

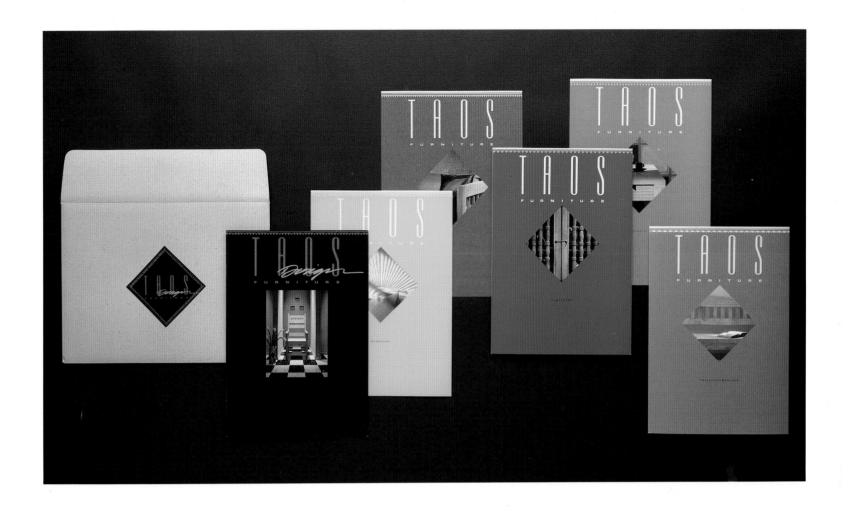

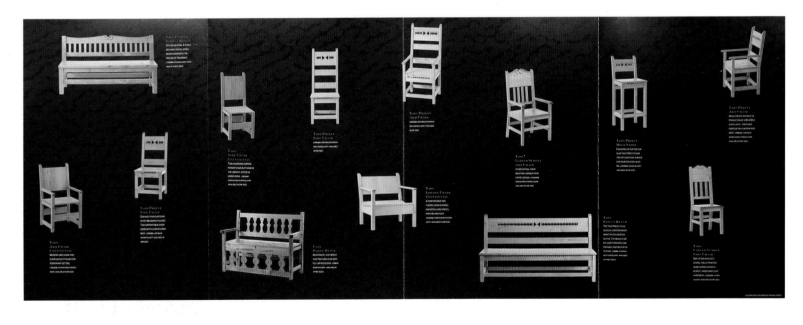

■ 185-188 Cover and double spreads taken from a largeformat brochure for a new line of furniture by Robert A.M. Stern for Hickory Business Furniture. The geometric pattern emphasizes the architectural style of the furniture. (USA)

■ 189, 190 Advertising material (brochure and folded pamphlets) distributed by Taos Furniture. The diamond shape is repeated on most of the pages. (USA)

■ 185-188 Umschlag und Doppelseiten einer grossformatigen Broschüre für eine Möbel-Linie von Robert A.M. Stern für Hickory Business Furniture. Das geometrische Muster entspricht dem architektonischen Stil der Möbel. (USA)

■ 189, 190 Werbematerial (Broschüre und Faltprospekte) für Taos-Möbel. Das Quadrat auf dem Umschlag für die Dokumentation taucht immer wieder auf. (USA)

■ 185-188 Couverture et doubles pages d'une brochure de grand format sur les nouveaux meubles conçus par Robert A. M. Stern pour Hickory Business Furniture. La sobriété du décor souligne le caractère architectural des formes. (USA)

■ 189, 190 Matériel publicitaire (brochure et prospectus dépliants) distribué par les meubles Taos. L'enveloppe qui contient la documentation est ornée d'une étiquette. (USA)

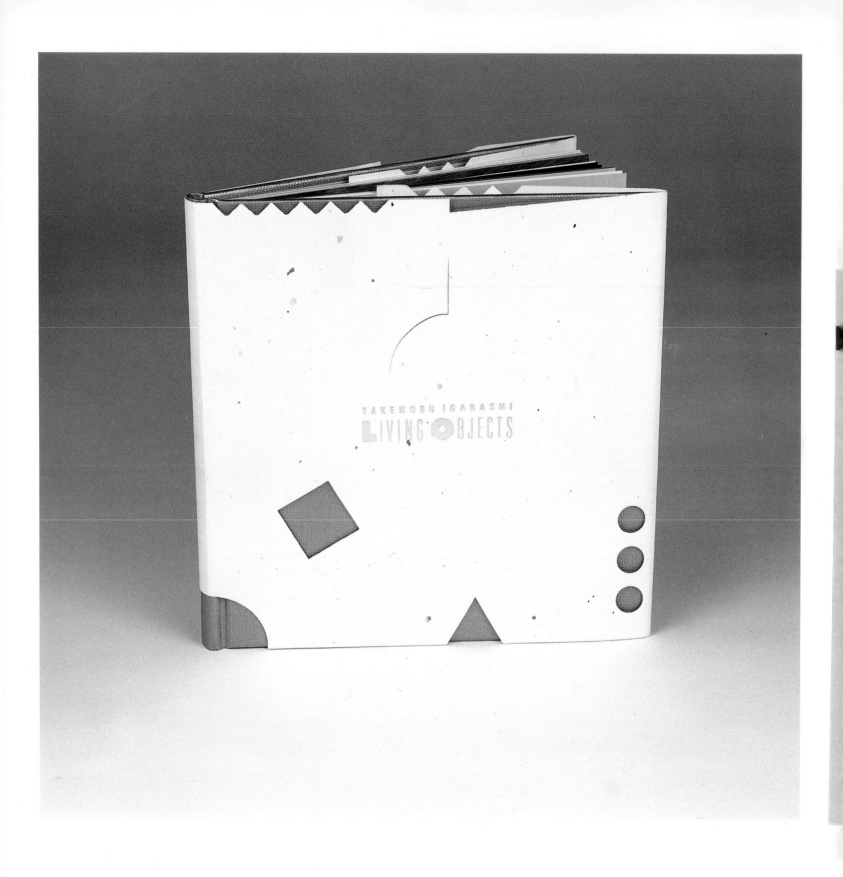

TAKENOBU IGARASHI
LIVING OBJECTS

■ 191-195 Cover and interior pages taken from a catalog realised for a touring exhibition of "Living Objects" designed and created by Takenobu Igarashi. The jacket is decorated with unusual cut-outs. (JPN)

■ 191-195 Umschlag und Innenseiten eines Katalogs für eine Wanderausstellung von Gebrauchsgegenständen («Living Objects»), entworfen von Takenobu Igarashi. Der Schutzumschlag hat ungewöhnliche Ausstanzungen. (JPN)

■ 191-195 Couverture et pages intérieures d'un catalogue de Takenobu Igarashi, réalisé à l'occasion d'une exposition itinérante des objets créés par ce designer. La couverture est ornée par des motifs en découpe. (JPN)

STOOL
Cast iron

ART DIRECTOR:
TAKENOBU IGARASHI
DESIGNER:
TAKENOBU IGARASHI
AGENCY:
IGARASHI STUDIO
CLIENT:
IGARASHI STUDIO
■ 191-195

FLATWARE
Stainless steel

STATIONERY TOOLS
ABS resin, others

TELEPHONE
ABS resin

ART DIRECTOR:
Finn Nygaard

DESIGNER:
Finn Nygaard

PHOTOGRAPHER:
Erik Zappon

AGENCY:
Finn Nygaard Design

CLIENT:
Randers

■ 196-201

The Series 3000 comprises a stackable conference chair, an easy chair, two and three seater sofas, as well as coffee and conference tables.

Great importance has been attached to the comfort of the lounge furniture. The shape and dimensions of seat and back cushions, constructed with fire-retardant highly flexible foam offer an excellent seating posture. To facilitate long-distance transportation body and frame can be totally dismantled. All legs are finished with a plastic-covered disc, giving protection to the floor surface.

The simple construction of the table top has been stabilised by the insertion of a steel core. The assembly of the legs is easily done with a threaded bolt into the steel structure. Apart from the quarter loose leaf, all table tops and two leaves are identical. Hanging of loose leaves is done by means of a robust connector. By means of loose leaves and connectors arrangements of tables can be easily changed and adapted to individual needs.

As with the lounge furniture, the steel frame structure for the conference chair is made of 16 mm steel tube, also finished with a disc foot. Stackability and a linking device, on which chair No's can be placed, make the chair suitable for assembly halls and auditoriums. The seat and back are made of moulded, laminated beech, comfortably upholstered in such a way that the chair keeps its slim form. The shape of the back assures excellent lumbar support in both working and relaxed positions.

The exposed steel frame of the seating is made of 16 mm epoxy powder coated steel tube available in 7 colours and chrome-satin. Upholstery is available in toning colours to the steel frames and black leather. The table legs are made from 60 mm steel tube, finished in the same epoxy powder colours and chrome-satin.
Table tops are 34 mm thick, veneered and lacquered. They are available in grey-lacquered mahogany, natural lacquered mahogany and natural lacquered maple.

Steelframe colours
Burgundy (RAL 3005)
Anthracite grey (RAL 7016)
Grey (RAL 7023)
Navy blue (RAL 5002)
White (RAL 9010)
Black (RAL 9005)
Honey yellow (RAL 1005)
Chrome-satin

Table tops
Grey-lacquered mahogany
Lacquered mahogany
Lacquered maple

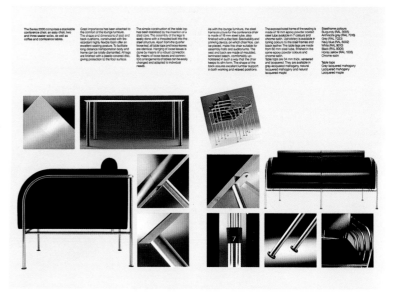

FORM FOLLOWS FEELING.

AGNES BOURNE

ART DIRECTOR:
CRAIG FRAZIER
DESIGNER:
CRAIG FRAZIER
PHOTOGRAPHER:
JOCK MCDONALD
COPYWRITER:
MICHEAL WRIGHT
AGENCY:
FRAZIER DESIGN
CLIENT:
AGNES BOURNE
■ 202-207

■ 196-201 Cover and double spreads taken from Randers' furniture brochure. The new furniture line created by architects Friis & Moltke is predominately produced for businesses, hotels and conference rooms. (DEN)

■ 202-207 Self-promotional catalog created by furniture designer Agnes Bourne. Her initials appear on the cover page as cut-outs. (USA)

■ 196-201 Umschlag und Doppelseiten aus einer Broschüre für Randers-Möbel. Die von den Architekten Friis & Moltke kreierte neue Linie ist vor allem für Büros, Hotels und Konferenzräume bestimmt. (DEN)

■ 202-207 Eigenwerbungskatalog der Möbel-Designerin Agnes Bourne. Ihre Initialen erscheinen ausgestanzt auf dem Umschlag. (USA)

■ 196-201 Couverture et pages intérieures d'une brochure du fabricant de meubles Randers. La nouvelle ligne, créée par les architectes Friis & Moltke, a tout d'abord été conçue pour des bureaux, hôtels ou salles de conférence. (DEN)

■ 202-207 Prospectus autopromotionnel de la créatrice de meubles Agnes Bourne. La chemise cartonnée est ornée des initiales en découpe. (USA)

ART DIRECTOR:
Michael Vanderbyl
DESIGNER:
Michael Vanderbyl
PHOTOGRAPHER:
Thomas Heinser
AGENCY:
Vanderbyl Design
CLIENT:
Bernhardt Furniture
■ 208-213

■ 208-213 Cover and double spreads from a large-format brochure in which a new collection of furnishings by Brian Krane for Bernhardt furniture-makers is shown. The designer introduces his work personally. The contrasting black and white underscores the furniture style. (USA)

■ 208-213 Umschlag und Doppelseiten aus einer grossformatigen Broschüre, in der eine neue Kollektion von Brian Krane für den Möbelhersteller Bernhardt gezeigt wird. Der Designer stellt sein Werk persönlich vor. Das kontrastreiche Schwarzweiss unterstreicht den Stil der Möbel. (USA)

■ 208-213 Couverture et doubles pages d'une brochure de grand format présentant une nouvelle ligne de mobilier dessinée par Brian Krane pour les meubles Bernhardt. Le créateur présente personnellement son œuvre. Les photos en noir et blanc contrastées soulignent l'aspect formel. (USA)

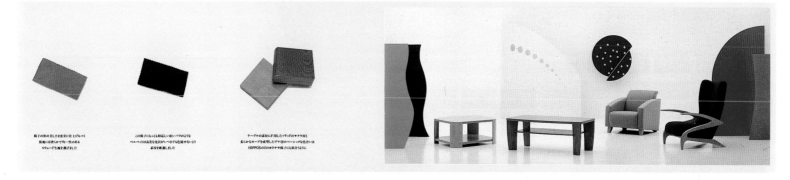

■ 214-217 Cover and three double spreads from a brochure in unusual horizontal format which presents a new furnishing range known as "Hippos". (JPN)

■ 218-221 Cover and double spreads from a brochure presenting mirrored cupboards. Reflections, light and shadow form the theme for the photographs. (USA)

■ 214-217 Umschlag und drei Doppelseiten aus einer Broschüre in ungewöhnlichem Querformat. Vorgestellt wird eine neue Möbel-Linie, «Hippos» genannt. (JPN)

■ 218-221 Umschlag und Doppelseiten aus einer Broschüre, in der Spiegelschränke vorgestellt werden. Reflektionen, Licht und Schatten sind das Thema der Photos. (USA)

■ 214-217 Couverture et trois doubles pages d'une brochure au format très allongé présentant une nouvelle ligne de meubles appelée «Hippos». (JPN)

■ 218-221 Couverture et doubles pages d'une brochure pour une nouvelle ligne d'armoires à glace. Les photos mettent en relief l'ambiguité et l'étrangeté du jeu des reflets. (USA)

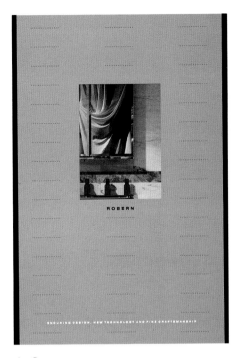

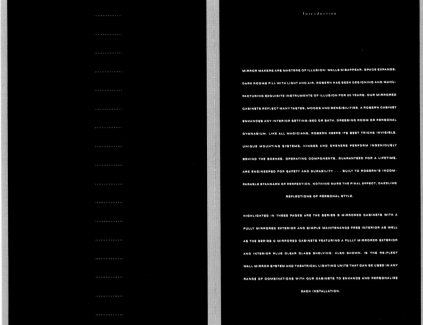

ART DIRECTOR:
Takaaki Matsumoto /
Michael McGinn

DESIGNER:
Takaaki Matsumoto /
Reiko Nogami

PHOTOGRAPHER:
Takashi Sekiguchi

STYLIST:
Harumi Tsuda

COPYWRITER:
Harumi Tsuda / Mark Tamura

AGENCY:
M Plus M Incorporated

CLIENT:
Sazaby, Inc.

◀■ 214-217

ART DIRECTOR:
Kerry Polite

DESIGERN:
Kerry Polite

PHOTOGRAPHER:
Tom Crane

STYLIST:
Barbara Pietsch

COPYWRITER:
Ann de Forest

CLIENT:
Robern, Inc.

►■ 218-221

Two Door Cabinet and Theatrical Light Strip

Two Door/Sliding and Four Door Cabinets

One Door Cabinet

ART DIRECTOR:
DITI KATONA / JOHN PYLYPCZAK
DESIGNER:
DITI KATONA
PHOTOGRAPHER:
DAVID WHITTAKER
COPYWRITER:
ROBERT YOUNG
AGENCY:
CONCRETE DESIGN
COMMUNICATIONS INC.
CLIENT:
REEBOK CANADA
■ 222

ART DIRECTOR:
THOM MARCHIONNA
DESIGNER:
THOM MARCHIONNA /
GEORGE STEINMETZ /
MICHAEL O'BRIEN
AGENCY:
APPLE CREATIVE SERVICES
CLIENT:
APPLE COMPUTER, INC.
■ 223

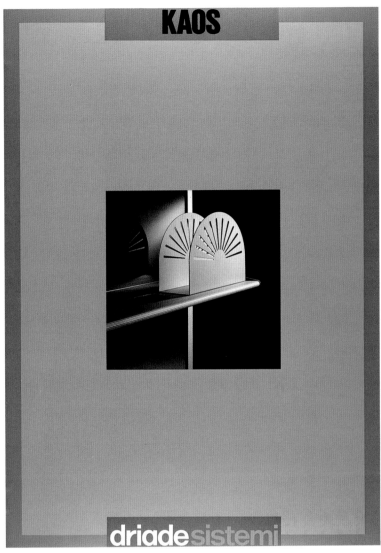

KAOS

driadesistemi

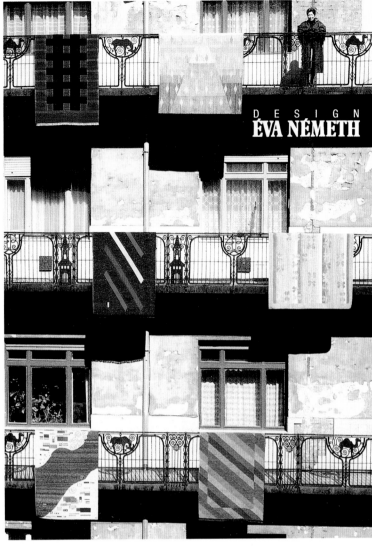

DESIGN
ÉVA NÉMETH

ART DIRECTOR:
Adelaide Acerbi
PHOTOGRAPHER:
Tom Vack / Corinne Pfister
AGENCY:
Studio Acerbi
CLIENT:
Driade
■ 224

DESIGNER:
György Kara
PHOTOGRAPHER:
Géza Molnar
COPYWRITER:
Miklos Peternak
CLIENT:
*Artex Hungarian
Foreign Trading Co.*
■ 225

■ 222 Cover of a brochure designed to assist retailers in presenting clothing, sports shoes and accessories made by Reebok. (CAN)

■ 223 Cover of a large-size brochure in which various persons talk about all the advantages of their most preferred computer in the Macintosh range. (USA)

■ 224 Cover of a brochure for "Kaos" – the modular furnishing system consisting mainly of combinations of aluminum and mirrors. (ITA)

■ 225 Cover of a catalog for an exporter of Hungarian carpets. The colors and motifs stand out from the hand-colored, almost monochrome background. (HUN)

■ 222 Umschlag einer Broschüre, mit deren Hilfe dem Einzelhandel gezeigt wird, wie Kleidung, Sportschuhe und Accessoires von Reebok präsentiert werden sollen. (CAN)

■ 223 Umschlag einer grossformatigen Broschüre, in der verschiedene Personen über die Vorteile des von ihnen bevorzugten Macintosh-Computer-Modells sprechen. (USA)

■ 224 Umschlag einer Broschüre für das Möbel-Kombisystem «Kaos», das vor allem aus Kombinationen von Aluminium und Spiegeln besteht. (ITA)

■ 225 Umschlag eines Katalogs für einen Exporteur von Teppichen. Die Farben und Motive heben sich von den sanften Tönen des handkolierten Hintergrunds ab. (HUN)

■ 222 Couverture d'un dépliant publicitaire pour un nouveau présentoir spécialement étudié pour les vêtements, chaussures de sport et accessoires de Reebok. (CAN)

■ 223 Couverture d'une brochure de grand format dans laquelle diverses personnalités expliquent quelles sont les qualités du Macintosh qu'elles apprécient surtout. (USA)

■ 224 Couverture d'une brochure présentant un système modulable de rayonnage et d'éléments combinant aluminium et miroirs. (ITA)

■ 225 Couverture d'un prospectus pour un exportateur de tapis hongrois. Les couleurs et les motifs se détachent sur un fond presque monochrome, coloré à la main. (HUN)

■ 226, 227 Covers of two catalogs in which new models by Nissan are presented. The luxury of this Japanese automobile marque is associated with the extravagant beauty and force of nature. (USA)

■ 228-232 Cover and double spreads of a brochure presenting various new sports automobiles by Nissan. The format underscores the elegance of the automobile line. Technical drawings on transparent sheets give information on the position of certain technical parts. (USA)

■ 226, 227 Umschläge für zwei Kataloge, in denen neue Modelle von Nissan vorgestellt werden. Der Luxus dieser japanischen Autos wird mit der verschwenderischen Schönheit und Kraft der Natur assoziiert. (USA)

■ 228-232 Umschlag und Doppelseiten einer Broschüre, die verschiedene neue Sportautos von Nissan vorstellt. Das Format unterstreicht die Eleganz der Form. Technische Zeichnungen auf transparenten Seiten informieren über die Position der verschiedenen Teile. (USA)

■ 226, 227 Couvertures de deux brochures de présentation de deux nouveaux modèles de Nissan. Le luxe de ces voitures japonaises est associé à la somptueuse beauté et à la force de la nature. (USA)

■ 228-232 Couverture et doubles pages d'une brochure présentant divers modèles de voitures de sport Nissan. Le format permet de souligner l'élégance de la ligne. Des dessins techniques imprimés sur feuille transparente, permettent de localiser certaines pièces. (USA)

ART DIRECTOR:
VIC CEVOLI
DESIGNER:
JOHN AVERY
PHOTOGRAPHER:
CLINT CLEMENS
COPYWRITER:
NEILL RAY
AGENCY:
HILL, HOLLIDAY
CLIENT:
NISSAN MOTOR CORP.
■ 226, 227

M30

THE POWER OF NATURE IS THAT

Q45

THE BEAUTY OF NATURE IS THAT

ART DIRECTOR:
Lynne Court / Paul Ison /
Lisa Langhoff

DESIGNER:
Lynne Court

PHOTOGRAPHER:
Kevin Hulsey / Bob Grigg

COPYWRITER:
Tony Assenza

AGENCY:
The Designory, Inc.

CLIENT:
Nissan Motor Corp.

■ 228-232

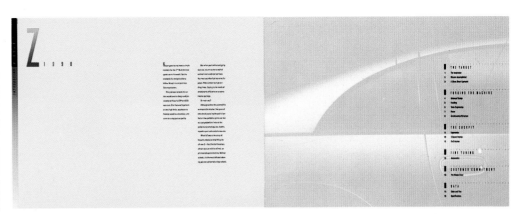

ART DIRECTOR:
Flett Henderson & Arnold

DESIGNER:
Flett Henderson & Arnold

PHOTOGRAPHER:
James Cant

STUDIO:
Flett Henderson & Arnold

CLIENT:
Rydges Hotel Group

■ 233

ART DIRECTOR:
Leslie Fried van Auken

DESIGNER:
Leslie Fried van Auken

ILLUSTRATOR:
Kurt Pakan

PHOTOGRAPHER:
Forest McMullan

COPYWRITER:
Liz Cunningham

AGENCY:
Stites & Roeding

CLIENT:
Sylvania

▼■ 234, 235

ART DIRECTOR:
KEN THOMPSON
DESIGNER:
KEN THOMPSON
COPYWRITER:
LINDA MORSE
CLIENT:
IDEAS INC.
►■ 236

CREATIVE DIRECTOR:
GERT MÜLLER
ART DIRECTOR:
DIETER WOLFF / ULI DEPPE
PHOTOGRAPHER:
MICHAEL MÖSCH
AGENCY:
SPIESS ERMISCH ABELS
CLIENT:
BMW MOTORRAD GMBH
▼■ 237, 238

■ 233 Two versions of a folding prospectus designed for a small hotel with exclusive interiors. (AUS)

■ 234, 235 Cover and double spread of a brochure publicizing a new transport and freight system which connects up the large cities of the United States. (USA)

■ 236 "A boxful of ideas" mailed by Ideas, an advertising agency based in Atlanta. (USA)

■ 237, 238 Cover and inside page of a brochure for BMW motorcycles. It defines the lifestyle of motorcycle enthusiasts – action and creation. (GER)

■ 233 Varianten eines Faltprospekts für ein kleines Hotel mit besonderer Innenausstattung. (AUS)

■ 234, 235 Umschlag und Doppelseite eines Prospektes über ein Transportsystem, durch das die grossen Städte der USA miteinander verbunden sind. (USA)

■ 236 «Eine Schachtel voller Ideen», verschickt von Ideas, einer Werbeagentur in Atlanta. (USA)

■ 237, 238 Umschlag und Innenseite eines Prospekts für BMW-Motorräder, in dem es um den Lebensstil der Motorrad-Fans geht. (GER)

■ 233 Prospectus publicitaire pour un petit hôtel dont les chambres sont individualisées. (AUS)

■ 234, 235 Couverture et double page d'un prospectus annonçant la mise en service d'un nouveau système de distribution reliant les grandes villes américaines. (USA)

■ 236 Une «boîte à idées» distribuée par Ideas, une agence de publicité d'Atlanta. (USA)

■ 237, 238 Action et création, tels sont les deux mots qui définissent le style de vie des amoureux de la moto. Dépliant publicitaire pour les motos BMW. (GER)

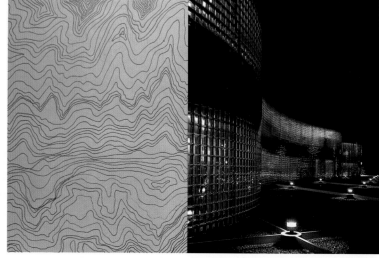

■ 239-241 Catalog issued for the twentieth anniversary of an architect office in Detroit. *239* shows the catalog with its slipcase, and the front of an envelope containing invitation cards. This envelope – as also the cover of the catalog – is ornamented with punched out motifs. *240, 241*: Double spreads from the catalog in which the most important buildings designed by these architects are presented. (USA)

■ 242-244 Cover and two double spreads from an ad brochure for Designcorp, specialists in the interior design of corporate offices. (USA)

■ 239-241 Anlässlich des 20jährigen Bestehens eines Architekturbüros in Detroit herausgegebener Katalog. *239:* Der Katalog mit Schuber sowie ein Umschlag mit Einladungskarten. Wie der Umschlag des Katalogs ist dieses Couvert mit Ausstanzungen versehen. *240, 241*: Doppelseiten des Katalogs, auf denen die wichtigsten Bauten der Firma vorgestellt werden. (USA)

■ 242-244 Umschlag und zwei Doppelseiten aus einer Werbebroschüre für Designcorp, Spezialisten für die Innengestaltung von Geschäftshäusern. (USA)

■ 239-241 Catalogue publié à l'occasion du 20e anniversaire d'un bureau d'architectes de Detroit. *239:* le catalogue et son emboîtage, ainsi que la pochette contenant les cartes d'invitation. La couverture du catalogue et la pochette sont ornées de motifs en découpe. *240, 241*: doubles pages du catalogue présentant les principales réalisations architecturales de Rossetti Associates. (USA)

■ 242-244 Couverture et deux doubles pages de la brochure publicitaire de Designcorp, une firme spécialisée dans l'aménagement intérieur des centres commerciaux. (USA)

ART DIRECTOR:
SCOTT TAYLOR / PAUL CAMPBELL
DESIGNER:
PAUL CAMPBELL
PHOTOGRAPHER:
RON BAXTER SMITH
AGENCY:
TAYLOR & BROWNING
DESIGN ASSOCIATES
CLIENT:
DESIGNCORP LTD.
▲■ 242-244

ART DIRECTOR:
MIHO
DESIGNER:
MIHO
CLIENT:
ROSSETTI
ASSOCIATES / ARCHITECTS
◄■ 239-241

BEDFORD PROPERTIES

HAWAII

Hawaii—one of the world's most prestigious resort areas is also one of the most desirable locales for doing business. Here is abundant beauty, yet boundless opportunity.

Today Hawaii offers more than super weather and luxury resorts. The economic climate couldn't be better. As a prime population and job growth market, Hawaii's retail, commercial and residential properties are burgeoning, boosted by increased tourism and an influx of investment capital both domestic and foreign. Construction on the islands has doubled and the outlook is for continued economic activity.

Launching an ambitious program to keep pace with Hawaii's accelerating economy, Bedford Properties, with an eye to long-range strategy and lasting value, has stepped up the development of diverse projects on Hawaii's Big Island and Oahu. These developments will be significant, substantial, trend-setting. Highly visible, easily accessible, geared to the needs of tenants and the community. And all in a setting found nowhere else on earth.

Hawaii Kai Towne Center, the first of two promotional shopping centers in the state of Hawaii and the commercial centerpiece for the master-planned community of Hawaii Kai.

Pearl Plantation Center, a major promotional center located just minutes from Honolulu's financial district and situated in the middle of a demographic area of 369,200 people.

Kona Coast Shopping Center Phase I and Phase II on the Big Island of Hawaii's Kona Coast, one of the state's hottest tourist destination areas.

Kalama Village Center providing convenient services to the community of Kalama Valley in Hawaii Kai.

Bedford Properties brings nearly three decades of know-how to the challenge of real estate investment, development and management. Tenants can rely on a team of professionals with experience, expertise and a commitment to creating and maintaining properties of the highest quality.

ART DIRECTOR:
Michael Vanderbyl
DESIGNER:
Michael Vanderbyl
AGENCY:
Vanderbyl Design
CLIENT:
Bedford Properties
■ 245-248

ART DIRECTOR:
Lowell Williams
DESIGNER:
*Lowell Williams / Lana
Rigsby*
PHOTOGRAPHER:
*Andy Dearwater /
Nick Merrick*
COPYWRITER:
JoAnn Stone
AGENCY:
Lowell Williams Design, Inc.
CLIENT:
Maguire Thomas Partners
■ 249-254

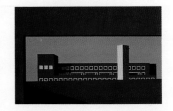

■ 245-248 Cover and three double spreads of a brochure for Bedford Properties, a company that builds and sells corporate buildings in Hawaii. (USA)

■ 249-254 Cover and double spreads from a brochure in which offices and apartments in the new town of Solana, west of Dallas, Texas, are presented. This urban project associates work and living. (USA)

■ 245-248 Umschlag und drei Doppelseiten einer Broschüre für Bedford Properties, eine Firma, die Geschäftshäuser auf Hawaii baut und verkauft. (USA)

■ 249-254 Umschlag und Doppelseiten aus einer Broschüre, in der Büros und Apartments in dem neuen Ort Solana, im Westen von Dallas, vorgestellt werden. Es geht um die Kombination von leben und arbeiten. (USA)

■ 245-248 Couverture et trois doubles pages d'une brochure publiée par Bedford Properties, une société qui construit des centres commerciaux à Hawaii. (USA)

■ 249-254 Couverture et doubles pages d'une brochure de leasing pour des bureaux et des appartements du nouveau village de Solana, à l'ouest de Dallas. Le projet d'urbanisme associe travail et détente. (USA)

ART DIRECTOR:
Scott Barsuhn
DESIGNER:
Scott Barsuhn /
Bruce Macindoe
ILLUSTRATOR:
Margaret Huber
COPYWRITER:
Julie Yanson / Kyia Downing
AGENCY:
Barsuhn Design
CLIENT:
Minneapolis College
of Art & Design
■ 255-258

DESIGNER:
Michael Mabry
PHOTOGRAPHER:
Leslie Flores / Monica Lee /
John DeGroot
COPYWRITER:
Virginia Porter
STUDIO:
Michael Mabry Design
CLIENT:
California College
of Arts and Crafts
■ 259-262

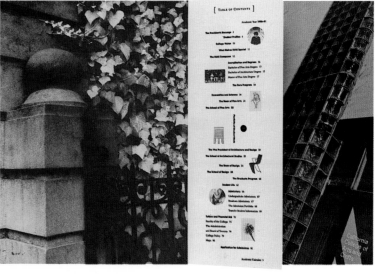

VINCENT
James
JOAN M.
& Soranno
TROY
Kampa
HELENA
Espinosa
KEVIN
Flynn

This is only a dream.

A dream about a dead city springing back to life. A city in which there is no "life safety" and invention is the only rule.

In this city new structures exist at the expense of others, but it is not a question of morality. It is a study of a parasitic relationship between an existing convention and a new order.

In this dream the unfamiliar is juxtaposed against the familiar; old and new tissue. Here dwellings struggle upward, dependent on other structures for materials and support. It is the overwhelming desire to ascend and command like a vine having found its way to the base of a tree.

house ('haüz) vb: to provide with living quarters; to serve as shelter for; to take shelter

An illegal house is any act which serves to facilitate the lifestyle and/or needs of the disenfranchised.

"The word 'homeless' is applied to so many different kinds of people, with so many different histories, that it is almost meaningless."

[There exists] "a marginal world inhabited by all those unable to find a place in 'our' world... a world not without its own rules and rituals."

"Marginal men and women hold a special significance; they remind us of the narrowness of received truths we take for granted... 'beyond the pale,' they somehow redefine the pale..."

"A society needs its margins as much as it needs art and literature."

"We owe them at least a place... [we have] an existential obligation."

"Compassion is little more than the passion for control."

Peter Marin in "Helping and Hating the Homeless; The Struggle as the Margins of America," *Harper's*, January, 1987.

Through an examination of what is considered abandoned by our society, this project attempts to assemble a framework for re-evaluating our current urban environment and the codes that have shaped it.

It was said that while on the bench the Judge used to dabble in Cartesian ethics. Some say he went mad, others smile quietly. Whichever it was, he left the bench the day a fly was trapped in the space between his panel and the block it fell upon.

The Judge lives exiled in a house with no entry or exit, located on the islands of green space formed by the highway's cloverleafs. He has become a public hermit in response to his concerns for spiritual safety, as opposed to the bodily safety which society's codes protect. Enclosed in a world of contemplation whose medium is thought (a weightless, silent thing whose intangibility often calls its presence into doubt), the Judge's thoughts and dreams are what mold his environment.

The house consists of a wall and tower. The tower is composed of stacking rooms, each molded by recurring ideas in his thought. The rooms redefine the Judge's personal codes as he contemplates his position outside society. The wall establishes the physical link to the land and between rooms by providing vertical circulation.

These two axes—the horizontal or physical world vs. the vertical or mental world—establish the new crossroads the Judge finds himself at. The objective viewpoint he held as a judge in society has changed to a subjective one, locating him at the origin of these two axes. No longer does he feel the mind and body separate. The yearning for their union is explored in the courtship between the wall and tower, and their longing for that infinitely dense point, coordinate 0,0.

This project began as an exploration of the idea of windows. The greatest question to be answered within this framework was: How can anything so small as the placement of a window affect a house, a street, a neighborhood or a city? How can it possibly affect the way we live?

I wondered, why can't a house have only one window? Why do they have to be certain sizes? Does a window really need to have glass in it? Could my windows be really, really tiny and high up on the walls? What if I don't want any windows at all? Are windows for looking in or looking out?

Presently, let's say I don't really change the shape or size of an ordinary window, but instead, alter its placement. Perhaps 'my' window is not really in my 'house' at all, but is, in fact, built into another person's home. Maybe I use their window; I use it not to receive air or light, but to look in upon them and record their actions for the expressed interest of the accumulation of experience and knowledge. I have then become an enlightened Peeping Tom. I am a Gnostic Voyeur.

The placement of this house and its window would violate zoning and building codes, as well as a universal social more. So it is not only a statement on the idea of window, but is also largely emblematic of our society as a whole, wherein people spend far too much time watching others perform rather than concentrating on their own progress, development and actions.

The window I look into could be your own; whose are you looking through?

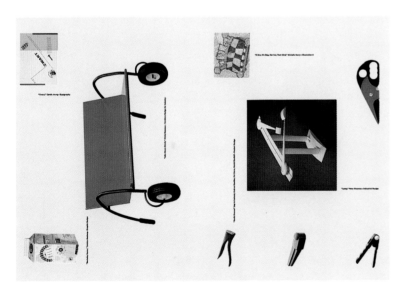

■ 255-258 "Illegal Houses" is the title of this exhibition catalog. Architectural projects are shown which purposely go against the accepted rules. The cover, in corrugated cardboard, is appropriate to the experimental character of this architecture. (USA)

■ 259-262 Cover and double spreads from an information brochure for the California College of Arts and Crafts, San Francisco. The program is illustrated by works of students from various classes. *260:* the first double spread with the timetable. (USA)

■ 255-258 «Illegale Häuser», so der Titel dieses Ausstellungskatalogs, in dem Architekturprojekte gezeigt werden, die bewusst den geltenden Regeln widersprechen. Der Umschlag aus Wellkarton entspricht dem experimentellen Charakter dieser Architektur. (USA)

■ 259-262 Umschlag und Doppelseiten einer Informationsbroschüre des California College of Arts and Crafts, San Francisco. Das Programm ist mit Arbeiten von Studenten der verschiedenen Klassen illustriert. *260:* erste Doppelseite mit dem Stundenplan. (USA)

■ 255-258 «Maisons illégales», tel est le titre de ce catalogue d'exposition regroupant des projets d'architectes qui violent délibérément les règles de la profession. La couverture de carton ondulé souligne le caractère expérimental d'une telle architecture. (USA)

■ 259-262 Couverture et doubles pages d'une brochure d'informations du California College of Arts and Crafts de San Francisco. Le programme est illustré de travaux réalisés par des élèves des diverses sections. *260:* première double page avec l'encart du sommaire. (USA)

■ 263 Cover of a brochure issued by the Zoological Society of Houston, publicizing a new program for their members for fund-raising activities. (USA)

■ 264 Invitation to the opening of a disco club. (SPA)

■ 265-267 Small poster as advertising for the film "Indiana Jones", produced by Lucasfilms. (USA)

■ 263 Umschlag einer Broschüre der zoologischen Gesellschaft von Houston, die ihren Mitgliedern ein neues Subventionsprogramm erläutert. (USA)

■ 264 Einladung für die Eröffnung eines Disco-Clubs. (SPA)

■ 265-267 Kleinplakate als Werbung für den Film «Indiana Jones», produziert von Lucasfilms. (USA)

■ 263 Couverture d'une brochure de la Société zoologique de Houston invitant ses membres à participer à un nouveau programme de souscription. (USA)

■ 264 Affichette pour l'ouverture d'un disco-club. (SPA)

■ 265-267 Trois affichettes pour la promotion du film «Indiana Jones», produit par Lucasfilms. (USA)

ART DIRECTOR:
LOWELL WILLIAMS
DESIGNER:
LANA RIGSBY
PHOTOGRAPHER:
ARTHUR MEYERSON
COPYWRITER:
HOLLY QUINN
AGENCY:
LOWELL WILLIAMS DESIGN, INC.
CLIENT:
ZOOLOGICAL SOCIETY OF
HOUSTON
■ 263

ART DIRECTOR:
PATI NUNEZ
DESIGNER:
PATI NUNEZ
SONSOLES LLORENS
AGENCY:
PATI NUNEZ
CLIENT:
LOUIE VEGA
■ 264

The Zoological Society of Houston

Corporate Conservators Program

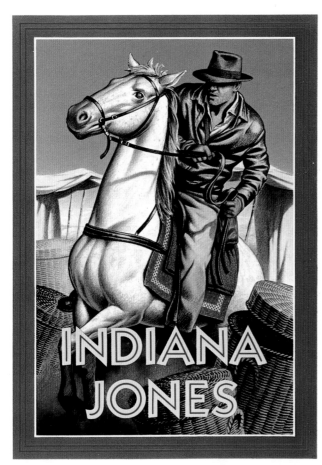

ART DIRECTOR:
DAVID EDELSTEIN /
LANNY FRENCH / ERIC HAGGARD
DESIGNER:
DAVID EDELSTEIN /
LANNY FRENCH / ERIC HAGGARD
ILLUSTRATOR:
LARRY JOST
AGENCY:
EDELSTEIN ASSOCIATES ADV. INC.
CLIENT:
LUCASFILMS
■ 265-267

ART DIRECTOR:
MICHAEL BIERUT
DESIGNER:
MICHAEL BIERUT
AGENCY:
VIGNELLI ASSOCIATES
CLIENT:
*AMERICAN INSTITUTE OF
GRAPHIC ARTS*
■ 268

ART DIRECTOR:
SCOTT PEDERSEN
DESIGNER:
BENNETT PEJI
ILLUSTRATOR:
BENNETT PEJI
COPYWRITER:
SCOTT PEDERSEN
AGENCY:
BENNET PEJI DESIGN
CLIENT:
SCOTTLAND CONCERTS
■ 269

■ 268 Invitation to an event organized by AIGA, New York, to benefit Diffa, a foundation established by graphic designers for assisting AIDS victims. (USA)

■ 269 Promotional leaflet for the announcement of a series of concerts of the Soviet rock group Vladimir Kuzmin & Dinamik. The star is cut out. (USA)

■ 270, 271 Two self-promotional cards for a designer and illustrator based in California. (USA)

■ 268 Einladung zu einer Veranstaltung des AIGA, New York, zugunsten der Diffa, einer von Graphikern gegründeten Stiftung für AIDS-Kranke. (USA)

■ 269 Handzettel für die Ankündigung einer Konzertreihe der sowjetischen Rockgruppe Vladimir Kuzmin & Dinamik. Der Stern ist ausgestanzt. (USA)

■ 270, 271 Zwei Eigenwerbungskarten eines Designers/ Illlustrators aus Kalifornien. (USA)

■ 268 Carte d'invitation à une fête organisée par l'AIGA de New York au profit de la Diffa, une fondation des industries graphiques pour le SIDA. (USA)

■ 269 Feuillet publicitaire annonçant une série de concerts du groupe de rock soviétique Vladimir Kuzmin & Dinamik. L'étoile est découpée. (USA)

■ 270-271 Deux cartes autopromotionnelles d'un graphiste-illustrateur californien. (USA)

ART DIRECTOR:
JEFF KOEGEL
DESIGNER:
JEFF KOEGEL
ILLUSTRATOR:
JEFF KOEGEL
STUDIO:
KOEGEL DESIGN
CLIENT:
KOEGEL DESIGN STUDIO
■ 270, 271

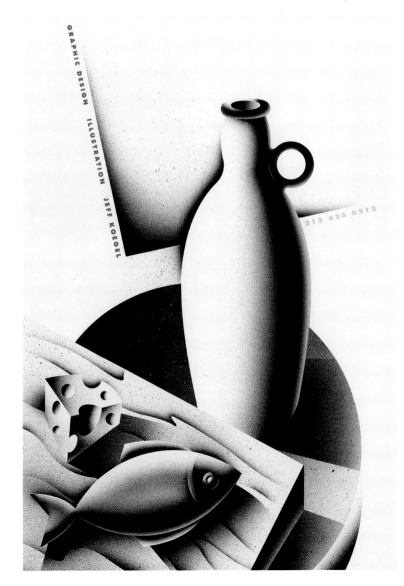

■ 272, 273 Self promotion portfolio for an advertising agency. The pockets on both inside pages contain two brochures that can be looked at simultaneously. (AUT)

■ 274, 275 Cover and double spread from a brochure for photographer Ron Baxter. (CAN)

■ 276 New Year card in concertina form for two graphic designers/illustrators. (SWI)

■ 277-279 Cover and two double spreads from the self-promotional brochure of an Italian illustrator. (ITA)

■ 272, 273 Eigenwerbungsmappe einer Werbeagentur. Die Taschen an den beiden Innenseiten enthalten zwei Prospekte, die man gleichzeitig anschauen kann. (AUT)

■ 274, 275 Umschlag und Doppelseite aus einer Broschüre des Photographen Ron Baxter. (CAN)

■ 276 Neujahrskarte in Leporello-Form von zwei Graphikern/Illustratoren. (SWI)

■ 277-279 Umschlag und zwei Doppelseiten der Eigenwerbungsbroschüre einer italienischen Illustratorin. (ITA)

■ 272, 273 Dossier autopromotionnel d'une agence de publicité. Les deux volets de la chemise cartonnée s'ouvrent sur deux brochures présentées symétriquement. (AUT)

■ 274, 275 Couverture et double page d'une brochure autopromotionnelle du photographe Ron Baxter. (CAN)

■ 276 Dépliant envoyé au Nouvel An par deux graphistes-illustrateurs représentés internationalement. (SWI)

■ 277-279 Couverture et deux doubles pages de la brochure autopromotionnelle d'une illustratrice italienne. (USA)

ART DIRECTOR:
JUSTINE FRANZISKA SCHÖRGEL
DESIGNER:
FREUND WERBEAGENTUR
PHOTOGRAPHER:
STASNY FOTOSTUDIO
AGENCY:
FREUND WERBEAGENTUR
◀■ 272, 273

ART DIRECTOR:
ENZO MESSI / URS SCHMIDT
ILLUSTRATOR:
ENZO MESSI / URS SCHMIDT
STUDIO:
MESSI & SCHMIDT
CLIENT:
ENZO MESSI / URS SCHMIDT
■ 276

ART DIRECTOR:
PIERA GRANDESSO
DESIGNER:
PIERA GRANDESSO
ILLUSTRATOR:
PIERA GRANDESSO
COPYWRITER:
PIERA GRANDESSO
AGENCY:
PIERA GRANDESSO
CLIENT:
PIERA GRANDESSO
✏ 277-279
▼

DESIGNER:
DEL TERRELONGE
PHOTOGRAPHER:
RON BAXTER SMITH
AGENCY:
TERRELONGE DESIGN
CLIENT:
RON BAXTER SMITH
PHOTOGRAPHER LTD.
◀■ 274, 275

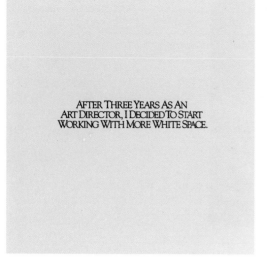

AFTER THREE YEARS AS AN
ART DIRECTOR, I DECIDED TO START
WORKING WITH MORE WHITE SPACE.

SO I MOVED TO MINNEAPOLIS.

Doug Trapp 3531 Harriet Ave #1 Minneapolis, MN 55408 612-822-3986

ART DIRECTOR:
DOUG TRAPP
DESIGNER:
DOUG TRAPP
PHOTOGRAPHER:
PAUL SINKLER
COPYWRITER:
JAN PETTIT/DOUG TRAPP
AGENCY:
McCOOL & COMPANY
CLIENT:
DOUG TRAPP
▲■ 280, 281

ART DIRECTOR:
RANDY PALMER
DESIGNER:
RANDY PALMER
PHOTOGRAPHER:
PAUL LOVEN
CLIENT:
*PAUL LOVEN
PHOTOGRAPHY, INC.*
▼■ 282, 283

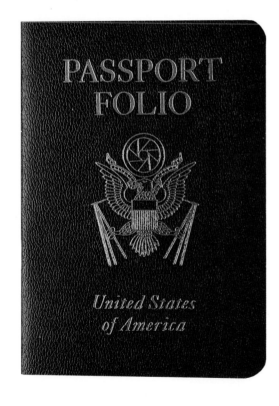

PASSPORT
FOLIO

*United States
of America*

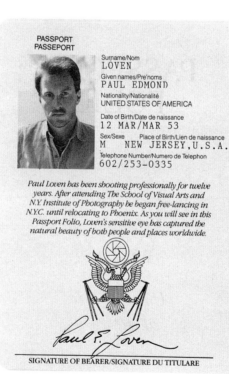

PASSPORT
PASSEPORT

Surname/Nom
LOVEN
Given names/Pre'noms
PAUL EDMOND
Nationality/Nationalité
UNITED STATES OF AMERICA
Date of Birth/Date de naissance
12 MAR/MAR 53
Sex/Sexe   Place of Birth/Lien de naissance
M   NEW JERSEY, U.S.A.
Telephone Number/Numero de Telephon
602/253-0335

*Paul Loven has been shooting professionally for twelve
years. After attending The School of Visual Arts and
N.Y. Institute of Photography be began free-lancing in
N.Y.C. until relocating to Phoenix. As you will see in this
Passport Folio, Loven's sensitive eye has captured the
natural beauty of both people and places worldwide.*

SIGNATURE OF BEARER/SIGNATURE DU TITULARE

Machu Picchu, Peru

■ 280, 281 Cards announcing an art director's change of
address who decided "to start working with more white
space." (USA)

■ 282, 283 Self-promotional brochure for a photographer
designed in the form of a passport. The photographs orig-
inate from all parts of the globe. (USA)

■ 284-287 Invitation to take part in the competition organized by the Society of Typographic Arts. (USA)

■ 280, 281 Karte für die Bekanntgabe einer Adressänderung
eines Art Directors «auf der Suche nach grösseren weissen
Flächen». (USA)

■ 282, 283 Als Pass konzipierte Eigenwerbungsbroschüre
eines Photographen. Die Photos stammen aus allen Teilen
der Welt. (USA)

■ 284-287 Einladung zur Teilnahme am Wettbewerb der
Society of Typographic Arts. (USA)

■ 280, 281 Carte annonçant le changement d'adresse d'un
directeur artistique «à la recherche de plus grands espaces
blancs». (USA)

■ 282, 283 Dossier autopromotionnel d'un photographe,
présenté sous forme de passeport. Les photos proviennent
de toutes les contrées du monde. (USA)

■ 284-287 Prospectus invitant les candidats à participer au
concours organisé par la Society of Typographic Arts. (USA)

ENTER

ART DIRECTOR:
RICK VALICENTI
DESIGNER:
RICK VALICENTI/
MICHAEL GIAMMANCO
PHOTOGRAPHER:
VARIOUS
COPYWRITER:
TODD LIEF
AGENCY:
THIRST
CLIENT:
SOCIETY OF TYPOGRAPHIC ARTS

■ 284-287

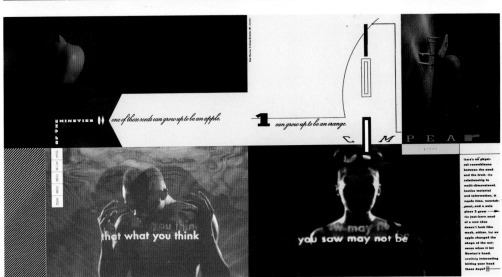

ART DIRECTOR:
Leslee Avchen / Laurie Jacobi

DESIGNER:
Leslee Avchen / Laurie Jacobi

PHOTOGRAPHER:
*John Vasiliou /
Terry Heffernan /
Jonathan Poor*

COPYWRITER:
Cynthia Zwirn

AGENCY:
Avchen & Jacoby, Inc.

CLIENT:
Consolidated Papers, Inc.

■ 288-294

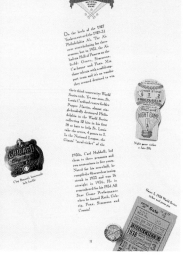

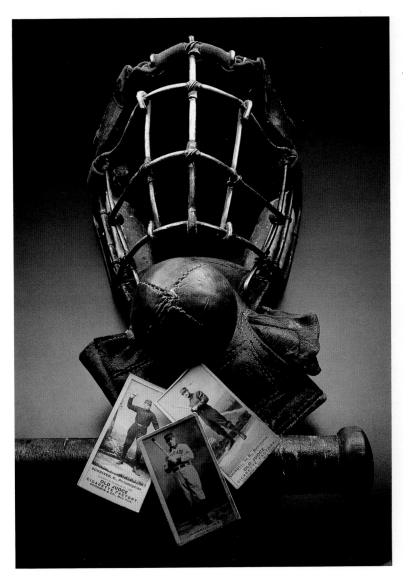

Many baseball fans believe the game was invented in 1839 by an American, Abner Doubleday and was first played on American soil at Cooperstown, New York. In recent years, however, advanced theories indicate that baseball had its origins in more primitive games played long before 1839. The ancient Egyptians "games of ball" were immortalized in temple wall carvings and tomb inscriptions. Later, in medieval Europe and Elizabethan England — as well as in early America — games using a ball were played. These ancient games are the true ancestors of America's favorite sport. A noted pioneer is Alexander J. Cartwright who organized the New York Knickerbockers in 1845. He introduced classic rules including foul ball and dropped third strike still used today!

Detroit ticket book c. 1890's

Umpire's Indicator kept record of balls, strikes and outs, still used today

Commemorative pin for the Baltimore Nationals

2

■ 288-294 Cover and pages from the inside of an advertising brochure for a paper producer. The subject is the history of baseball. Highlighted is the print quality on simple paper, without high gloss. The typography is specially adapted to fit the illustrations and gives each double spread its own individual character. (USA)

■ 288-294 Umschlag und Seiten aus dem Inneren einer Werbebroschüre für einen Papierhersteller. Thema ist die Geschichte des Baseballs. Hier soll die Druckqualität auf einfachem Papier ohne Hochglanz demonstriert werden. Die Typographie ist den Bildern angepasst und gibt jeder Doppelseite einen speziellen Charakter. (USA)

■ 288-294 Couverture et pages intérieures d'une brochure publicitaire retraçant l'histoire du base-ball pour un fabricant de papiers. Les qualités d'un papier sans vernis sont ici mises en valeur. La typographie reprend les grandes lignes de l'image, donnant à chaque double page un caractère et un rythme particuliers. (USA)

ART DIRECTOR:
DAVID POCKNELL
DESIGNER:
ROY HAGUE
PHOTOGRAPHER:
MATTHEW PRINCE
AGENCY:
POCKNELL & CO.
CLIENT:
Q B FACTORY
■ 295

■ 295 Catalog establishing a new identity for the Q B Factory – typesetters and printers. There is a negative and a positive version of the cover. (GBR)

■ 296-302 Brochures issued by paper producers James River Corp. with samples of tinted papers from the "Terra and Tuscan Antique" range. The special spiral binding allows a comparison of various paper qualities. 296: the closed brochure (USA)

■ 295 Katalog für eine neue Firmenidentität der Setzerei und Druckerei QB Factory. Vom Umschlag existieren eine Negativ- und eine Positiv-Version. (GBR)

■ 296-302 Broschüre des Papierherstellers James River Corp. mit Mustern getönter Papiersorten der Linie «Toskanische Erde». Die besondere Spiralbindung erlaubt einen Vergleich der verschiedenen Papiermuster. *296:* die geschlossene Broschüre. (USA)

■ 295 Catalogue d'une imprimerie spécialisée dans la typographie, QB Factory. La couverture a été imprimée en négatif et en positif. (GBR)

■ 296-302 Brochure du fabricant de papiers James River Corp. présentant les papiers teintés de la ligne «Terre toscane». Le système de reliure à spirale permet de comparer les différents échantillons imprimés. *296:* la brochure refermée. (USA)

ART DIRECTOR:
Nancy Skolos
DESIGNER:
Nancy Skolos
ILLUSTRATOR:
Thomas Wedell
COPYWRITER:
Neal Kane
AGENCY:
Skolos Wedell + Raynor
CLIENT:
James River Corporation
■ 296-302

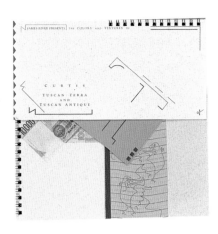

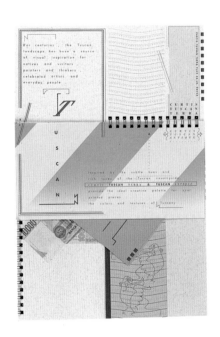

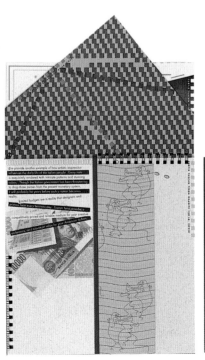

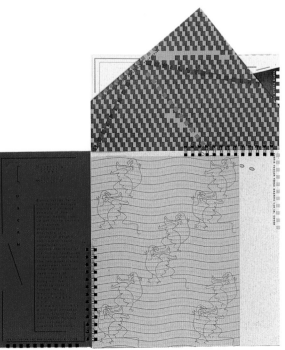

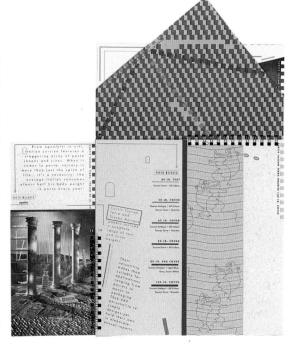

■ 303-306 Cover and double spreads of a small book entitled *The Voyage of All Time* and published for promotional purposes by a paper producer. It tells the story of a designer who travels through time searching for new ideas. (USA)

■ 307-313 Cover and double spreads from a brochure issued by the Mead Corporation, paper manufacturers. Each style of shoe corresponds to a paper quality. (USA)

■ 303-306 Umschlag und Doppelseiten eines kleinen Buches als Werbung für Papierhersteller. Erzählt wird die Geschichte eines Designers, der auf der Suche nach Ideen durch die Zeit reist. Die Farbillustrationen sind reliefartig im Aufdruck. (USA)

■ 307-313 Umschlag und Doppelseiten einer Broschüre für die Mead Corp., einen Papierhersteller. Jedem Schuhmodell ist eine Papiersorte zugeordnet. (USA)

■ 303-306 Couverture et doubles pages d'un petit livre de promotion publié par un fabricant de papiers, dans lequel nous est contée l'histoire d'un designer en mal d'inspiration qui voyage dans le temps. Les illustrations en couleurs sont gaufrées. (USA)

■ 307-313 Couverture et doubles pages d'une brochure pour Mead Corp., un fabricant de papiers. A chaque style de chaussures correspond une qualité de papier. (USA)

ART DIRECTOR:
SHARON WERNER
DESIGNER:
SHARON WERNER
ILLUSTRATOR:
SHARON WERNER /
CHARLES BURNS
COPYWRITER:
CHUCK CARLSON
AGENCY:
THE DUFFY DESIGN GROUP
CLIENT:
FOX RIVER PAPER CO.
■ 303-306

Those aren't "just shoes"
you put on in the morning
They're definitions.
They announce where you're from.
How you expect to be treated.
What you do for a living
and what you think is fun.
Even your gender.
In short, they say who you are.
Over time,
they'll become worn
to your personal specifications
and may as much about you
as your signature.
Just as your paper choices
make your professional attitudes clear,
Signature from Mead
says you take pride in your work.
Then it gives you work
to be proud of.

Straightforward.
Some people
claim passions
grow stronger
the more
you love them in.
Great-grandmother
must have been
something else.

Put Your Best Foot Forward on Signature from Mead

ART DIRECTOR:
John Van Dyke
DESIGNER:
John Van Dyke
PHOTOGRAPHER:
Terry Heffernan
COPYWRITER:
Jon Bell
AGENCY:
Van Dyke Company
CLIENT:
Mead Corporation
■ 307-313

Signature takes pressure in stride.
Today's presses, with their
five- and six-color processes,
bring out the worst
in lesser papers,
including distortion and wrinkles.
But Signature resists mechanical stretch,
surface pull of ink and
sheet-to-sheet misregistration.
Jobs tend to go smoother
tempers stay cooler
and waste is kept to a minimum.
Best of all, you'll see the difference
in your own color work.
While the presses hum,
the colors sing.

Seriously casual.

Born with style.
Some babies
are born with
silver spoons.
Maybe
the luckier ones
are born
with parents
who give them
a strong sense
of themselves.

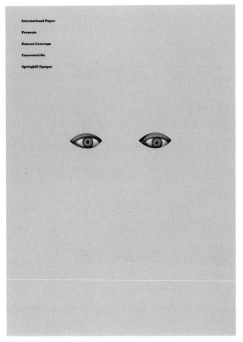

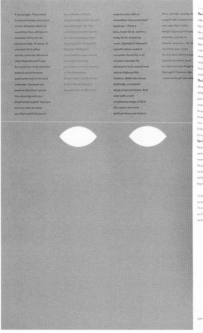

ART DIRECTOR:
REX PETEET
DESIGNER:
REX PETEET
ILLUSTRATOR:
JOHN EVANS / REX PETEET /
JACK UNRUH
COPYWRITER:
MARY LANGRIDGE / REX PETEET
AGENCY:
SIBLEY / PETEET DESIGN
CLIENT:
INTERNATIONAL PAPER CO.
■ 314-318

■ 314-318 Large-size brochure for a paper quality by the International Paper Co. *314:* the brochures in their respective envelopes. The punched out eyes are repeated on the cover *(315)* and the first double spread *(316)*. The subject of masking and demasking "coverups" runs throughout the brochure. (USA)

■ 314-318 Grossformatige Broschüre für eine Papierqualität der International Paper Co. *314:* die Broschüre im dazugehörigen Couvert. Die Ausstanzung wiederholt sich auf dem Umschlag *(315)* und auf der ersten Doppelseite *(316)*. Das Thema der Maskierung und Demaskierung zieht sich durch die gesamte Broschüre. (USA)

■ 314-318 Brochure de grand format réalisée pour le fabricant de papiers International Paper Co. *314:* la brochure dans son enveloppe. Le motif en découpe se répète sur la couverture *(315)* et sur la première double page *(316)*. Ce jeu de superpositions se répète d'une page à l'autre, le sujet se démasquant ou se dévoilant. (USA)

The
Illustrious
Professor

If you had done your homework, you would know, Professor Joseph Abernathy Prissbiddy doffs his pants, his past and his persona to become (drum roll, please) –"Tattoo Joe and his Amazing Picture Show!" ☐ Known for a terrific vocabulary and a prodigious appetite for wine, women and witticisms. Tattoo Joe is a carny Casanova and a clown of renown. But what Joe is *really* famous for is his epic epidermis. For Joseph's favorite works have literally gotten under Joe's skin. Inscribed on *their* hide is comedy, tragedy, melodrama and farce. Freckles are used for punctuation, wrinkles work as plot lines, and characters seem so real that they literally jump off the page…er, skin. ☐ But as popular as Tattoo Joe's tableau always is, carny regulars can't help but wonder, Whatever does this colorful guy find to *do* in the off-season?

When you want a stock
with an A+ finish
that can help you save
on both postage
and paper costs, then
step right up, ladies
and gentlemen. Because
Springhill Opaque
will give you the Greatest
Show on Earth! (At a
price that won't take the
shirt off your back.)

■ 319-323 Envelope with an ad brochure for the paper quality "Strathmore Americana" which has a structured surface. Famous old stamps are shown. (USA)

■ 319-323 Umschlag mit einer Werbebroschüre für die Papiersorte «Strathmore Americana» mit strukturierter Oberfläche. Hier werden bekannte alte Marken gezeigt. (USA)

■ 319-323 Chemise renfermant le dossier publicitaire illustré d'anciennes marques devenues fameuses pour papier «Strathmore Americana» à surface structurée. (USA)

ART DIRECTOR:
MICHAEL MABRY
DESIGNER:
MICHAEL MABRY
ILLUSTRATOR:
MELISSA GRIMES/
STEVEN GUARNACCIA/
JOHN HERSEY
COPYWRITER:
LINDA PETERSON/
STEVEN HELLER/PHILIP MEGGS
AGENCY:
MICHAEL MABRY DESIGN
CLIENT:
STRATHMORE PAPER CO.
■ 319-323

W

Celebrating the Great American Icon

by Steven Heller

WHOSE MOUTH WOULDN'T WATER AT THE SIGHT OF THE FRESHLY BITTEN GOOD HUMOR ICE CREAM BAR EMBLAZONED ON THE SIDE OF A CREAMY WHITE TRUCK, AND WHO COULD RESIST A COLD REFRESHING ORANGE CRUSH AFTER BEING EXPOSED TO ITS SEDUCTIVELY SCULPTED BOTTLE? THESE AND OTHER GREAT AMERICAN TRADEMARKS ARE HYPNOTIC CUES TRIGGERING APPETITES, PASSIONS, AND EVEN MEMORIES. MOREOVER, THE MOST EFFECTIVE TRADE CHARACTERS (LITTLE MASCOTS WHO EMBODY A PRODUCT OR COMPANY) ARE NOT MERE COMMERCIAL SIGNPOSTS, BUT TOTEMS AS POTENT AS ANY REAL LIFE IDOL. HAD PAVLOV OBSERVED HUMAN BEINGS

John Hersey on Mount Dream White

Melissa Grimes on Nantucket Irony

MARKET MASCOTS

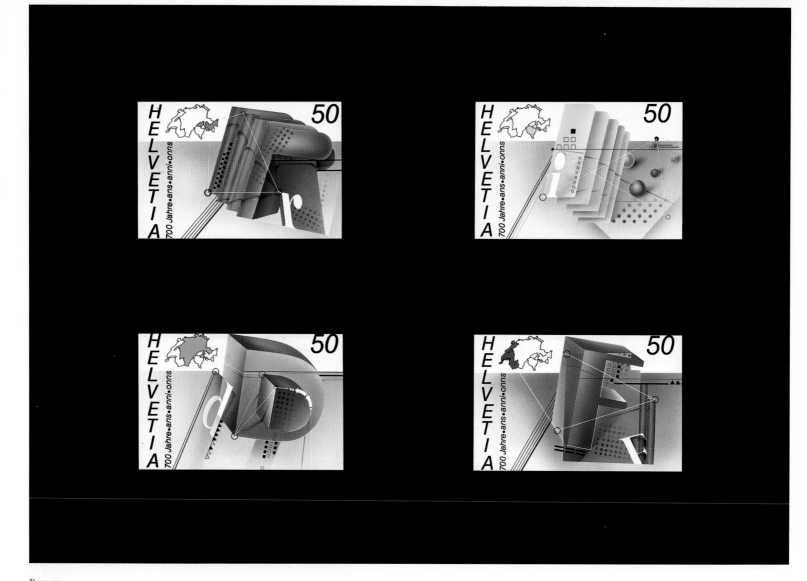

DESIGNER:
VLADISLAV M. CIMBUREK
ILLUSTRATOR:
VLADISLAV M. CIMBUREK
STUDIO:
VLADISLAV M. CIMBUREK
CLIENT:
PTT
■ 324

■ 324 Four postage-stamp designs to mark the 700th anniversary of Switzerland. The initials of the four national languages – German, French, Italian and Rhetoromansh – are the subject of the individual stamps. (SWI)

■ 324 Vier Briefmarkenentwürfe für die 700-Jahrfeier der Schweiz. Die Initialen der vier Landessprachen – deutsch, französisch, italienisch und rätoromanisch – sind das Thema der einzelnen Marken. (SWI)

■ 324 Quatre projets de timbres pour les 700 ans de la Confédération. Variations formelles sur les initiales de chaque région linguistique – français, italien, allemand («d» pour deutsch) et romanche – de la Suisse. (SWI)

DESIGN DE PÉRIODIQUES

REDAKTIONELLES DESIGN

DESIGN DE PÉRIODIQUES

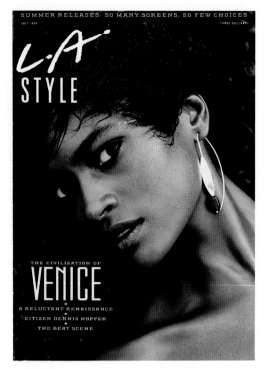

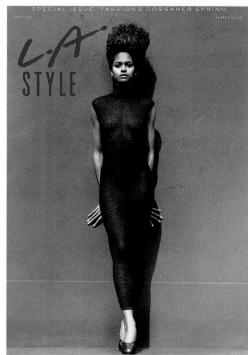

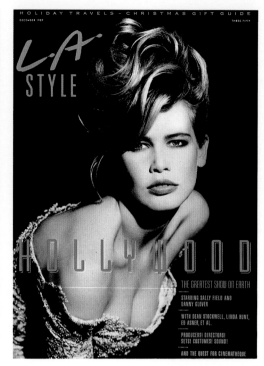

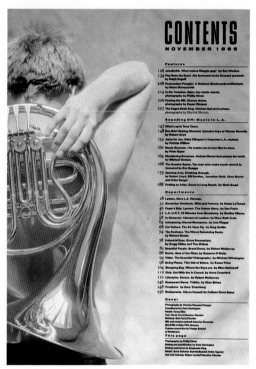

DESIGN DIRECTOR:
MICHAEL BROCK
ART DIRECTOR:
MICHAEL BROCK/
MARILYN BABCOCK
DESIGNER:
MICHAEL BROCK/
MARILYN BABCOCK
PHOTOGRAPHER:
HERB RITTS
STYLIST:
KATE HARRINGTON 326, 328
SHARON SIMONAIRE 327
AGENCY:
MICHAEL BROCK DESIGN
PUBLISHER:
L.A. STYLE
■ 325-328

DESIGN DIRECTOR:
MICHAEL BROCK
ART DIRECTOR:
MICHAEL BROCK/
MARILYN BABCOCK
DESIGNER:
MICHAEL BROCK/
MARILYN BABCOCK
PHOTO ILLUSTRATOR:
MALCOLM TARLOFSKY
AGENCY:
MICHAEL BROCK DESIGN
PUBLISHER:
L.A. STYLE
►■ 329

■ 325-328 Covers taken from three issues of the magazine *L.A. Style* and contents page for an issue with various articles on music from California. (USA)

■ 329 Surrealistic-inspired double spread taken from *L.A. Style*, announcing a series of articles on the history of Country Music. (USA)

■ 325-328 Umschläge von drei Ausgaben der Zeitschrift *L.A. Style* und Inhaltsseite für eine Ausgabe mit verschiedenen Beiträgen über die Musik in Kalifornien. (USA)

■ 329 Surrealistisch anmutende Doppelseite aus der Zeitschrift *L.A. Style*, mit der eine Serie über die Geschichte der Country-Musik angekündigt wird. (USA)

■ 325-328 Couvertures de trois numéros du magazine *L.A. Style* et table des matières d'un numéro qui comporte plusieurs articles sur la musique en Californie. (USA)

■ 329 Inspiration surréaliste pour cette double page du magazine *L.A. Style* annonçant une série d'articles consacrés à l'histoire de la musique «country». (USA)

135

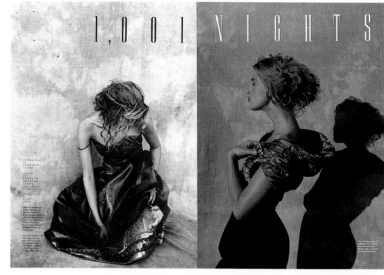

DESIGN DIRECTOR:
Michael Brock
ART DIRECTOR:
Michael Brock/
Marilyn Babcock
ARTIST:
Ray Eames
AGENCY:
Michael Brock Design
PUBLISHER:
L.A. Style
▲■ 330

DESIGN DIRECTOR:
Michael Brock
ART DIRECTOR:
Michael Brock/
Marilyn Babcock
PHOTOGRAPHER:
Patrick Demarchelier
AGENCY:
Michael Brock Design
PUBLISHER:
L.A. Style
▲■ 332

DESIGN DIRECTOR:
Michael Brock
ART DIRECTOR:
Michael Brock/
Marilyn Babcock
PHOTOGRAPHER:
Fabrizio Ferri
STYLIST:
Ernesto Massimo Serra
AGENCY:
Michael Brock Design
PUBLISHER:
L.A. Style
▲■ 331

DESIGN DIRECTOR:
Michael Brock
ART DIRECTOR:
Michael Brock/
Marilyn Babcok
PHOTOGRAPHER:
Franco Salmoiraghi
AGENCY:
Michael Brock Design
PUBLISHER:
L.A. Style
▲■ 333

■ 330-334 Examples of double spreads from an issue of *L.A. Style*. *330:* Collage by Ray Eames, originated in 1949, for an article written about the Avant-Garde designers Charles and Ray Eames. *331:* "1001 Nights". *332:* For an article about actress Glenn Close. *333:* About the adventure of sailing in Hawaii, a combination of blue water ocean sailing and coastal navigation. *334:* Introduction to an article about Avant Garde photography in Los Angeles. (USA)

■ 330-334 Doppelseiten aus *L.A. Style*. *330:* Collage von Ray Eames, 1949 entstanden, für einen Artikel über die beiden Avant-Garde-Designer Charles und Ray Eames. *331:* «1001 Nacht». *332:* für einen Beitrag über die Schauspielerin Glenn Close. *333:* «Alle Segel gesetzt» – Artikel über die verschiedenen Landschaften, die man vom Wasser aus entdecken kann. *334:* Einleitung für einen Artikel über die Avant-Garde-Photographie in Los Angeles. (USA)

■ 330-334 Exemples de doubles pages du magazine *L.A. Style*. *330:* collage de Ray Eames réalisé en 1949 introduisant un article sur les designers d'avant-garde Charles et Ray Eames. *331:* «1001 nuits». *332:* une «approche» de l'actrice Glenn Close. *333:* «Toutes voiles dehors» – l'article évoque la vision différente des pays que l'on découvre en bateau. *334:* début d'un article sur la photographie d'avantgarde à Los Angeles. (USA)

UNCONVENTIONAL

IN THE 150 YEARS SINCE PHOTOGRAPHY WAS INVENTED, THE PHOTO IMAGE HAS THOROUGHLY INFILTRATED OUR CULTURE. FROM THE BARRAGE OF STILL AND MOVING PICTURES WE CONFRONT DAILY, TO THE MOST ARCANE OF GALLERY FARE, THE RECORDED IMAGE, FOR BETTER OR WORSE, HAS IN LARGE PART SUPPLANTED THE WORD AS THE PRIMARY METHOD OF COMMUNICATION. NOWHERE IS THAT MORE TRUE THAN IN LOS ANGELES, WHERE MANIPULATION OF IMAGE (IN ALL SENSES) IS A CENTRAL ACTIVITY AND A SIGNIFICANT CONTRIBUTION TO THE NATION'S IDENTITY. ⌀ SO IN CELEBRATION OF THE 150TH ANNIVERSARY OF PHOTOGRAPHY AND THE FOURTH ANNIVERSARY OF *L.A. STYLE*, WE DECIDED TO EXPLORE THE STATE OF PHOTOGRAPHY IN OUR CITY IN 1989. WE ASKED HISTORIAN AND PHOTOGRAPHER MARK JOHNSTONE TO PROVIDE A CHRONICLE OF LOS ANGELES PHOTOGRAPHY, AND GROUNDBREAKING PHOTOGRAPHER ROBERT HEINECKEN OFFERED HIS PERSPECTIVE ON THE ESSENTIAL PHOTOGRAPHIC IMPULSE AND HOW IT ACTUALLY CHANGED SEEING. WE ASKED A GROUP OF PHOTO INSIDERS FOR THEIR COMMENTS ON THE L.A. PHOTO SCENE AND ASKED NUMEROUS IMPORTANT PHOTOGRAPHERS TO DISPLAY THEIR WORK. AND WE'VE TAKEN A LOOK AT ROBERT SHAPAZIAN'S EXTRAORDINARY COLLECTION OF EARLY AND AVANT-GARDE IM- *Photography* AGES, PROFILED THE BLACK GALLERY, AND ASSEMBLED A PORTFOLIO OF CONTEMPO- *in* RARY PHOTOGRAPHS, SOME OF THEM MAKING THEIR DEBUT PUBLIC APPEARANCE IN *L.A.* THESE PAGES. ELSEWHERE IN THE ISSUE, WE OFFER A LOOK AT L.A. PIONEER EDMUND TESKE ("IN CHARACTER"), AT MASTER FRAMER STEVE JOSEFSBERG ("STYLEMAKERS"), AT THE BEST IN EASY-TO-USE CAMERAS ("EQUIPMENT") AND AT MOCA'S GARRY WINOGRAND SHOW ("DATEBOOK"). ⌀ NATURALLY, OUR SELECTION IS REPRESENTATIVE. WE COULD NOT HAVE INCLUDED ALL THE WORTHY ARTISTS IN A BOOK MANY TIMES THE SIZE OF OUR MAGAZINE. ALSO, IT IS FAIR TO POINT OUT THAT WE HAVE APPROACHED THIS PROJECT WITH AT LEAST TWO CURATORIAL PREJUDICES: FIRST, WE DO NOT BELIEVE THAT THE DISTINCTION BETWEEN "ART" AND "PHOTOGRAPHY" MAKES ANY SENSE AT ALL, BUT OUR SELECTION OF PICTURES, PARTICULARLY IN "THE EMERGING IMAGE" PORTFOLIO, LEANS TO WORK THAT REMAINS FIRMLY ROOTED IN PHOTOGRAPHY (RATHER THAN ART THAT MIGHT BEST BE DESCRIBED AS "PHOTO-DERIVED"). SECOND, WHEN THERE WAS A CHOICE TO BE MADE, WE FREQUENTLY ELECTED TO SHOW LESSER-KNOWN WORK OR PHOTOGRAPHS BY LESSER-KNOWN ARTISTS RATHER THAN FAMOUS IMAGES BY WORLD-RENOWNED PHOTOGRAPHERS THAT ARE ROUTINELY USED TO REPRESENT PHOTOGRAPHY IN LOS ANGELES. WE APOLOGIZE IN ADVANCE TO ALL THOSE WHO ARE OFFENDED BY OUR INCLUSIONS AND EXCLUSIONS. —MICHAEL LASSELL AND GARRETT WHITE

PERSPECTIVES

Rod Baer

VISIONS FROM FLATLAND: RUSTED HEAP #1, 1986-88, WELDED STEEL, 54" x 42" x 42"

DESIGN DIRECTOR:
MICHAEL BROCK
ART DIRECTOR:
MICHAEL BROCK/
MARILYN BABCOCK
DESIGNER:
MICHAEL BROCK
PHOTOGRAPHER:
ROD BAER
AGENCY:
MICHAEL BROCK DESIGN
PUBLISHER:
L.A. STYLE
■ 334

DESIGN DIRECTOR:
Michael Brock
ART DIRECTOR:
Michael Brock/
Marilyn Babcock
DESIGNER:
Michael Brock
PHOTOGRAPHER:
Stuart Watson 335, 338
Penny Wolin 337
STYLIST:
Stephanie King 335
AGENCY:
Michael Brock Design
PUBLISHER:
L.A. Style
■ 335–338

DESIGN DDIRECTOR:
Michael Brock
ART DIRECTOR:
Michael Brock/
Marilyn Babcock
PHOTOGRAPHER:
Albert Watson
STYLIST:
Kate Harrington
AGENCY:
Michael Brock Design
PUBLISHER:
L.A. Style
►■ 339

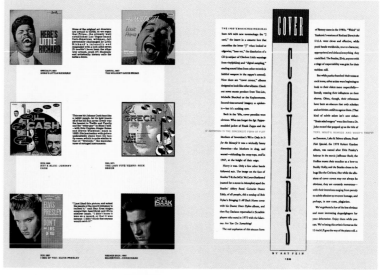

■ 335-338 Double spreads taken from *L.A. Style*. *335:* A sleek stretch knit dress (Azzedine Alaia) and a sheer lamé blouse (Issey Miyake). *336:* An article about the making of L.P. album covers. *337:* An old photograph showing a replica of Venice as an amusement park in the United States as built by an American millionaire. *338:* Introduction to an article about actor Danny Glover. (USA)

■ 339 First double spread from a fashion report in *L.A. Style*. (USA)

■ 335-338 Doppelseiten aus *L.A. Style*. *335:* «Leicht verschleiert» – zwei Modelle von Modeschöpfern, die mit der Transparenz spielen. *336:* Für einen Artikel über die Gestaltung von Schallplattenhüllen. *337:* Eine alte Aufnahme des von einem Millionär geschaffenen amerikanischen Venedig, eine Art Amusement Park. *338:* Einführung zu einem Beitrag über den Schauspieler Danny Glover. (USA)

■ 339 «Rot sehen» – erste Doppelseite einer Mode-Reportage in der Zeitschrift *L.A. Style*. (USA)

■ 335-338 Doubles pages de *L.A. Style*. *335:* «Légèrement voilées» – deux modèles de couturiers jouant sur la transparence. *336:* il s'agit d'un article sur le design des pochettes de disques. *337:* atmosphère rétro pour cet article retraçant brièvement l'histoire de la Venise américaine, un parc d'attractions créé par un millionnaire. *338:* début d'un article sur l'acteur Danny Glover. (USA)

■ 339: «Voir rouge» – première page d'un reportage de mode paru dans le magazine *L.A. Style*. (USA)

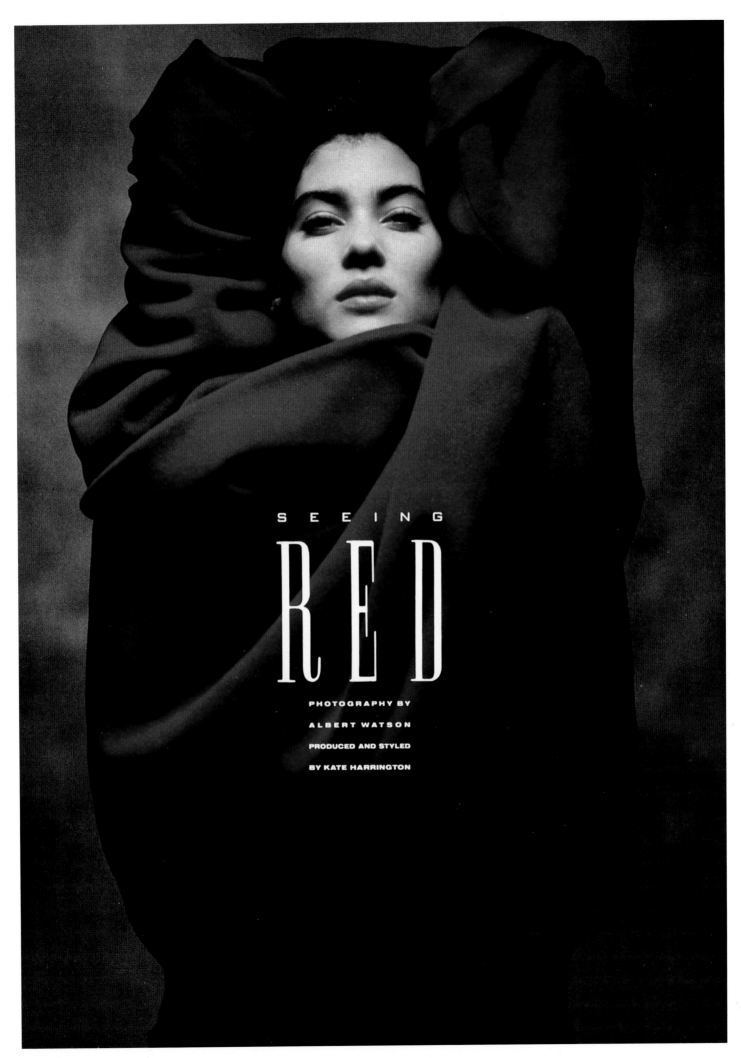

SEEING

RED

PHOTOGRAPHY BY

ALBERT WATSON

PRODUCED AND STYLED

BY KATE HARRINGTON

Art Director:
Fabien Baron
Photographer:
Steven Meisel
Client:
Vogue Italia
Publisher:
Edizioni Condé Nast S.P.A.
■ 340-342

nurejev

JOHN ZIMMERMAN – AGENZIA PIGNOTTI

ART DIRECTOR:
FABIEN BARON
PHOTOGRAPHER:
JOHN ZIMMERMAN/
AGENZIA PIGNOTTI
CLIENT:
VOGUE ITALIA
PUBLISHER.
EDIZIONI CONDÉ NAST S.P.A.
■ 343

■ 340-342 Covers for three issues of *Vogue Italia*. Reported are the lastest colorful fashion ideas, the expensive materials and the extravagant fashions of the '90s. (ITA)

■ 343 Double spread from an article about ballet star Rudolf Nurejev in *Vogue Italia*. (ITA)

■ 340-342 Umschläge von drei Ausgaben der italienischen *Vogue*, in denen über die neue farbige Mode, kostbare Stoffe und extravagante Mode 1990 berichtet wird. (ITA)

■ 343 Doppelseite aus einem in *Vogue Italia* erschienenen Artikel über Ballett-Star Rudolf Nurejev. (ITA)

■ 340-342 Couvertures de trois numéros de l'édition italienne de *Vogue*, ayant pour sujet la mode en couleurs, les tissus précieux et la mode extravagante 90. (ITA)

■ 343 Double page d'un article consacré au danseur étoile Rudolf Nurejev publié dans *Vogue Italia*. (ITA)

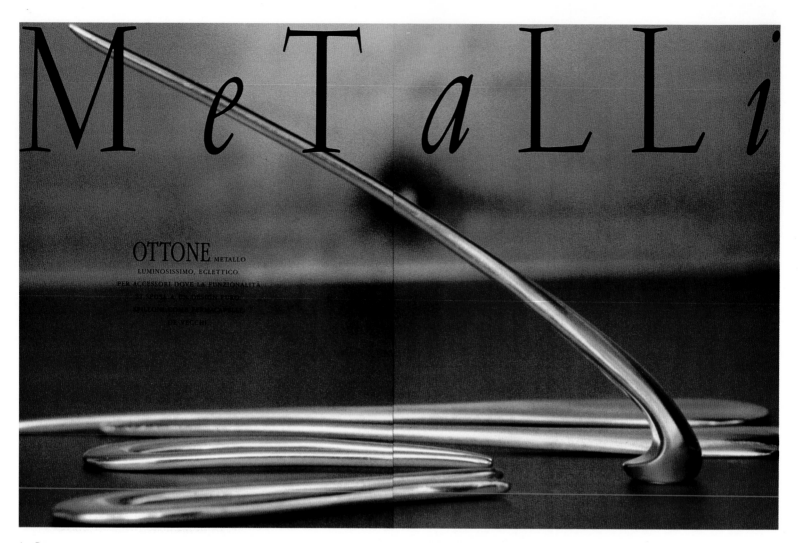

OTTONE METALLO
LUMINOSISSIMO, ECLETTICO.
PER ACCESSORI DOVE LA FUNZIONALITÀ
SI COSA A UN DESIGN PURO,
SPILLONE COME FERMACAPELLO
DE VECCHI

ART DIRECTOR:
Fabien Baron
PHOTOGRAPHER:
Sheila Metzner
CLIENT:
Vogue Italia
PUBLISHER:
Edizioni Condé Nast S.p.A.
■ 344

■ 344 Double spread taken from Italian *Vogue*. Shown are pieces of jewelry and fashion accessories made out of precious metals. (ITA)

■ 345-347 Double spreads from *Vogue Italia*. 345: People that have become contemporary myths. 346: Painted-on tatoos as a fashion statement. 347: Report about K.D. Lang, a young country singer. (USA)

■ 344 Doppelseite aus *Vogue Italia*. Vorgestellt werden Schmuck und Modezubehör aus verschiedenen Edelmetallen. (ITA)

■ 345-347 Doppelseiten aus *Vogue Italia*. 345: Menschen, die zu Mythen unserer Zeit wurden. 346: Gemalte Tätowierungen als Mode-Botschaft. 347: Reportage über K.D. Lang, eine jungenhafte Country-Sängerin. (USA)

■ 344 Double page de *Vogue Italia*. On présente ici des bijoux et accessoires de mode réalisés dans des métaux précieux. (ITA)

■ 345-347 Doubles pages de l'édition italienne de *Vogue*. 346: les figures mythologiques de l'époque contemporaine. 347: la mode-message des tatouages peints. 348: reportage consacré à K.D. Lang, une chanteuse «country». (ITA)

ART DIRECTOR:
JUAN GATTI
DESIGNER:
ANNA PIAGGI
PHOTOGRAPHER:
GIAMPAOLO BARBIERI
CLIENT:
VOGUE ITALIA
PUBLISHER:
EDIZIONI CONDÉ NAST S.P.A.
■ 345

ART DIRECTOR:
JUAN GATTI
PHOTOGRAPHER:
HERB RITTS
CLIENT:
VOGUE ITALIA
PUBLISHER:
EDIZIONI CONDÉ NAST S.P.A.
■ 346

ART DIRECTOR:
JUAN GATTI
PHOTOGRAPHER:
VARIOUS
CLIENT:
VOGUE ITALIA
PUBLISHER:
EDIZIONI CONDÉ NAST S.P.A.
■ 347

■ 348-352 Cover and four double spreads taken from Italian *Vogue*. *348:* An issue concerning silk garments. *349:* A beauty feature on how to protect skin and hair from the sun. *350:* The photo is an interpretation of Willem de Kooning's statement on the importance of female mouths. *351:* Masks and jesting are the objects of this fashion report. *352:* The first pages taken from an article about actress Silvana Mangano. (ITA)

■ 348-352 Umschlag und vier Doppelseiten aus *Vogue Italia*. *348:* Eine Ausgabe, in der es um Kleidung aus Seide geht. *349:* Wie man Haut und Haare vor der Sonne schützt. *350:* Die Aufnahme zitiert Willem de Kooning, für den der Mund einer Frau besondere Wichtigkeit hat. *351:* Maske und Gestik sind Gegenstand dieser Mode-Reportage. *352:* Erste Seiten eines Artikels über die Schauspielerin Silvana Mangano. (ITA)

■ 348-352 Une couverture et quatre doubles pages de *Vogue Italia*. *348:* ce numéro est consacré à la soie dans l'habillement. *349:* comment protéger la peau et les cheveux du soleil. *350:* la photo illustre une citation du peintre Willem de Kooning qui insiste sur l'importance de la bouche chez une femme. *351:* le masque et la gestualité sont évoqués dans ce reportage de mode. *352:* premières pages d'un article sur l'actrice Silvana Mangano. (ITA)

ART DIRECTOR:
JUAN GATTI
PHOTOGRAPHER:
STEVEN MEISEL
CLIENT:
VOGUE ITALIA
PUBLISHER:
EDIZIONI CONDÉ NAST S.P.A.
■ 348

ART DIRECTOR:
FABIEN BARON
PHOTOGRAPHER:
HERB RITTS
CLIENT:
VOGUE ITALIA
PUBLISHER:
EDIZIONI CONDÉ NAST S.P.A.
■ 349

ART DIRECTOR:
Juan Gatti
PHOTOGRAPHER:
Nick Knight
CLIENT:
Vogue Italia
PUBLISHER:
Edizioni Condé Nast S.P.A.
■ 350

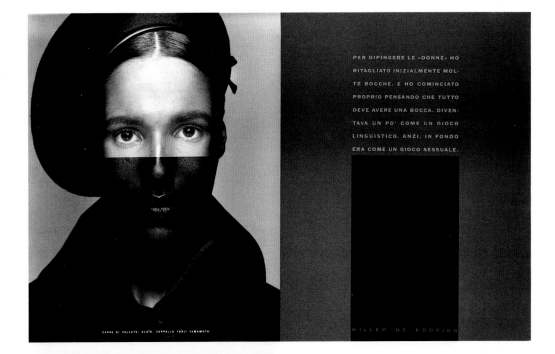

PER DIPINGERE LE «DONNE» HO RITAGLIATO INIZIALMENTE MOL-TE BOCCHE. E HO COMINCIATO PROPRIO PENSANDO CHE TUTTO DEVE AVERE UNA BOCCA. DIVEN-TAVA UN PO' COME UN GIOCO LINGUISTICO, ANZI, IN FONDO ERA COME UN GIOCO SESSUALE.

WILLEM DE KOONING

ART DIRECTOR:
Juan Gatti
PHOTOGRAPHER:
Albert Watson
CLIENT:
Vogue Italia
PUBLISHER:
Edizioni Condé Nast S.P.A.
■ 351

SI PENSA GENERALMENTE CHE LA MASCHERA E LA GESTUALITÀ AD ESSA COLLEGATA, IN ALTRE PAROLE IL SENSO DEL TRAVESTIMENTO, SIA UN PATRIMONIO CULTURALE FRANCESE. È INVECE UN FATTO TUTTO ITALIANO, UNA TRADIZIONE CON RADICI PROFONDE E REMOTE: DOBBIA-MO FARLA RISALIRE ADDIRITTURA AL TEATRO DEI ROMANI. LA STORIA CONTINUA POI PER TUTTO IL MEDIOEVO E NELLE CORTI RINASCIMENTALI, FINO ALL'EVENTO PIÙ IMPORTANTE, LA NASCITA A FIRENZE DEL MELO-DRAMMA E DEL BALLETTO. COL MATRIMONIO FRANCESE DI CATERINA DE' MEDICI, IL BARICENTRO DI TUTTO IL MONDO ARTISTICO SI TRASFERÌ IN FRANCIA: SI VERIFICÒ UNO STILLICIDIO DI TALENTO ITALIANO. E IL GESTO SPONTANEO VENNE CODIFICATO CON UNA TERMINOLOGIA LOCA-LE, TANTO CHE ANCORA OGGI LA LINGUA UFFICIALE DELLA DANZA È IL FRANCESE. LE SCUOLE, FORMATESI SU UNA BASE DI CULTURA ITALIANA, ACQUISTARONO CONNOTAZIONI SEMPRE PIÙ ARISTOCRATICHE E SUBIRONO L'INFLUENZA DEL FERVORE ROMANTICO CHE PERMEAVA LA SOCIETÀ PARIGINA DELL'OTTOCENTO. ARRICCHITE ANCHE DALLA «TRASFUSIONE DEL GESTO» CHE SI EBBE DALLA PIAZZA AI TEATRI, FLUIRONO POI NELL'ESTREMO EST EUROPEO FINO IN RUSSIA. ORIGINARIA-MENTE IL GESTO DELLA MASCHERA È QUASI VIOLENTO, MA IL GRANDE MOVIMENTO ARTISTICO DÉCO LO RIVISITÒ FORMALMENTE E GRAFICAMEN-TE NEL TEATRO DI QUEST'ULTIMO SECOLO E PIÙ «SENTITO», ADDOLCITO E SUBLIMATO, HA ASSUNTO LE CARATTERISTICHE DI SENTIMENTO E DI RAFFINATEZZA CHE LO CONNOTANO NELLE GRANDI COREOGRAFIE DI OGGI. L'EVOLUZIONE DELLA MASCHERA È CONTINUA, NON SI È ANCORA ARRESTATA, PERCHÉ SEGUE IL SUO TEMPO. NE È UN ESEMPIO IL PULCINEL-LA DI EDUARDO DE FILIPPO, CHE CORRISPONDE PERFETTAMENTE AI SENTIMENTI E AL LINGUAGGIO CONTEMPORANEI. CARLA FRACCI

"CAMICIA YOHJI YAMAMOTO; COLLARETTA DI PENTELLE.

ART DIRECTOR:
Fabien Baron
PHOTOGRAPHER:
Gilles Tapie
CLIENT:
Vogue Italia
PUBLISHER:
Edizioni Condé Nast S.P.A.
■ 352

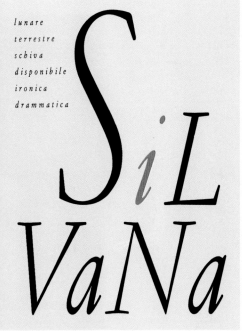

lunare
terrestre
schiva
disponibile
ironica
drammatica

SiL VaNa

ART DIRECTOR:
Fred Woodward

PHOTO EDITOR:
Laurie Kratochvil

PHOTOGRAPHERS:
Glenn Erler 353
Timothy White 354, 355
Walter Chin 356

PUBLISHER:
Rolling Stone

■ 353-356

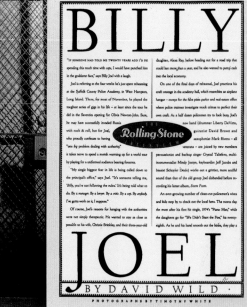

■ 353-357 Double spreads and cover taken from *Rolling Stone* magazine. *353:* Upon the beginning of a new day, musician Bob Mould decided to record his own album as seen by this article. *354, 355:* In this issue, Billy Joel talks about his problems with the police, with its uniform. *356:* Getting fit. *357:* Excerpt from a novel which is be published in 1990. (USA)

■ 353-357 Doppelseiten und Umschlag der Zeitschrift *Rolling Stone*. *353:* «Ein neuer Tag beginnt» – gemeint ist der Tag, an dem Bob Mould beschloss, eine eigene Platte aufzunehmen. *353, 354:* In dieser Ausgabe spricht Billy Joel über seine Probleme mit der Polizei, mit der Uniform. *356:* Conditions-Training. *357:* Auszug aus einer Science-Fiction-Geschichte mit dem Titel «Osten ist Osten». (USA)

■ 353-357 Doubles pages et couverture du magazine *Rolling Stone*. *353:* «Un nouveau jour se lève» – l'article fait allusion au jour où le musicien Bob Mould a décidé de produire son propre album. *354, 355:* Billy Joel parle de ses relations difficiles avec la police, avec l'uniforme. *356:* les sports de mise en condition. *357:* début d'une nouvelle de science-fiction intitulée «L'est est l'est». (USA)

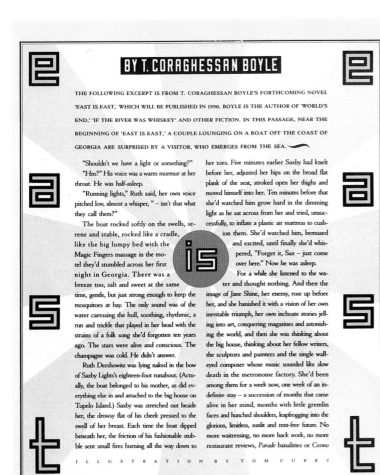

BY T. CORAGHESSAN BOYLE

THE FOLLOWING EXCERPT IS FROM T. CORAGHESSAN BOYLE'S FORTHCOMING NOVEL 'EAST IS EAST,' WHICH WILL BE PUBLISHED IN 1990. BOYLE IS THE AUTHOR OF 'WORLD'S END,' 'IF THE RIVER WAS WHISKEY' AND OTHER FICTION. IN THIS PASSAGE, NEAR THE BEGINNING OF 'EAST IS EAST,' A COUPLE LOUNGING ON A BOAT OFF THE COAST OF GEORGIA ARE SURPRISED BY A VISITOR, WHO EMERGES FROM THE SEA.

"Shouldn't we have a light or something?"

"Hm?" His voice was a warm murmur at her throat. He was half-asleep.

"Running lights," Ruth said, her own voice pitched low, almost a whisper, " – isn't that what they call them?"

The boat rocked softly on the swells, serene and stable, rocked like a cradle, like the big lumpy bed with the Magic Fingers massage in the motel they'd stumbled across her first night in Georgia. There was a breeze too, salt and sweet at the same time, gentle, but just strong enough to keep the mosquitoes at bay. The only sound was of the water caressing the hull, soothing, rhythmic, a run and trickle that played in her head with the strains of a folk song she'd forgotten ten years ago. The stars were alive and conscious. The champagne was cold. He didn't answer.

Ruth Dershowitz was lying naked in the bow of Saxby Lights's eighteen-foot runabout. (Actually, the boat belonged to his mother, as did everything else in and attached to the big house on Tupelo Island.) Saxby was stretched out beside her, the drowsy flat of his cheek pressed to the swell of her breast. Each time the boat dipped beneath her, the friction of his fashionable stubble sent small fires burning all the way down to her toes. Five minutes earlier Saxby had knelt before her, adjusted her hips on the broad flat plank of the seat, stroked open her thighs and moved himself into her. Ten minutes before that she'd watched him grow hard in the dimming light as he sat across from her and tried, unsuccessfully, to inflate a plastic air mattress to cushion. She'd watched him, bemused and excited, until finally she'd whispered, "Forget it, Sax – just come over here." Now he was asleep.

For a while she listened to the water and thought nothing. And then the image of Jane Shine, her enemy, rose up before her, and she banished it with a vision of her own inevitable triumph, her own inchoate stories jelling into art, conquering magazines and astonishing the world, and then she was thinking about the big house, thinking about her fellow writers, the sculptors and painters and the single walleyed composer whose music sounded like slow death in the metronome factory. She'd been among them for a week now, one week of an indefinite stay – a succession of months that came alive in her mind, months with little gremlin faces and hunched shoulders, leapfrogging into the glorious, limitless, sunlit and rent-free future. No more waitressing, no more hack work, no more restaurant reviews, *Parade* banalities or *Cosmo*

ILLUSTRATION BY TOM CURRY

126 · ROLLING STONE, OCTOBER 5TH, 1989

FROM 'EAST IS EAST,' TO BE PUBLISHED BY VIKING PENGUIN IN 1990. COPYRIGHT © 1989 BY T. CORAGHESSAN BOYLE.

ROLLING STONE, OCTOBER 5TH, 1989 · 127

ART DIRECTOR:
FRED WOODWARD
ILLUSTRATOR:
TOM CURRY
PUBLISHER:
ROLLING STONE
■ 357

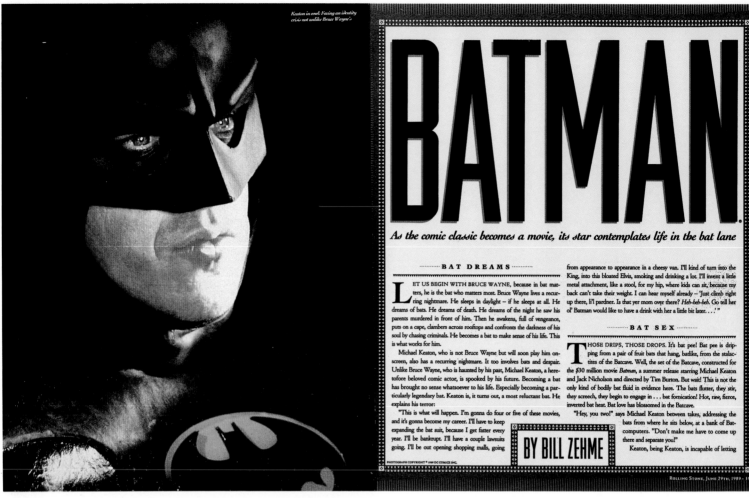

Keaton in cowl: Facing an identity crisis not unlike Bruce Wayne's

BATMAN.

As the comic classic becomes a movie, its star contemplates life in the bat lane

BAT DREAMS

LET US BEGIN WITH BRUCE WAYNE, because in bat matters, he is the bat who matters most. Bruce Wayne lives a recurring nightmare. He sleeps in daylight – if he sleeps at all. He dreams of bats. He dreams of death. He dreams of the night he saw his parents murdered in front of him. Then he awakens, full of vengeance, puts on a cape, clambers across rooftops and confronts the darkness of his soul by chasing criminals. He becomes a bat to make sense of his life. This is what works for him.

Michael Keaton, who is not Bruce Wayne but will soon play him on-screen, also has a recurring nightmare. It too involves bats and despair. Unlike Bruce Wayne, who is haunted by his past, Michael Keaton, a heretofore beloved comic actor, is spooked by his future. Becoming a bat has brought no sense whatsoever to his life. Especially becoming a particularly legendary bat. Keaton is, it turns out, a most reluctant bat. He explains his terror:

"This is what will happen. I'm gonna do four or five of these movies, and it's gonna become my career. I'll have to keep expanding the bat suit, because I get fatter every year. I'll be bankrupt. I'll have a couple lawsuits going. I'll be out opening shopping malls, going

from appearance to appearance in a cheesy van. I'll kind of turn into the King, into this bloated Elvis, smoking and drinking a lot. I'll invent a little metal attachment, like a stool, for my hip, where kids can sit, because my back can't take their weight. I can hear myself already – 'Just climb right up there, li'l pardner. Is that yer mom over there? *Heh-heh-heh.* Go tell her ol' Batman would like to have a drink with her a little bit later. . . .'"

BAT SEX

THOSE DRIPS, THOSE DROPS. It's bat pee! Bat pee is dripping from a pair of fruit bats that hang, batlike, from the stalactites of the Batcave. Well, the set of the Batcave, constructed for the $30 million movie *Batman*, a summer release starring Michael Keaton and Jack Nicholson and directed by Tim Burton. But wait! This is not the only kind of bodily bat fluid in evidence here. The bats flutter, they stir, they screech, they begin to engage in . . . bat fornication! Hot, raw, fierce, inverted bat heat. Bat love has blossomed in the Batcave.

"Hey, you two!" says Michael Keaton between takes, addressing the bats from where he sits below, at a bank of Bat-computers. "Don't make me have to come up there and separate you!"

Keaton, being Keaton, is incapable of letting

BY BILL ZEHME

PHOTOGRAPH COPYRIGHT © 1989 DC COMICS INC.

ROLLING STONE, JUNE 29TH, 1989 · 39

ART DIRECTOR:
Fred Woodward
PHOTOGRAPHY:
© *1989 DC Comics Inc.*
PHOTO EDITOR:
Laurie Kratochvil
PUBLISHER:
Rolling Stone
■ 358

■ 358 Double spread from *Rolling Stone* magazine regarding "Batman". Actor Michael Keaton speaks about his role as Batman and what this means for his career. (USA)

■ 359, 360 Double spreads from *Rolling Stone* magazine. Both portraits can be used as posters. *359:* A portrait of actress Uma Thurman who has to cope with all the attention she is getting because of her sex-appeal. *359:* Photograph for an interview with musician Elvis Costello. (USA)

■ 358 Für einen Beitrag in *Rolling Stone* über eine «Batman»-Verfilmung. Michael Keaton macht sich hier Gedanken, was die Rolle für ihn bedeutet. (USA)

■ 359, 360 Doppelseiten aus *Rolling Stone*. Beide Portraits lassen sich als Poster verwenden. *359:* Uma Thurman, eine Schauspielerin, die wegen ihres Sex-Appeals zu plötzlichem Ruhm gelangte. *359:* Aufnahme für die Einleitung eines Interviews mit Elvis Costello. (USA)

■ 358 Double page de *Rolling Stone* sur le thème de Batman. L'acteur Michael Keaton qui incarne la célèbre chauve-souris s'interroge sur l'avenir de sa carrière. (USA)

■ 359, 360 Doubles pages du magazine *Rolling Stone*. Chaque portrait, pris dans le sens de la hauteur, forme une affiche. *359:* Uma Thurman, une starlette célèbre pour son sex-appeal qui garde la tête froide devant le succès. *359:* photo d'une interview du musicien Elvis Costello. (USA)

ART DIRECTOR:
Fred Woodward
PHOTO EDITOR:
Laurie Kratochvil
PHOTOGRAPHER:
Matthew Rolston
PUBLISHER:
Rolling Stone
■ 359

ART DIRECTOR:
Fred Woodward
PHOTO EDITOR:
Laurie Kratochvil
PHOTOGRAPHER:
Matt Mahurin
PUBLISHER:
Rolling Stone
■ 360

HOT COVER Inspiring lust in audiences, Sylvester Stallone and gossip columnists alike, starlet Uma Thurman tries to cope with all the attention while keeping her sense of Uma… Photographs by MATTHEW ROLSTON

THE ROLLING STONE INTERVIEW

Elvis Costello may be thought of as the angry young man of the British New Wave, but as he and his wife, Cait O'Riordan, greet me in the elegant piano bar of the Four Seasons Clift Hotel, BY DAVID WILD *photograph by matt mahurin*

ART DIRECTOR:
Fred Woodward
PHOTO EDITOR:
Laurie Kratochvil
PHOTOGRAPHER:
E.J. Camp
PUBLISHER:
Rolling Stone
■ 361

ART DIRECTOR:
Fred Woodward
PHOTO EDITOR:
Laurie Kratochvil
PHOTOGRAPHER:
Herb Ritts
PUBLISHER:
Rolling Stone
■ 362

ART DIRECTOR:
Fred Woodward
PHOTO EEDITOR:
Laurie Kratochvil
LETTERING:
Anita Karl
PHOTOGRAPHER:
Albert Watson
PUBLISHER:
Rolling Stone
■ 363

ART DIRECTOR:
FRED WOODWARD
PHOTO EDITOR:
LAURIE KRATOCHVIL
PHOTOGRAPHER:
HERB RITTS
PUBLISHER:
ROLLING STONE
■ 364

ART DIRECTOR:
FRED WOODWARD
LETTERING:
DENNIS ORTIZ-LOPEZ
ILLUSTRATOR:
TERRY ALLEN
PUBLISHER
ROLLING STONE
■ 365

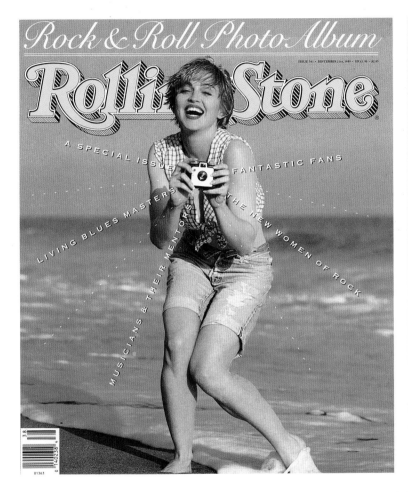

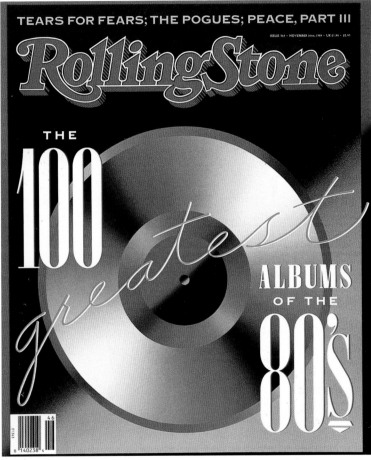

■ 361-363 Three double spreads from *Rolling Stone* magazine describing show business and the stars' future. *361:* In spite of his success, musician John Mellencamp is unhappy. *362:* Can Paul McCartney make it to the top again? *363:* Referring to the difficulties of the Rolling Stones; shown are Keith Richards and Mick Jagger. (USA)

■ 364, 365 Two covers taken from *Rolling Stone* magazine. *364:* A presentation of the new generation of Ladies in Rock. *365:* The best record albums of the 1980's. (USA)

■ 361-363 Auf diesen Doppelseiten aus *Rolling Stone* geht es um das Show-Geschäft und die Zukunft der Stars. *361:* John Mellencamp, der trotz seines Erfolges nicht glücklich ist. *362:* «Schafft Paul McCartney den Weg zurück an die Spitze?» *363:* Anspielung auf Schwierigkeiten der Rolling Stones, hier Keith Richards und Mick Jagger. (USA)

■ 364, 365 Zwei Umschläge von *Rolling Stone. 364:* Eine Ausgabe, die der neuen Generation der Rock-Ladies gewidmet ist. *365:* Die 100 besten Platten der 80er Jahre. (USA)

■ 361-363 Ces trois doubles pages de *Rolling Stone* s'interrogent sur le monde du show business et sur l'avenir des stars. *361:* le vague à l'âme d'une star du rock désabusée, John Mellencamp. *362:* «Paul Mc Cartney peut-il revenir en arrière?» *363:* allusion aux conflits au sein du groupe des Rolling Stones. (USA)

■ 364, 365 Deux couvertures du magazine *Rolling Stone. 364:* numéro consacré aux nouvelles chanteuses de rock. *365:* les 100 meilleurs albums des années 80. (USA)

Von Christopher Schwarz
Fotos Susan Lamèr

WENN
SCHÖNHEIT
PRUNKT

ART DIRECTOR:
HANS-GEORG POSPISCHIL
ILLUSTRATOR:
PETER KRÄMER 366
PHOTOGRAPHER:
SUSAN LAMÈR 367
LILLIAN BIRNBAUM 368
PUBLISHER:
FRANKFURTER ALLGEMEINE
ZEITUNG GMBH
■ 366-368

■ 366-368 Cover and double spreads taken from the *Frankfurter Allgemeine* magazine. *366:* With the closing of one door, another one opens – the 1990's begin. *367:* Showing off beauty, an article about decolletés. *368:* Fringes and their place in Haute Couture. (GER)

■ 369 Cover of the Sunday supplement of the *Figaro* meant for its female readership. (FRA)

■ 370 Cover of *Omni* magazine: keeping the mind fit helps keep the immune system fit. (USA)

■ 366-368 Umschlag und zwei Doppelseiten aus dem *Frankfurter Allgemeine Magazin*. *366:* Eine Tür schliesst sich, eine andere öffnet sich – die 90er-Jahre beginnen. *367:* Grosse Inszenierung des Dekolletés. *368:* Beitrag über Fransen in der Haute Couture. (GER)

■ 369 Umschlag der für die weibliche Leserschaft bestimmten Sonntagsbeilage des *Figaro*. (FRA)

■ 370 Umschlag der Zeitschrift *Omni*: geistiges Training stärkt das Immunsystem. (USA)

■ 366-368 Couverture et deux doubles pages du *Frankfurter Allgemeine Magazin*. *366:* «Une porte se ferme, une autre s'ouvre» – les promesses des années 90. *367:* «Quand la beauté s'étale»: titre d'un article sur les décolletés. *368:* les franges dans la haute couture. (GER)

■ 369 Couverture du supplément dominical du journal *Le Figaro*, destiné au public féminin. (FRA)

■ 370 Couverture du magazine *Omni* sur «des exercices spirituels qui renforcent votre système immunitaire». (USA)

ART DIRECTOR:
Martin Schmollgruber
PHOTOGRAPHER:
Pierre Berdoy
PUBLISHER:
Madame Figaro
■ 369

CREATIVE DIRECTOR:
Frank DeVino
ART DIRECTOR:
Dwayne Flinchum
ILLUSTRATOR:
Nicholas Gaetano
PUBLISHER:
General Media International
■ 370

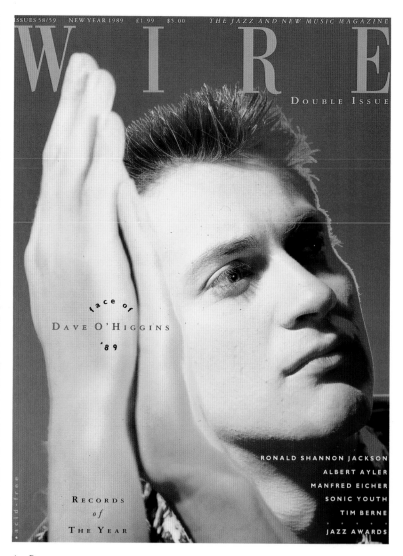

ART DIRECTOR:
CLAUDE CRAPLET
PHOTOGRAPHER:
AL RUBIN
PUBLISHER:
ZOOM
■ 371

ART DIRECTOR:
LUCY WARD
PHOTOGRAPHER:
NICK WHITE
PUBLISHER:
THE NAMARA GROUP
■ 372

DESIGN DIRECTOR:
ROBERT BEST
ART DIRECTOR:
JOSH GOSFIELD
PHOTOGRAPHER:
TORKIL GUDNASON
PUBLISHER:
NEW YORK MAGAZINE
►■ 375

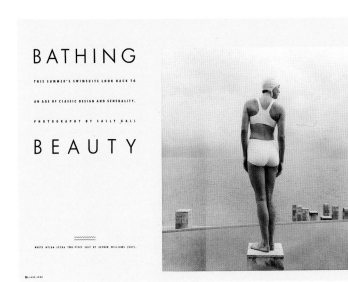

BATHING

THIS SUMMER'S SWIMSUITS LOOK BACK TO

AN AGE OF CLASSIC DESIGN AND SENSUALITY.

PHOTOGRAPHY BY SALLY GALL

BEAUTY

WHITE NYLON LYCRA TWO-PIECE SUIT BY ESTHER WILLIAMS ($47).

Taking Panes

Architect Peter Wheelwright consulted with artist-technician James Carpenter, guru of glass to the architectural elite, on the windows for this Chelsea penthouse. Designed as a poet's writing room, the pink stucco structure is punctured at odd intervals with windows of bicolored glass—one pane shifts from yellow to purple, depending on the light, another from green to vermilion. The glass is transparent when backlit, reflective when the light is brighter in front.

ART DIRECTOR:
D.J. Stout
DESIGNER:
D.J. Stout
PHOTOGRAPHER:
Sally Gall
AGENCY:
Texas Monthly
PUBLISHER:
Texas Monthly
■ 373

DESIGN DIRECTOR:
Robert Best
PHOTOGRAPHER:
Andrew Garn
PUBLISHER:
New York Magazine
■ 374

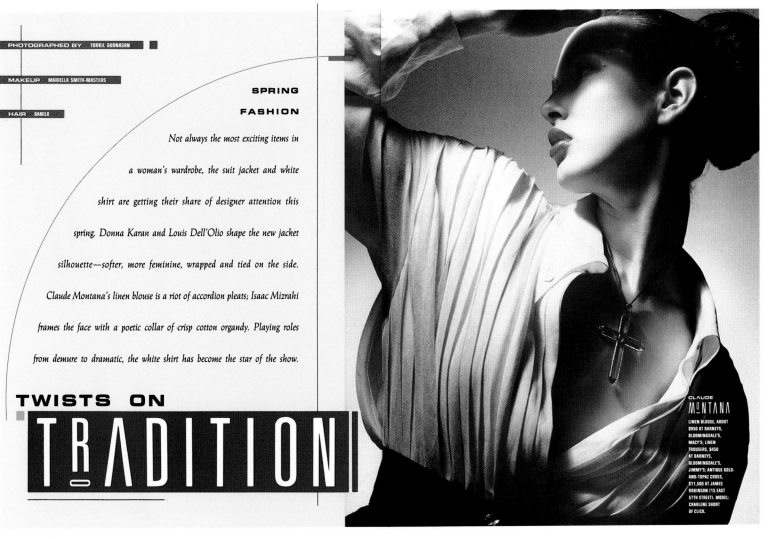

PHOTOGRAPHED BY TORKIL GUDNASON

MAKEUP MARIELLA SMITH-MASTERS

HAIR DANILO

SPRING FASHION

Not always the most exciting items in

a woman's wardrobe, the suit jacket and white

shirt are getting their share of designer attention this

spring. Donna Karan and Louis Dell'Olio shape the new jacket

silhouette—softer, more feminine, wrapped and tied on the side.

Claude Montana's linen blouse is a riot of accordion pleats; Isaac Mizrahi

frames the face with a poetic collar of crisp cotton organdy. Playing roles

from demure to dramatic, the white shirt has become the star of the show.

TWISTS ON
TRADITION

CLAUDE MONTANA
LINEN BLOUSE, ABOUT $950 AT BARNEYS, BLOOMINGDALE'S, MACY'S; LINEN TROUSERS, $450 AT BARNEYS, BLOOMINGDALE'S, JIMMY'S; ANTIQUE GOLD-AND-TOPAZ CROSS, $11,500 AT JAMES ROBINSON (15 EAST 57TH STREET). MODEL: CHARLENE SHORT OF CLICK.

FEBRUARY 1989 · $1.95

How Texas Begs for Jobs · Valentines From Texas Artists

Texas Monthly

THE LOST TRIBE

"**T**he Comanches were the wildest people that the plains had ever produced. They were an emblem of barbaric splendor, and it was tempting to believe that they had not been subdued but had merely vanished like a prairie wind. But the Comanches did not vanish…"

BY STEPHEN HARRIGAN

OCTOBER 1989 · $1.95

Why the World Cares About Austin's Treaty Oak, by Stephen Harrigan

Texas Monthly

THE SOUL OF EAST TEXAS

IMAGES BY
KEITH CARTER
ME•MORIES BY
PRUDENCE MACKINTOSH

ART DIRECTOR:
D.J. STOUT
DESIGNER:
D.J. STOUT
PHOTOGRAPHER:
KURT MARKUS
AGENCY:
TEXAS MONTHLY
PUBLISHER:
TEXAS MONTHLY
■ 376

ART DIRECTOR:
D.J. STOUT
DESIGNER:
D.J. STOUT
PHOTOGRAPHER:
KEITH CARTER
AGENCY:
TEXAS MONTHLY
PUBLISHER:
TEXAS MONTHLY
■ 377

■ 376, 377 Covers taken from two issues of *Texas Monthly* magazine, one dealing with a religious sect in East Texas and the other with the Comanches. (USA)

■ 378, 379 Covers for *New York* magazine. At left, a special fall issue on cultural events. At right, an issue on Christmas gifts. (USA)

■ 376, 377 Für zwei Ausgaben der Zeitschrift *Texas Monthly.* In der einen geht es um eine religiöse Sekte im Osten von Texas, in der anderen um Komantschen. (USA)

■ 378, 379 Umschläge der Zeitschrift *New York.* Links eine Spezialausgabe über das kulturelle Angebot im Herbst; rechts eine Ausgabe über Weihnachtsgeschenke. (USA)

■ 376, 377 Pour deux numéros du *Texas Monthly.* Dans le premier, on parle de la vie religieuse à l'est du Texas, dans le second de la tribu des Indiens Comanches. (USA)

■ 378, 379 Couvertures du magazine *New York.* A gauche, un numéro consacré aux programmes culturels en automne; à droite, numéro des cadeaux de Noël. (USA)

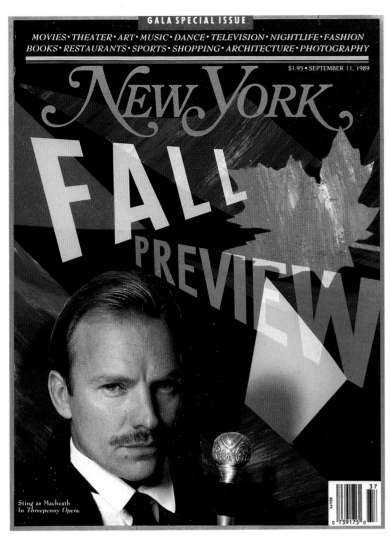

DESIGN DIRECTOR:
ROBERT BEST
PHOTOGRAPHER:
TERRY O'NEILL/SYGMA
PUBLISHER:
NEW YORK MAGAZINE
■ 378

DESIGN DIRECTOR:
ROBERT BEST
ARTIST:
MAX GINSBURG
PUBLISHER:
NEW YORK MAGAZINE
■ 379

■ 380, 381 Cover for the Italian magazine *King*. *380:* "The Return of the Witches". *381:* "Three Men and a Mascot", an issue dedicated to the football championship. (ITA)

■ 382 Cover for a French photography magazine with an article about animal photography. The photo entitled "Monsieur Lester" was taken by Robert Doisneau (Agence Rapho) in 1947. (FRA)

■ 380, 381 Für italienische Zeitschrift *King*. *380:* «Die Rückkehr der Hexen». *381:* «Drei Männer und ein Maskottchen» – Ausgabe zur Fussball-Weltmeisterschfaft. (ITA)

■ 382 Umschlag einer Photo-Fachzeitschrift mit einer Reportage über die Tierphotographie. Die Aufnahme mit dem Titel "Monsieur Lester" machte Robert Doisneau (Agence Rapho) 1947. (FRA)

■ 380, 381 Pour le mensuel italien *King*. *380:* «Les sorcières reviennent». *381:* «Trois hommes et une mascotte» – numéro consacré au championnat du monde de football. (ITA)

■ 382 Couverture d'une revue professionnelle de photographie qui présente un reportage sur «la photo animalière». La photo intitulée "Monsieur Lester" était prise par Robert Doisneau (Agency Rapho) en 1947. (FRA)

ART DIRECTOR:
SERGIO SARTORI
DESIGNER:
NIGEL SMITH/MARIAPIA COPPIN/CLAUDIA FIORI/ NADIA DONA
ILLUSTRATOR:
EDIMAGE 380
STUDIO:
SERGIO SARTORI
PUBLISHER:
NUOVA ERI-EDIZIONI RAI
■ 380, 381

ART DIRECTOR:
AGNES PROPECK
PHOTOGRAPHER:
ROBERT DOISNEAU/RAPHO
PUBLISHER:
PHOTOGRAPHIES MAGAZINE
►■ 382

PHOTOGRAPHIES
m a g a z i n e

SALON 89. JEANLOUP SIEFF. DAVID
SEIDNER. LA PHOTO ANIMALIÈRE

ART DIRECTOR:
ROSS RENWICK
DESIGNER:
ROSS RENWICK
PUBLISHER:
BILLY BLUE GROUP
■ 383, 384

■ 383, 384 Covers taken from a magazine published on a quarterly basis by a graphics company. (AUS)

■ 385-387 Cover for the trade magazine *Industrial Launderer*. *385:* Two different companies supplying trains with towels and linens, celebrate their 100th birthday. *386:* Bar coding and its usage in identifying garments. *387: Industrial Launderer* produces in-house materials with desk top publishing equipment. (USA)

■ 388 Double spread from *Bandwagon*, in-house magazine of *Frito Lay*, an American snack food company. The article deals with northern regional truck drivers. (USA)

■ 383, 384 Umschläge einer von Graphikern vierteljährlich herausgegebenen Zeitschrift. (AUS)

■ 385-387 Umschlag der Wäschereifachzeitschrift *Industrial Launderer*. *385:* Zwei Firmen, die ihr 100jähriges Bestehen feiern und mit dem Wäschedienst in Zügen begannen. *385:* Computer-Codes helfen bei der Identifizierung der Kleidungsstücke. *385:* Ein Computer-System erleichtert die betriebliche Organisation. (USA)

■ 388 Doppelseite aus *Bandwagon*, Hauszeitschrift von Frito Lay, einem amerikanischen Unternehmen. Hier geht es um einen Artikel über die Fahrer im Norden der USA. (USA)

■ 383, 384 Couvertures d'une revue publiée par The Billy Blue Group, une association de graphistes. (AUS)

■ 385-387 Couvertures de la revue de blanchisserie industrielle *Industrial Launderer*. *385:* deux compagnies qui ont débuté dans le secteur ferroviaire fêtent leur 100e anniversaire. *386:* les codes à barres permettent d'identifier les vêtements. *387:* un bon matériel informatique garantit une meilleure communication. (USA)

■ 388 Double page de *Bandwagon*, publiée par Frito Lay, une entreprise américaine. Ici, un article sur les chauffeurs des Montagnes Rocheuses. (USA)

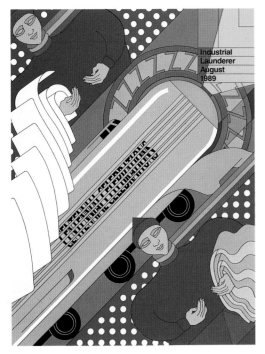

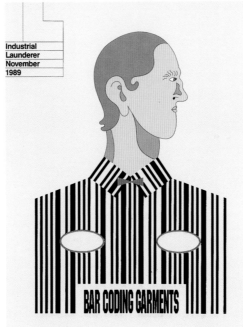

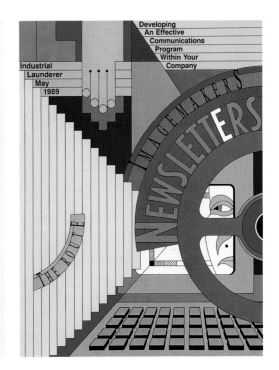

DESIGNER:
JACK LEFKOWITZ
ILLUSTRATOR:
BOB WASILOWSKI 385
PAM LEFKOWITZ/
BOB WASILOWSKI 386
PAM LEFKOWITZ 387
PUBLISHER:
INSTITUTE OF INDUSTRIAL
LAUNDERERS
▲■ 385-387

ART DIRECTOR:
SCOTT RAY
DESIGNER:
SCOTT RAY
PHOTOGRAPHER:
PETER LACKER
AGENCY:
PETERSON & COMPANY
PUBLISHER:
FRITO-LAY, INC.
▼■ 388

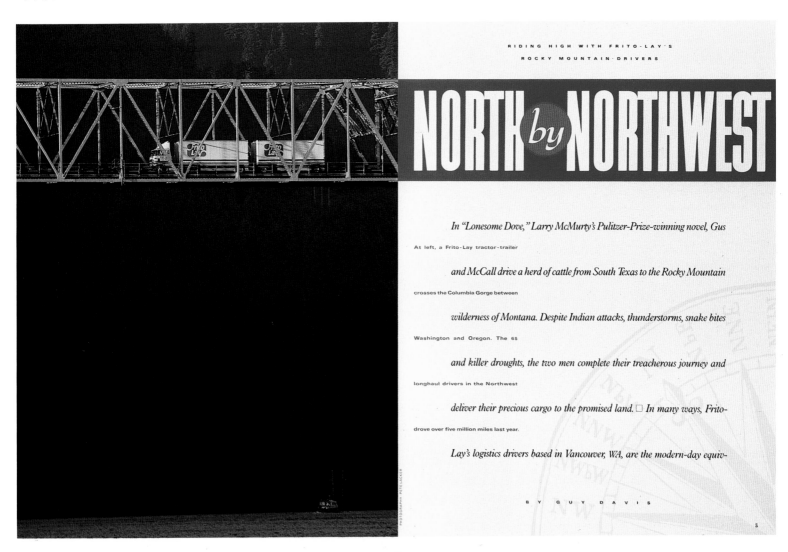

RIDING HIGH WITH FRITO-LAY'S
ROCKY MOUNTAIN DRIVERS

NORTH *by* NORTHWEST

In "Lonesome Dove," Larry McMurtry's Pulitzer-Prize-winning novel, Gus

At left, a Frito-Lay tractor-trailer

and McCall drive a herd of cattle from South Texas to the Rocky Mountain

crosses the Columbia Gorge between

wilderness of Montana. Despite Indian attacks, thunderstorms, snake bites

Washington and Oregon. The 65

and killer droughts, the two men complete their treacherous journey and

longhaul drivers in the Northwest

deliver their precious cargo to the promised land. □ In many ways, Frito-

drove over five million miles last year.

Lay's logistics drivers based in Vancouver, WA, are the modern-day equiv-

BY GUY DAVIS

161

ELEKTRA

ART DIRECTOR:
PETER HARRISON/HAROLD BURCH

DESIGNER:
HAROLD BURCH

AGENCY:
PENTAGRAM DESIGN, NEW YORK

PUBLISHER:
WARNER COMMUNICATIONS INC.

■ 389-391

ART DIRECTOR:
STEPHEN HALL
PHOTOGRAPHER:
CHARLES PURVIS
AGENCY:
RUMRILL-HOYT, INC.
PUBLISHER:
EASTMAN KODAK COMPANY
■ 392, 393

■ 389-391 Cover and double spreads from *Currents*, Warner Communications' internal employee newsletter. *389:* "With apologies to El Lissitsky". *390* tells the success story of the Elektra record company, *391* refers to film director Tim Burton's new hit: *Batman.* (USA)

■ 392, 393 Covers taken from *International Photography*, a magazine published bi-annually by Kodak. Its intention is to act as a gallery, in print exhibiting works by famous photographers, as well as works from newer talents. At right Julia Margaret Cameron's carbon print from wet collodion negative (c. 1867) for the issue on 150 years of photography. (USA)

■ 389-391 Umschlag und Doppelseiten aus *Currents*, Hauszeitschrift der Warner Communications. *389:* «Verzeihung, El Lissitski.» *390:* Artikel über die Erfolgs-Story der Plattenfirma Elektra. *391:* *Batman*, der neuste Hit des Filmregisseurs Tim Burton. (USA)

■ 392, 393 Umschläge von *International Photography*, einer zweimal jährlich von Kodak herausgebenen Zeitschrift. Sie wird zu einer Art Galerie für die Photos von bekannten Photographen und neuen Talenten. Rechts die Ausgabe zum 150. Geburtstag der Photographie mit einer Aufnahme (Kohledruck von Kollodium-Negativ, Nassverfahren, ca. 1867) von Julia Margaret Cameron. (USA)

■ 389-391 Couverture et doubles pages de *Currents*, magazine destiné aux employés de Warner Communications. *389:* «Avec excuses à El Lissitski.» *390:* l'histoire du succès de la companie de disques Elektra; *391:* *Batman*, le nouveau film du directeur Tim Burton. (USA)

■ 392-393 Couvertures de *International Photography*, un magazine publié deux fois par an par Kodak. La présentation des photos de professionnels ou de nouveaux talents évoque une galerie d'exposition. A droite, numéro sur 150 ans de photographie avec une photo de Julia Margaret Cameron (impression sur papier carbone d'un négatif de collodium humide). (USA)

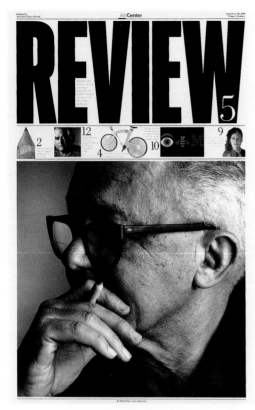

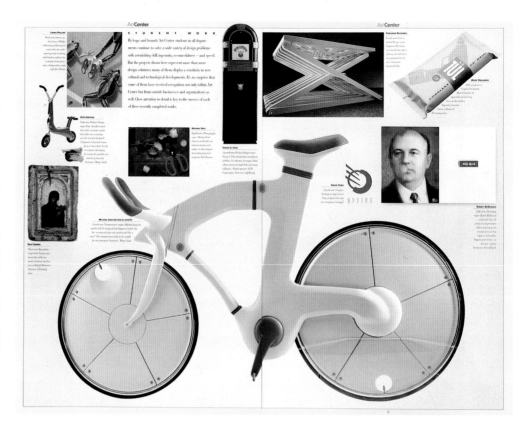

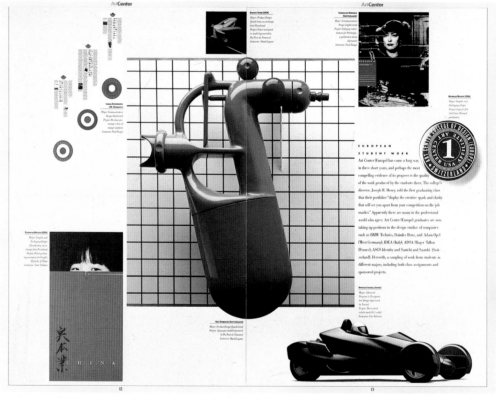

ART DIRECTOR:
KIT HINRICHS

DESIGNER:
KIT HINRICHS/TERRI DRISCOLL

ILLUSTRATOR:
ALEXEY BRODOVITCH 396

PHOTOGRAPHER:
STEVEN HELLER/
DENNIS POTOKAR

AGENCY:
PENTAGRAM

PUBLISHER:
ART CENTER COLLEGE OF
DESIGN, PASADENA

■ 394-397

■ 394-397 Covers and double spreads taken from two issues of the magazine published by the Art Center College of Design in San Francisco. *394:* Paul Rand at his first visit. *395:* Works of several students; *396:* Alexey Brodovitch, the first modern art director. *397:* Student work from the Art Center in Europe. (USA)

■ 398 Cover taken from *Six*, customer magazine of fashion makers Comme des Garçons. The bird's body is coated with black varnish while the background has a mat finish. (JPN)

■ 399 Cover taken from an in-house magazine from Audi of America, Inc. A still life with oars. (USA)

■ 394-397 Umschläge und Doppelseiten von zwei Ausgaben der Hauszeitschrift des Art Center College of Design in San Francsico. *394:* Paul Rand bei seinem ersten Besuch. *395, 397:* die Arbeiten verschiedener Studenten aus den USA und Europa. *396:* Alexey Brodovitch, der erste moderne Art Direktor. (USA)

■ 398 Umschlag von *Six*, Kundenzeitschrift von Comme des Garçons. Der Körper des Vogels wurde schwarz lackiert und hebt sich plastisch vom matten Hintergrund ab. (JPN)

■ 399 Umschlag der Hauszeitschrift von Audi of America, Inc.: Ruderblätter werden zu einem Stilleben. (USA)

■ 394-397 Couvertures et doubles pages de deux numéros de la revue trimestrielle du Art Center College of Design de San Francisco. *394:* Paul Rand visite pour la première fois cette école. *395, 397:* quelques créations des étudiants designers aux Etats-Unis et en Europe. *396:* Alexey Brodovitch, le premier directeur artistique moderne. (USA)

■ 398 Couverture de *Six*, magazine destiné aux clients de Comme des Garçons. Le corps de l'oiseau est imprimé en noir brillant et en relief sur le fond mat de l'image. (JPN)

■ 399 Couverture de la revue d'entreprise du fabricant de voitures Audi: des rames pour l'aviron. (USA)

ART DIRECTOR:
TSUGUYA INOUE/BEANS CO. LTD.
DESIGNER:
TSUGUYA INOUE
AGENCY:
COMME DES GARÇONS/SERVICE DE PUBLICITÉ
PUBLISHER:
COMME DES GARÇONS
■ 398

ART DIRECTOR:
MILES ABERNETHY
DESIGNER:
MILES ABERNETHY
PHOTOGRAPHER:
BRIAN HILL
AGENCY:
SHR DESIGN COMMUNICATIONS
PUBLISHER:
AUDI OF AMERICA, INC.
■ 399

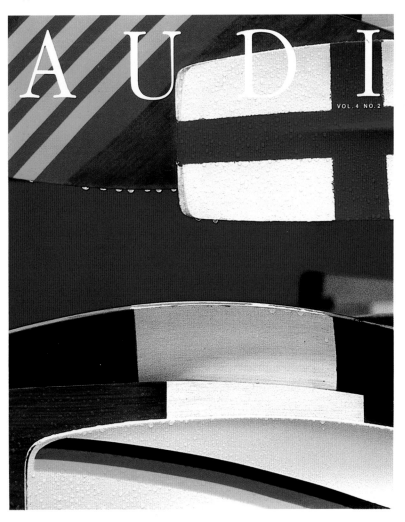

■ 400-405 Covers and double spreads taken from *HQ* magazine published by a manufacturer of printing machines in Heidelberg. The covers' themes are: "Contrasts", "1839" (the year in which daguerreotype became known), "Periphical Phenomenons". *403, 404*: two double spreads presenting the contrast phenomenon. *405*: "Stairway to Heaven" a high-built house with many steps which is made out of clay. It was built in Morocco's desert by artist Hannsjorg Voth of Munich. (GER)

■ 400-405 Umschläge und Doppelseiten der Zeitschrift *HQ (High Quality/Heidelberger Quality)*, herausgegeben von der Heidelberger Druckmaschinen AG. Die Umschläge beziehen sich auf folgende Themen: «Kontraste», «1839» (das Jahr, in dem die Daguerreotypie zum Allgemeingut wurde), «Randerscheinungen». *403, 404*: zwei Doppelseiten über das Phänomen der Kontraste. *405*: Die von dem Münchener Künstler Hannsjörg Voth in der Wüste Marokkos aus Lehm erbaute «Himmelstreppe», ein hohes Haus aus Stufen. (GER)

■ 400-405 Couvertures et doubles pages de *HQ*, revue professionnelle d'un constructeur de machines à imprimer. Ici, les couvertures illustrent les sujets suivants: «Contrastes», «1839» (date à laquelle la daguerréotypie devint un domaine public), «Phénomènes marginaux». *403, 404*: deux doubles pages illustrant des phénomènes de contraste. *405*: «Escalier vers le ciel», maison en terre en forme d'escalier construite par l'artiste munichois Hannsjörg Voth au milieu du désert du Maroc. (GER)

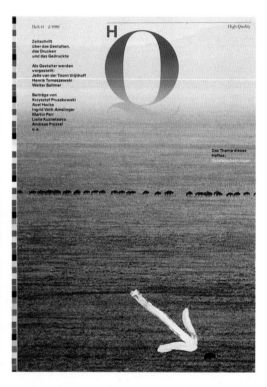

ART DIRECTOR:
ROLF MÜLLER
DESIGNER:
ROMAN LORENZ/BARBARA MIEDANER
ILLUSTRATOR:
CLAUDE KUHN-KLEIN 403
TYPOGRAPHER:
HANS-RUDOLF LUTZ 405
PHOTOGRAPHER:
INGRID VOTH-AMSLINGER 405
AGENCY:
BÜRO ROLF MÜLLER
PUBLISHER:
HEIDELBERGER DRUCK-MASCHINEN AG
■ 400-405

INSTANT

INSTANT **ERWEITERT** den HORIZONT   Nr. 28

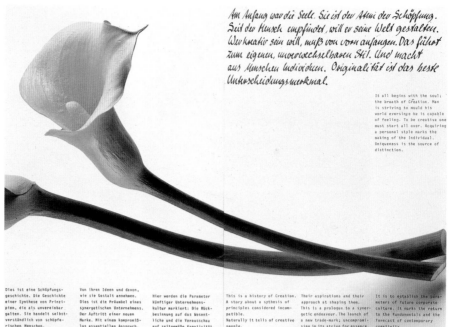

Am Anfang war die Seele. Sie ist der Atem der Schöpfung. Seit der Mensch empfindet, will er seine Welt gestalten. Wer kreativ sein will, muß von vorn anfangen. Das führt zum eigenen, unverwechselbaren Stil. Und macht aus Menschen Individuen. Originalität ist das beste Unterscheidungsmerkmal.

It all begins with the soul; the breath of Creation. Man is striving to mould his world eversince he is capable of feeling. To be creative one must start all over. Acquiring a personal style marks the making of the Individual. Uniqueness is the source of distinction.

Dies ist eine Schöpfungsgeschichte. Die Geschichte einer Synthese von Prinzipien, die als unvereinbar galten. Sie handelt selbstverständlich von schöpferischen Menschen.

Von ihren Ideen und davon, wie sie Gestalt annehmen. Dies ist die Präambel eines künftigen Unternehmens. Der Auftritt einer neuen Marke. Mit einem kompromißlos essentiellen Anspruch.

Hier werden die Parameter künftiger Unternehmenskultur markiert: Die Rückbesinnung auf das Wesentliche und die Vorausschau auf zeitgemäße Kreativität.

This is a history of Creation. A story about a sythesis of principles considered incompatible. Naturally it tells of creative people.

Their aspirations and their approach at shaping them. This is a prologue to a synergetic endeavour. The launch of a new trade-mark; uncompromising in its strive for essence.

It is to establish the parameters of future corporate culture. It marks the return to the fundamentals and the forecast of contemporary creativity.

ART DIRECTOR:
FRANZ AUMÜLLER/THOMAS FEICHT
DESIGNER:
UTE BEHRENDT
AGENCY:
TRUST
PUBLISHER:
INSTANT
■ 406-409

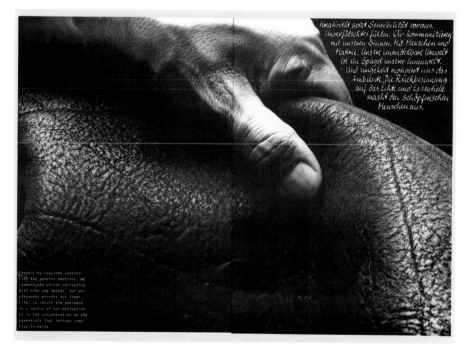

Kreativität setzt Sensibilität voraus. Unverfälscht fühlen. Wir kommunizieren mit unseren Sinnen. Mit Menschen und Materie. Unsere unmittelbare Umwelt ist ein Spiegel unserer Innenwelt. Und umgekehrt motiviert uns das Ambiente. Die Rückbesinnung auf das Echte und Essentielle macht den schöpferischen Menschen aus.

Creativity requires sensitivity and genuine emotions. We communicate whilst reflecting. With mind and matter. Our environment mirrors our inner life. In return the ambiance is a source of our motivation. It is the concentration on the essentials that defines creative thinking.

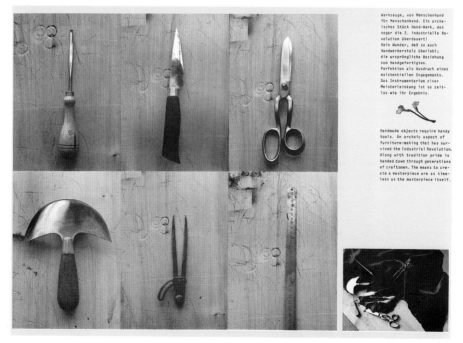

Werkzeuge, von Menschenhand für Menschenhand. Ein archaisches Stück Hand-Werk, das sogar die 2. industrielle Revolution überdauert! Kein Wunder, daß so auch Handwerkerstolz überlebt; die ursprüngliche Beziehung zum Handgefertigten. Perfektion als Ausdruck eines existentiellen Engagements. Das Instrumentarium einer Meisterleistung ist so zeitlos wie ihr Ergebnis.

Handmade objects require handy tools. An archaic aspect of furniture-making that has survived the Industrial Revolution. Along with tradition pride is handed down through generations of craftsmen. The means to create a masterpiece are as timeless as the masterpiece itself.

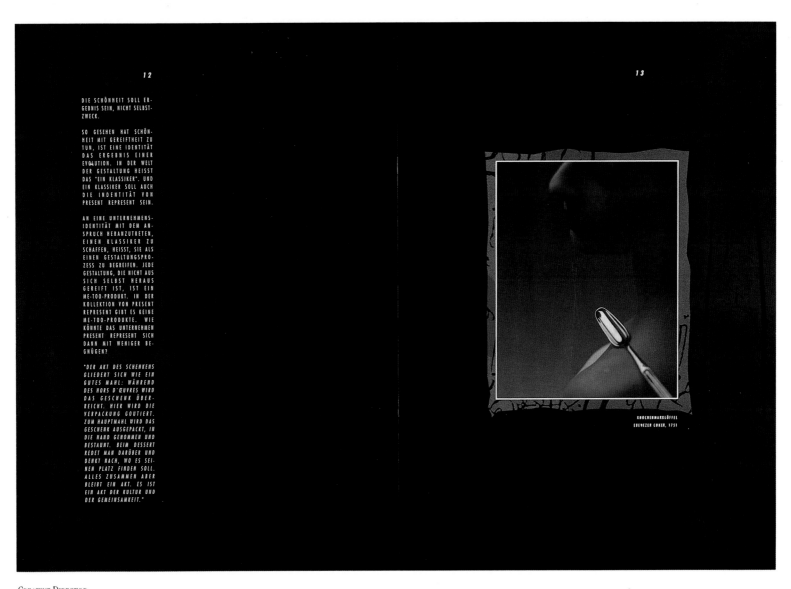

DIE SCHÖNHEIT SOLL ER-
GEBNIS SEIN, NICHT SELBST-
ZWECK.

SO GESEHEN HAT SCHÖN-
HEIT MIT GEREIFTHEIT ZU
TUN, IST EINE IDENTITÄT
DAS ERGEBNIS EINER
EVOLUTION. IN DER WELT
DER GESTALTUNG HEISST
DAS "EIN KLASSIKER". UND
EIN KLASSIKER SOLL AUCH
DIE INDENTITÄT VON
PRESENT REPRESENT SEIN.

AN EINE UNTERNEHMENS-
IDENTITÄT MIT DEM AN-
SPRUCH HERANZUTRETEN,
EINEN KLASSIKER ZU
SCHAFFEN, HEISST, SIE ALS
EINEN GESTALTUNGSPRO-
ZESS ZU BEGREIFEN. JEDE
GESTALTUNG, DIE NICHT AUS
SICH SELBST HERAUS
GEREIFT IST, IST EIN
ME-TOO-PRODUKT. IN DER
KOLLEKTION VON PRESENT
REPRESENT GIBT ES KEINE
ME-TOO-PRODUKTE. WIE
KÖNNTE DAS UNTERNEHMEN
PRESENT REPRESENT SICH
DANN MIT WENIGER BE-
GNÜGEN?

"DER AKT DES SCHENKENS
GLIEDERT SICH WIE EIN
GUTES MAHL: WÄHREND
DES HORS D'ŒUVRES WIRD
DAS GESCHENK ÜBER-
REICHT. HIER WIRD DIE
VERPACKUNG GOUTIERT.
ZUM HAUPTMAHL WIRD DAS
GESCHENK AUSGEPACKT, IN
DIE HAND GENOMMEN UND
BESTAUNT. BEIM DESSERT
REDET MAN DARÜBER UND
DENKT NACH, WO ES SEI-
NEN PLATZ FINDEN SOLL.
ALLES ZUSAMMEN ABER
BLEIBT EIN AKT. ES IST
EIN AKT DER KULTUR UND
DER GEMEINSAMKEIT."

KNOCHENMARKLÖFFEL
EBENEZER COKER, 1751

CREATIVE DIRECTOR:
FRANZ AUMÜLLER
ART DIRECTOR:
KLAUS MAI
PHOTOGRAPH:
WERNER PAWLOK
AGENCY:
TRUST
CLIENT:
*PRESENT REPRESENT,
GERD F. KLEIN*
PUBLISHER:
INSTANT
■ 410

■ 406-409 Cover and double spreads taken from *Instant magazine*. The examples shown are from an issue dedicated to the theme creativity. *406, 407:* Cover and first double spread which is typical of the particular style of the magazine. *408:* "Creativity requires sensitivity. Feel the real thing. We communicate with our senses." *409:* The importance of the tools for the crafts. (GER)

■ 410 Spread from an issue of the magazine *Instant*, dedicated to beauty. Shown is a bone marrow spoon designed by Ebenezer Coker in 1751. (GER)

■ 406-409 Umschlag und Doppelseiten der Zeitschrift *Instant*. Die gezeigten Beispiele stammen aus einer Ausgabe, die der Kreativität gewidmet ist. *406, 407:* Umschlag und erste Doppelseite, die bezeichnend für den besonderen Stil ist. *408:* «Wir kommunizieren mit unseren Sinnen.» *409:* Die Bedeutung des Werkzeugs, die Beziehung zum Handgefertigten. (GER)

■ 410 Doppelseite aus einer Ausgabe von *Instant*, die der Schönheit von Dingen gewidmet ist. Hier ein Knochen-marklöffel aus dem Jahre 1751 von Ebenezer Coker. (GER)

■ 406-409 Couverture et doubles pages du magazine Instant. «Instant élargit l'horizon» – Les exemples présentés ici sont tirés d'un numéro consacré à la créativité. *406, 407:* couverture et première double page illustrant le caractère unique de l'œuvre. *408:* l'émotion et la sensibilité sont nécessaires à la créativité. *409:* l'importance de l'outil dans la création. (GER)

■ 410 Double page d'un numéro du magazine *Instant*, dédié à la beauté des objects. Ici, une cuillère pour la moelle créée par Ebenezer Coker en 1751. (GER)

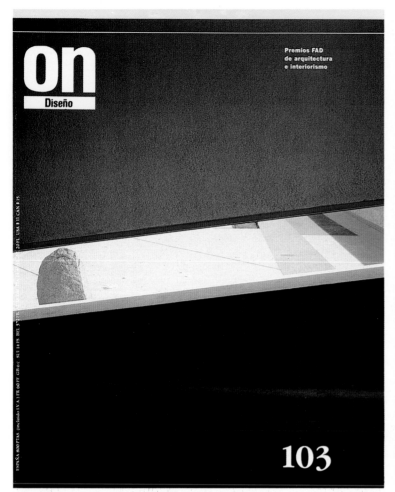

ART DIRECTOR:
JORDI AMBROS
DESIGNER:
STEPHAN WOLJACK
PHOTOGRAPHER:
LLUIS CASALS
AGENCY:
ESTUDIO ZIMMERMANN
PUBLISHER:
*ARAM EDICIONES,
S.A.*
■ 411, 412

■ 411, 412 Covers taken from the Spanish design magazine, *On Diseno.* (SPA)

■ 413, 414 Two covers of the Turkish design magazine, *Dekorayon* (Decoration) published monthly. (TUR)

■ 411, 412 Umschläge der spanischen Design-Zeitschrift *On Diseno.* (SPA)

■ 413, 414 Umschläge des monatlich erscheinenden türkischen Design-Magzins *Dekorasyon* (Dekoration). (TUR)

■ 411, 412 Couvertures du magazine de design espagnol *On Diseno.* (SPA)

■ 413, 414 Deux exemples de couvertures d'un magazine de décoration et de design paraissant chaque mois. (TUR)

ART DIRECTOR:
BÜLENT ERKMEN

DESIGNER:
BÜLENT ERKMEN

PUBLISHER:
ARREDAMENTO DEKORASYON

■ 413, 414

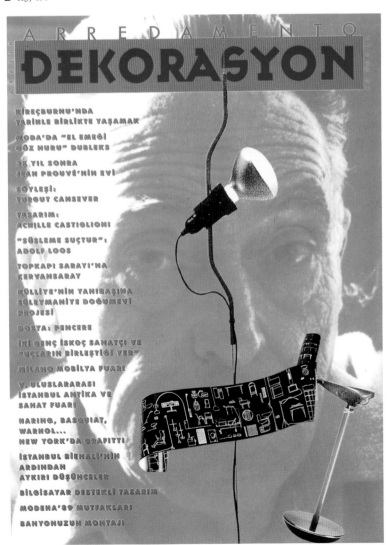

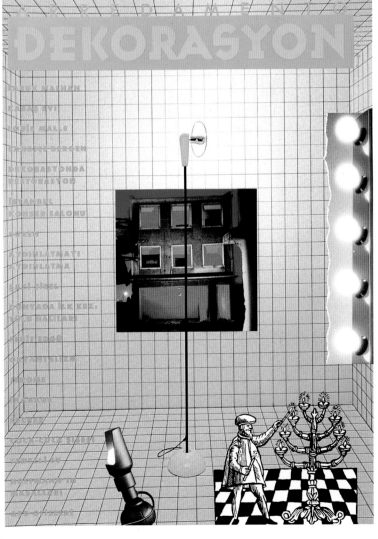

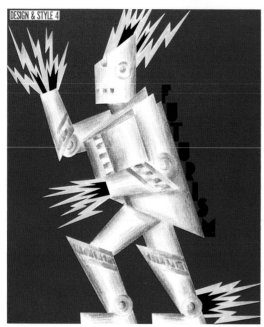

ART DIRECTOR:
Seymour Chwast

DESIGNER:
Roxanne Slimak/Seymour Chwast

ILLUSTRATOR:
Seymour Chwast

AGENCY:
The Pushpin Group

PUBLISHER:
Mohawk Paper Mills, Inc.

■ 415-419

■ 415-419 Two issues of *Design & Style* magazine published by Mohawk Paper Mills, Inc. Each issue is dedicated to a particular style. *415, 416, 419:* De Stijl, the Dutch avant-garde movement of the '20s. *417, 418:* Cover for an issue regarding Italian futurism, and double spread on the subject with cut-outs. (USA)

■ 415-419 Aus zwei Ausgaben von *Design & Style*, Zeitschrift eines Papierherstellers. Jede Nummer ist einer bestimmten Stilrichtung gewidmet. *415, 416, 419:* De Stijl, die holländische Avant-Garde-Bewegung der 20er Jahre. *417, 418:* Umschlag der Ausgabe über den italienischen Futurismus und Doppelseite mit Ausstanzungen. (USA)

■ 415-419 Deux exemples de *Design & Style*, magazine promotionnel d'un fabricant de papiers. *415, 416, 419:* numéro consacré au mouvement hollandais d'avant-garde des années 1920-1930, De Stijl. *417, 418:* couverture du numéro sur le futurisme italien et double page avec découpes. (USA)

ART DIRECTOR:
Oswaldo Miranda (Miran)
DESIGNER:
Oswaldo Miranda (Miran)
AGENCY:
Casa de Ideias
PUBLISHER:
Grafica Magazine
■ 420

■ 420 Double spread taken from an article about Russian graphic design in *Grafica Magazine*. The small brochure glued onto the page on the right contains signs and symbols. (BRA)

■ 421 Cover taken from *Picabia*, a Japanese magazine on culture. (JPN)

■ 422 Cover taken from Italian architecture and design magazine *Terrazzo*. (ITA)

■ 420 Doppelseite aus einem Artikel über russisches Graphik-Design in *Grafica Magazine*. Die kleine, auf die rechte Seite geklebte Broschüre enthält Markenzeichen und Symbole. (BRA)

■ 421 Umschlag von *Picabia*, einem japanischen Kulturmagazin. (JPN)

■ 422 Umschlag für *Terrazzo*, eine italienische Zeitschrift über Architektur und Design. (ITA)

■ 420 Double page de *Grafica Magazine* pour un article sur le graphic design russe. Une série de marques et emblèmes est présentée dans un petit livret collé sur la page de droite. (BRA)

■ 421 Couverture de *Picabia*, un magazine culturel japonais. (JPN)

■ 422 Couverture de *Terrazzo*, un magazine italien d'architecture et de design. (ITA)

ART DIRECTOR:
MASATOSHI TODA
DESIGNER:
MASANORI MIZUSHIMA
PHOTOGRAPHER:
JEAN-FRANÇOIS LEPAGE
PUBLISHER:
RIKUYO-SHA PUBLISHING, INC.
■ 421

DESIGNER:
CHRISTOPH RADL
PUBLISHER:
TERRAZZO
■ 422

ART DIRECTOR:
AUBREY BALKIND
DESIGNER:
DAVID SUH
PHOTOGRAPHER:
MICHAEL MELFORD/PAUL STEVENS
AGENCY:
FRANKFURT GIPS BALKIND
CLIENT:
REEVES COMMUNICATIONS CORP.
■ 423-426

■ 423-426 Cover and three double spreads taken from the 1988 annual report for RCC, an enterprise which produces entertainment programs for TV. (USA)

■ 423-426 Umschlag und drei Doppelseiten aus dem Jahresbericht 1988 für RCC, ein Unternehmen, das Unterhaltungsprogramme für das Fernsehen produziert. (USA)

■ 423-426 Couverture et trois doubles pages du rapport annuel 1988 de RCC, une entreprise qui produit des émissions récréatives pour la télévision. (USA)

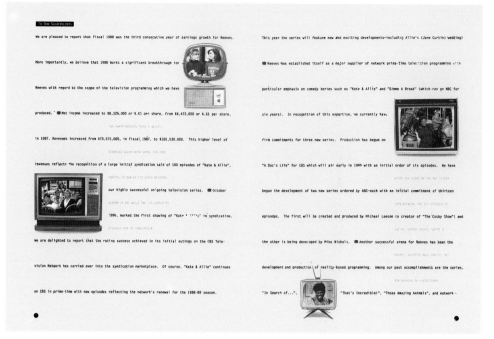

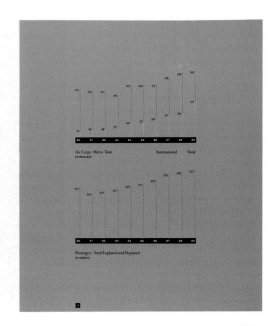

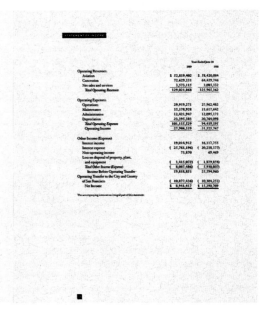

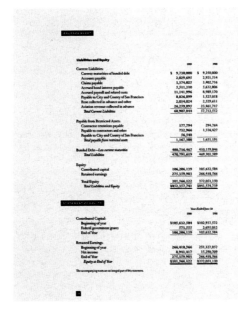

ART DIRECTOR:
JENNIFER MORLA
DESIGNER:
MARIANNE MITTEN
ILLUSTRATOR:
GUY BILLOUT
AGENCY:
MORLA DESIGN INC.
CLIENT:
SAN FRANCISCO INTERNATIONAL
AIRPORT
■ 427-430

■ 427-430 Cover and
double spreads taken from
the 1989 annual report of
the San Francisco International Airport, "Gateway to
the Pacific". The corner of
the cover's bottom right-
hand side is cut off. (USA)

■ 427-430 Umschlag und
Doppelseiten aus dem
Jahresbericht 1989 für den
internationalen Flughafen
von San Francisco, das «Tor
zum Pazifik». Rechts unten
ist der Umschlag schräg
abgeschnitten. (USA)

■ 427-430 Couverture et
doubles pages du rapport
annuel 1989 de l'aéroport
international de San Francisco, «Porte du Pacifique».
L'angle inférieur droit de la
couverture est taillé en
biseau. (USA)

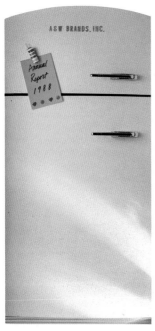

ART DIRECTOR:
LISA KLAUSING

DESIGNER:
LISA KLAUSING

PHOTOGRAPHER:
ERIC JACOBSEN/
STEVEN BEGLERTER

COPYWRITER:
MARGO CONTRUCCI

AGENCY:
HILL AND KNOWLTON, INC./
CORPORATE DESIGN GROUP

CLIENT:
A&W BRANDS, INC.

■ 431-435

■ 431-435 Annual report shaped in the form of a refrigerator for A&W, producers of soft drinks. The refrigerator's door serves as the cover illustration, the double spread presents the contents listing the assorted beverages and the year's balance sheet. The report's back page looks like the back of a refrigerator. (USA)

■ 436-439 Annual report of Skaggs Foundation, a charity organization which financed a study on the effects of mass media on human behavior. Here are some of the findings: television works like a drug; the positive and negative aspects of communication; the danger of political propaganda. (USA)

■ 431-435 Jahresbericht in Form eines Kühlschrankes Für A&W, Hersteller nicht-alkoholischer Getränke. Die Tür des Kühlschranks client als Umschlagillustration; die Doppelseiten präsentieren den Inhalt, d.h. das Getränkesortiment der Firma und die Bilanz des Jahres. Die Rückseite des Berichtes sieht wie die Rückseite eines Kühlschranks aus. (USA)

■ 436-439 Jahresbericht der Skaggs Foundation, eine karitative Einrichtung, die eine Studie über die Auswirkungen der Massenmedien auf menschliche Verhaltensnormen finanziert hat: Fernsehen wirkt wie eine Droge; die positiven und negativen Aspekte der Kommunikation; die Gefahren der politischen Propaganda. (USA)

■ 431-435 Rapport annuel en forme de frigidaire pour A&W, le leader dans la branche des boissons non alcoolisées. En couverture, la porte du frigidaire; les doubles pages présentent le contenu, c'est-à-dire la gamme des boissons commercialisées et le bilan financier de l'année. Le rapport se referme sur une photo de l'arrière du frigidaire. (USA)

■ 436-439 Rapport annuel de la Fondation Skaggs, une association caritative qui a financé une étude sur les effets des mass media sur le comportement humain. En voici quelques extraits: la TV agit comme une drogue, les aspects positifs et négatifs de la communication, les dangers de la propagande de masse. (USA)

ART DIRECTOR:
Michael Vanderbyl
DESIGNER:
Michael Vanderbyl
AGENCY:
Vanderbyl Design
CLIENT:
*The L.J. Skaggs and
Mary C. Skaggs Foundation*
■ 436-439

A D D I C T I O N

"IT IS, IN FACT, THE PARENTS FOR WHOM TELEVISION IS AN IRRESISTIBLE NARCOTIC, NOT THROUGH THEIR OWN VIEWING (ALTHOUGH FREQUENTLY THIS, TOO, IS THE CASE) BUT AT A REMOVE, THROUGH THEIR CHILDREN, PARKED OUT IN FRONT OF THE RECEIVER, STRANGELY QUIET. SURELY THERE CAN BE NO MORE INSIDIOUS A DRUG THAN ONE THAT YOU MUST ADMINISTER TO OTHERS IN ORDER TO ACHIEVE AN EFFECT YOURSELF."
—MARIE WINN
THE PLUG-IN DRUG

THE PARADOX OF COMMUNICATION

Shortly after the introduction of radio broadcasting in 1920, Lewis Mumford was putting the finishing touches to his now classic book, Technics and Civilization, the first history of the development of technology and its effect on social life, art, science, philosophy, customs and manners. In it, he discussed what he called "the paradox of communication." On the one hand, he said, there is a fabulous potential for telegraph, telephone, and telecommunications to bridge the gap in space and time, making person-to-person communications and widened discourse on a worldwide basis available instantaneously. On the other, he foresaw a magnified danger of mass regimentation, a reduction of quality in the more abstract forms of communication such as reading and writing, and a general fascination with—and addiction to—new telecommunications media regardless of real need or benefit. "As with all instruments of multiplication," he warned, "the critical question is as to the function and quality of the object one is multiplying." Sixty years later, his prescient ghost haunts the maze of newspapers, television game shows, radio commercials, videocassettes, sit-coms, cablevision, print ads, news clips, 60 second paid political announcements, Rambo films, billboards, magazines, children's cartoons, TV evangelists and even the reams of "documentary" and "independent" film produced annually. While there is no doubt that mass media communications play an important role in informing and entertaining people, it is clear we have now entered a new age of media pollution which may be as much a threat to our mental and physical health as environmental pollution has become.
Last year, the L.J. Skaggs and Mary C. Skaggs Foundation launched a new program

entitled "The Effect of Mass Media on Human Behavior and Decision-Making." The program rests on the assumption that while our society has developed an incredibly sophisticated media technology, we have neglected to develop the equally important capacity for analyzing how this media is affecting us. There is no doubt that it is. Scholars, researchers, advertising experts, and scientists all agree that media, and particularly the complex electronic mass media which has become so much a part of our lives now, helps to shape our thought processes, our value systems and ultimately our actions in the world. In fact, media has the power and the potential to shape both positive and negative social values. We know, for instance, that certain forms of advertising are very effective & convincing people to buy certain products, or to vote in a certain way, or to support a certain movement, lifestyle or belief system. We also know that media in general, and electronic mass media in particular, appeal so deep human emotions, and that clever technologists can—and do—play on public angst about sexuality, desire, love, fear, anger, pain, grief and years to convince people to behave in certain ways. What we don't know is how images and words and music used singly or in tandem work on the human mind to change it.
In Darkness at Noon, Arthur Koestler argued that every major technological innovation (such as the invention of the sea b. or later, the automobile, or later the airplane) transforms in this case not just transportation, but also society's entire way of thinking about time, about travel, about movement. We are now in the process of a complete communications revolution. The development of mass media technology, however, is progressing far more rapidly than our knowledge about the effects of these new technologies on individual human

R E G I M E N T A T I O N / P R O P A G A N D A

"Instantaneous personal communication over long distances is the mechanical symbol of those world-wide cooperations of thought and feeling which must emerge, finally, if our whole civilization is not to sink into ruin. The new avenues of communication have the characteristic features and advantages of the new technics: in the long run, they promise not to displace the human being but to refocus him and enlarge his capacities. But there is a proviso attached to this promise: Plato defined the limits of the size of a city as the number of people who could hear the voice of a single orator. Today those limits do not define a city but a civilization. The possibilities for good and evil here are immense: the secondary personal contact with the voice and image may increase the amount of mass regimentation. At the present moment, the dangers of the radio and the talking picture seem greater than the benefits."
—Lewis Mumford
Technics and Civilization

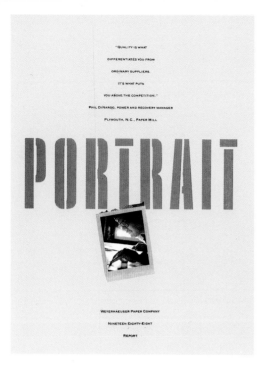

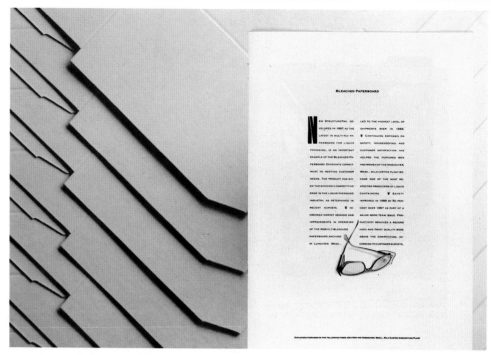

ART DIRECTOR:
John Van Dyke
DESIGNER:
John Van Dyke
PHOTOGRAPHER:
Jeff Corwin/Terry Heffernan
COPYWRITER:
Dan Koger
AGENCY:
Van Dyke Company
CLIENT:
*Weyerhaeuser Paper
Company*
■ 440-443

■ 440-443 Cover with
embossed title and glued-on
picture, as well as double
spreads taken from the
annual report of a paper
manufacturer. (USA)

■ 440-443 Umschlag mit
geprägtem Titel und
aufgeklebtem Bild sowie
Doppelseiten aus dem
Jahresbericht eines Papierherstellers. (USA)

■ 440-443 Couverture
avec effets de gaufrage et
doubles pages du rapport
annuel d'un fabricant de
papiers. Les pages de texte
sont insérées comme des
encarts. (USA)

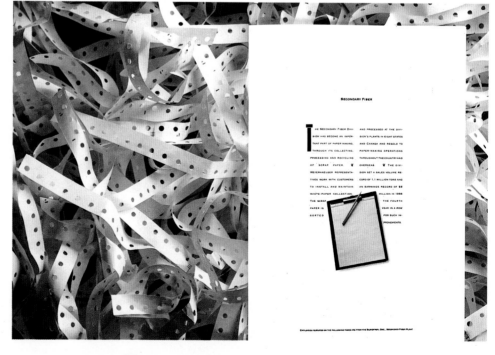

ILLUSTRATION

ILLUSTRATION

ILLUSTRATION

ONE·NINETY·ONE PEACHTREE TOWER
Architecture by John Burgee Architects
Design Consultant Philip Johnson
1990
A Joint Venture of Cousins Properties Incorporated,
Dutch Institutional Holding Company and
Gerald D. Hines Interests

ART DIRECTOR:
TOM MCNEFF
DESIGNER:
TOM MCNEFF
ILLUSTRATOR:
TOM MCNEFF
AGENCY:
HERRING DESIGN, INC.
CLIENT:
COUSINS PROPERTIES INC.
DUTCH INSTITUTIONAL
HOLDING CO.
GERALD D. HINES INTERESTS
■ 444

ART DIRECTOR:
RICHARD BLEIWEISS
DESIGNER:
RICHARD BLEIWEISS
ILLUSTRATOR:
LAURENCE GONZALES
PUBLISHER:
PENTHOUSE MAGAZINE
►■ 445

■ 444 The upper, south view of 191 Peachtree Tower, a building by the John Burgee architect office, design counselling by Philip Johnson. (USA)

■ 445 "Lynch Justice" – full-page illustration for a feature in *Penthouse*. (USA)

■ 444 Der obere, südliche Teil des 191 Peachtree Tower, ein Bauwerk des Architekturbüros John Burgee, Design-Beratung durch Philip Johnson. (USA)

■ 445 «Lynch-Justiz» – ganzseitige Illustration für einen Beitrag in *Penthouse*. (USA)

■ 444 Partie supérieure du côté sud de la 191 Peachtree Tower, un bâtiment construit par le studio d'architecture John Burgee, avec la collaboration de Philip Johnson. (USA)

■ 445 «La loi et les lynchages»: illustration de *Penthouse* au sujet des citoyens qui assassinent au nom de la justice. (USA)

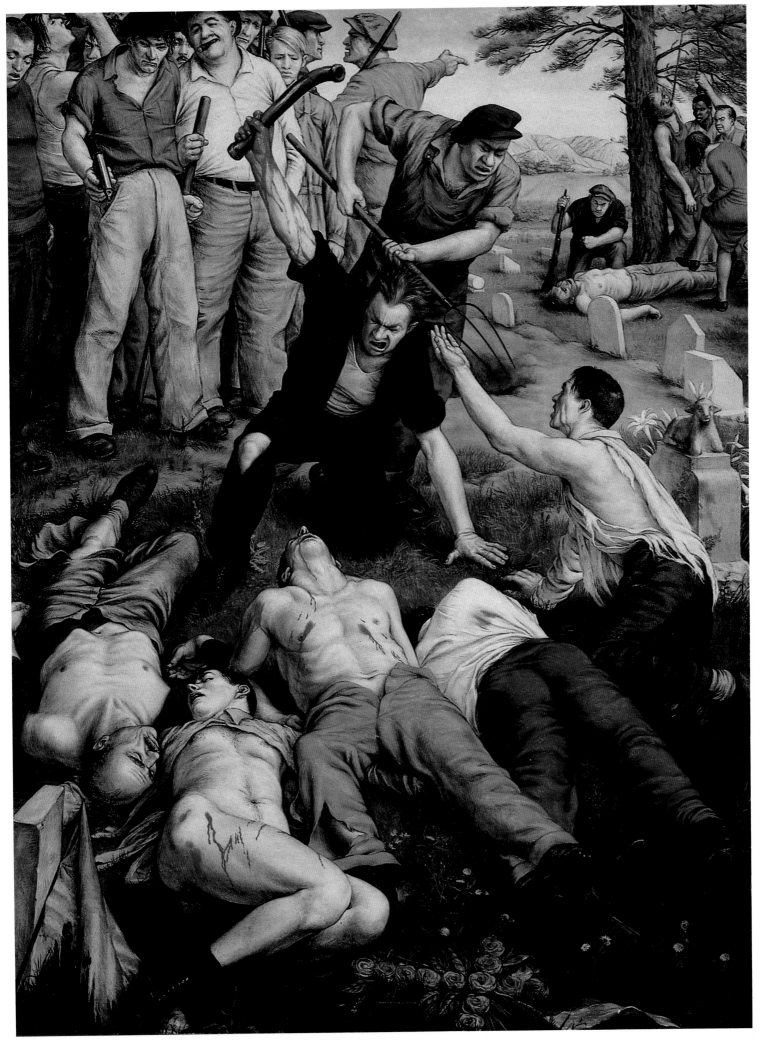

ART DIRECTOR:
SANDY DIPASQUA
ILLUSTRATOR:
GARY KELLEY
PUBLISHER:
CONNOISSEUR MAGAZINE
■ 446

ILLUSTRATOR:
JOHN KLEBER
AGENCY:
DESIGN RESOURCES
CLIENT:
CAL ARTS
■ 447

ART DIRECTOR:
CARON PERKAL
ILLUSTRATOR:
KAREL HAVLICEK
AGENCY:
ADVERTISING CONSORTIUM
CLIENT:
BERNINI
■ 448

■ 446 This illustration in pastels relates to a wild party given by Picasso in 1908 in his Paris studio in honour of painter Henri Rousseau. (USA)

■ 447 Illustration by American artist John Kleber for Cal Arts art college. (USA)

■ 448 Illustration from an advertisement for a man's outfitters. While nature tends to privilege the male animal, the human counterpart has *Bernini*. (USA)

■ 446 Diese Illustration in Pastell erzählt von einer wilden Party, die Picasso 1908 in seinem Pariser Atelier zu Ehren des Malers Henri Rousseau gab. (USA)

■ 447 Illustration von John Kleber für die Kunstschule Cal Arts. (USA)

■ 448 «Die männlichen Tiere werden von der Natur meistens recht elegant ausgestattet. Der Mann hat zum Glück *Bernini*.» Anzeige für einen Herrenausstatter. (USA)

■ 446 Cette illustration exécutée au pastel évoque la fête qui eut lieu dans l'atelier de Picasso en 1908, en l'honneur du peintre Henri Rousseau. (USA)

■ 447 Illustration par John Kleber pour l'école d'art Cal Arts. (USA)

■ 448 Illustration tirée d'une annonce pour un magasin de mode masculine. Le texte rappelle que chez les animaux, l'élégance est surtout le privilège du mâle. (USA)

ILLUSTRATOR:
HASHIM AKIB
■ 449, 450

■ 449, 450 Unpublished drawings from a series for the novel *The Great Gatsby* by Scott Fitzgerald. (GBR)

■ 451, 452 Two examples from a series for the advertising campaign of a jeans manufacturer. (POR)

■ 449, 450 Unveröffentliche Zeichnungen für den Roman *Der grosse Gatsby* von Scott Fitzgerald. (GBR)

■ 451, 452 Zwei Beispiele aus einer Serie für die Werbekampagne eines Jeans-Herstellers. (POR)

■ 449, 450 Dessins inédits tirés d'une série illustrant le roman de Scott Fitzgerald *Gatsby le Magnifique*. (GBR)

■ 451, 452 Deux exemples d'illustrations tirées d'une série conçue pour Jeans Generation. (POR)

ART DIRECTOR:
MANUEL PERES
ILLUSTRATOR:
MANUEL PERES
AGENCY:
LAGE STABEL
CLIENT:
JEANS JENEARATION
■ 451, 452

Art Director:
Hermann Roth
Illustrator:
Peter Krämer
Agency:
Deutsche Lufthansa
Presseabteilung
Publisher:
Deutsche Lufthansa AG
■ 453, 454

■ 453, 454 Airbrush illu-
strations for the inflight
magazine of the Lufthansa
airline. (GER)

■ 453, 454 Airbrush-Illu-
strationen für das *Bord-
buch*, Inflight-Magazin der
Deutschen Lufthansa. (GER)

■ 453, 454 Illustrations
réalisées à l'aérographe
pour le magazine de bord
de la Lufthansa. (GER)

Designer:
Michael Schwab
Illustrator:
Michael Schwab
Studio:
Michael Schwab
►■ 455

■ 455 Unpublished illustration by American illustrator
Michael Schwab. (USA)

■ 455 Unveröffentlichte
Illustration des amerikani-
schen Illustrators Michael
Schwab. (USA)

■ 455 Illustration inédite de
l'illustrateur américain
Michael Schwab. (USA)

ART DIRECTOR:
Danielle Gallo
DESIGNER:
Danielle Gallo
Laura Woods
ILLUSTRATOR:
Carlos Revilla
PUBLISHER:
Penthouse Letters
■ 456

■ 456 From a special edition of *Penthouse Letters* on the subjects of erotic and magic. The symbolic pictures by Carlos Revilla are reminiscent of Hieronymus Bosch. (USA)

■ 457 Unpublished illustration for a theater program. (USA)

■ 458 Illustration for an ad for Varitel Video. (USA)

■ 456 Aus einer Spezial-Edition von *Penthouse Letters* zum Thema Erotik und Magie. In ihrer Symbolik erinnern die Bilder von Carlos Revilla an Hieronymus Bosch. (USA)

■ 457 Illustration für ein Theaterprogramm. (USA)

■ 458 Illustration für ein Inserat von Varitel Video. (USA)

■ 456 Image tirée d'une série spéciale sur les pratiques magiques de l'érotisme, parue dans *Penthouse Letters*. La symbolique des images rappelle Hieronymus Bosch. (USA)

■ 457 Illustration pour un programme de théâtre. (USA)

■ 458 Illustration d'une annonce pour Varitel Video. (USA)

Art Director:
William Gin
Designer:
John Mattos
Illustrator:
John Mattos
Client:
Gin & Assoc.
■ 457

Art Director:
Michael Fitzgerald
Designer:
Kathy Broyles
Illustrator:
John Mattos
Agency:
B.G.F & C.
Client:
Varitel Video
■ 458

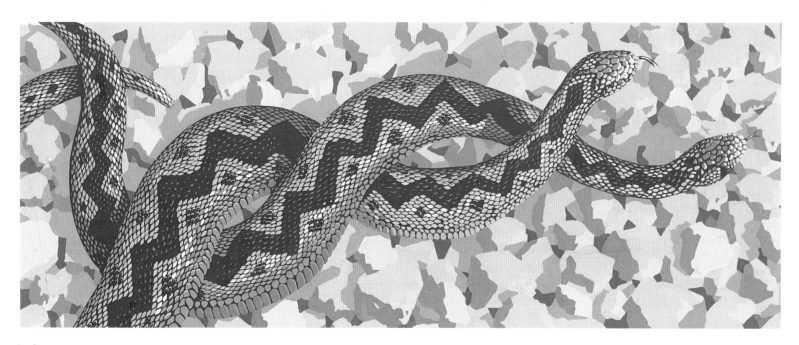

ART DIRECTOR:
Pedro Silmon
DESIGNER:
Pedro Silmon
ILLUSTRATOR:
Andrew Davidson
PUBLISHER:
Sunday Times Magazine
▲■ 459

ILLUSTRATOR:
Sergio Martinez
▼■ 460

ART DIRECTOR:
D.J. STOUT
DESIGNER:
D.J. STOUT
ILLUSTRATOR:
BRALDT BRALDS
AGENCY:
TEXAS MONTHLY
PUBLISHER:
TEXAS MONTHLY
■ 461

■ 459 Illustration from the *Sunday Times Magazine*. (GBR)

■ 460 Personal work of a Spanish illustrator. (SPA)

■ 461 From a series of illustrations for cowboy songs in the *Texas Monthly* magazine. (USA)

■ 459 Illustration aus dem *Sunday Times Magazine*. (GBR)

■ 460 Freie Arbeit eines spanischen Illustrators. (SPA)

■ 461 Aus einer Reihe von Illustrationen für Cowboy-Songs in der Zeitschrift *Texas Monthly*. (USA)

■ 459 Illustration pour le *Sunday Times Magazine*. (GBR)

■ 460 Illustration personnelle d'un artiste espagnol. (SPA)

■ 461 L'une des images illustrant des chansons de cowboys, publiées dans le *Texas Monthly*. (USA)

ART DIRECTOR:
JAYME ODGERS
DESIGNER:
JAYME ODGERS
ILLUSTRATOR:
JAYME ODGERS
◀■ 462

ART DIRECTOR:
DEBORAH FLYNN HANRAHAN
DESIGNER:
SANDRA HENDLER
ILLUSTRATOR:
SANDRA HENDLER
PUBLISHER:
LOTUS PUBLISHING CO.
▲■ 463

■ 462 A combination of photography and painting as self-promotion for American Jayme Odgers. (USA)

■ 463 Illustration for an article about the growth of investments. (USA)

■ 462 Eine übermalte Photographie als Eigenwerbung des Amerikaners Jayme Odgers. (USA)

■ 463 Illustration für einen Artikel über das Wachsen von Investitionen. (USA)

■ 462 Photographie peinte comme autopromotion d'un illustrateur américain. (USA)

■ 463 Illustration conçue pour un article concernant la croissance des investissements. (USA)

464 Promotional piece for a costume shop.

464 Werbung für einen Kostümverleih. (USA)

464 Pour une firme de location de costumes. (USA)

465 This illustration relates to a true historic event. During an attempted attack on a fort, Native Americans were driven off by a pack of dogs. (USA)

465 Diese Illustration bezieht sich auf eine wahre Begebenheit: Bei einem Angriff auf ein Fort liessen sich Indianer von einigen Hunden in die Flucht schlagen. (USA)

465 Cette illustration fait allusion à un événement historique: quelques chiens mirent en fuite les Indiens lors d'une attaque contre un fort. (USA)

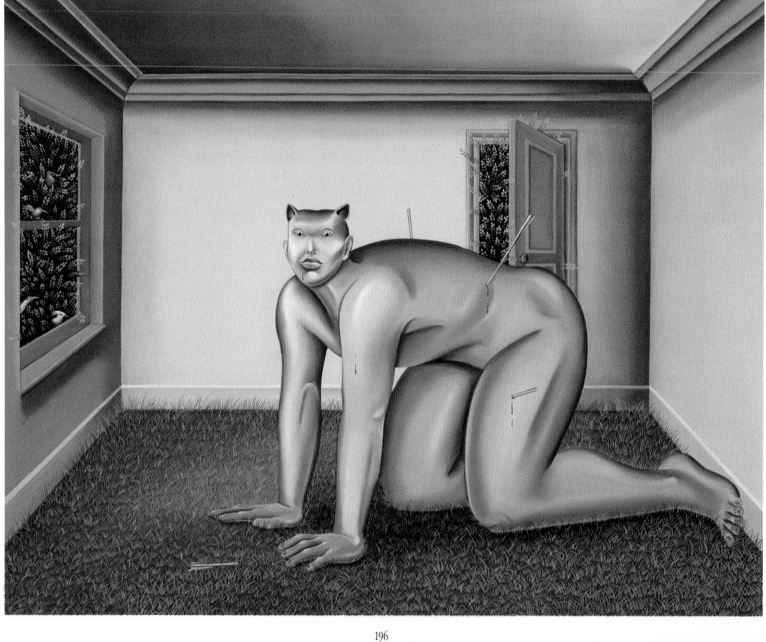

ART DIRECTOR:
SANDRA HENDLER
DESIGNER:
SANDRA HENDLER
ILLUSTRATOR:
SANDRA HENDLER
CLIENT:
STUDIO DIABOLIQUE
◄■ 464

ART DIRECTOR:
MARY WORKMAN
DESIGNER:
TIM BROWN
ILLUSTRATOR:
SANDRA HENDLER
PUBLISHER:
WHITTLE COMMUNICATIONS
▲■ 465

ART DIRECTOR:
DAVID PEARCE
DESIGNER:
JULIE FELLOWES
ILLUSTRATOR:
GUY BILLOUT
AGENCY:
TATHAM PEARCE LTD.
CLIENT:
ASSURANCEFORENINGEN
GARD
■ 466

ART DIRECTOR:
ELLEN ZIEGLER
DESIGNER:
ELLEN ZIEGLER
KRIS MORGAN
ILLUSTRATOR:
GUY BILLOUT
AGENCY:
ELLEN ZIEGLER DESIGN
CLIENT:
PERKINS COIE
■ 467

ART DIRECTOR:
EDWIN FOSTER
DESIGNER:
EDWIN FOSTER
ILLUSTRATOR:
GUY BILLOUT
AGENCY:
FOSTER DESIGN GROUP
CLIENT:
CAPITAL
◄■ 468

ART DIRECTOR:
James Sebastian
Margaret Wollenhaupt
DESIGNER:
Margaret Wollenhaupt
ILLUSTRATOR:
Guy Billout
AGENCY:
Designframe Inc.
CLIENT:
The Hillier Group
Architect
■ 469

■ 466 Illustration for the cover of the annual report of an insurance company for ship owners. The text closes with the same illustration. (NOR)

■ 467 Example of the illustrations from the company brochures of a legal firm. Shown here are the intellectual abilities and demands made on the partners. (USA)

■ 468 Full-page illustration from a brochure for an investment company. (USA)

■ 469 From a brochure for a group of architects showing that construction can be quite an adventure. (USA)

■ 466 Illustration für den Umschlag des Jahresberichtes einer Versicherungsgesellschaft für Schiffseigner. Der Textteil schliesst mit der gleichen Illustration ab. (NOR)

■ 467 Beispiel der Illustrationen aus der Firmenbroschüre einer Anwaltsfirma. Hier geht es um die intellektuellen Fähigkeiten und Anforderungen an die Partner. (USA)

■ 468 Ganzseitige Illustration aus einer Broschüre für eine Investment-Firma. (USA)

■ 469 «Der Bau als Abenteuer» – doppelseitige Illustration aus der Firmenbroschüre eines Architekturbüros. (USA)

■ 466 Illustration ornant la couverture du rapport annuel d'une société d'assurances pour des propriétaires de bateaux. (NOR)

■ 467 L'une des illustrations figurant dans une brochure conçue pour un bureau d'avocats. Les juristes y ont la possibilité de développer leurs capacités intellectuelles. (USA)

■ 468 Illustration tirée d'une brochure pour une compagnie d'investissements financiers. (USA)

■ 469 «Quand la construction est une aventure». Illustration pour la brochure d'un groupe d'architectes. (USA)

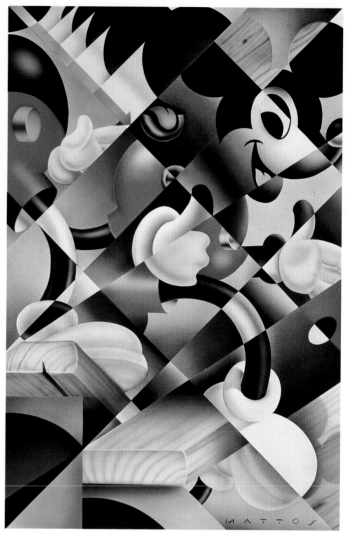

ILLUSTRATOR:
JOEL PETER JOHNSON
■ 470

ART DIRECTOR:
JOHN MATTOS
DESIGNER:
JOHN MATTOS
ILLUSTRATOR:
JOHN MATTOS
▲■ 471

ART DIRECTOR:
DAVID CARSON
DESIGNER:
DAVID CARSON
ILLUSTRATOR:
MATT MAHURIN
PUBLISHER:
BEACH CULTURE MAGAZINE
►■ 472

■ 470 Illustration entitled "Portrait of an Art Director", used as self promotion. (USA)

■ 471 Illustration used to promote a book. Featured is the most famous mouse of all time. (USA)

■ 472 Portrait of surfer Tom Curren who became a legend on account of his forceful personality. It appeared in *Beach Culture Magazine*. (USA)

■ 470 Als Eigenwerbung verwendete Illustration mit dem Titel «Porträt eines Art Direktors». (USA)

■ 471 «Mickey in der Kunst» – für eine Buchpromotion verwendete Illustration (gespritzte Tusche). (USA)

■ 472 In der Zeitschrift *Beach Culture Magazine* erschienenes Porträt des Surfers Tom Curren, der durch seine starke Persönlichkeit zur Legende wurde. (USA)

■ 470 «Portrait d'un directeur artistique» – autopromotion d'un illustrateur américain. (USA)

■ 471 «Mickey dans l'art»: ici, Mickey descendant un escalier. Illustration pour la promotion d'un livre. (USA)

■ 472 Illustration pleine page parue dans *Beach Culture Magazine*. On y évoque la figure d'un grand surfer qui était aussi une très forte personnalité. (USA)

ART DIRECTOR:
NANCY RUENZEL
ILLUSTRATOR:
BRAD HOLLAND
PUBLISHER:
STEP-BY-STEP GRAPHICS
■ 473

ART DIRECTOR:
MILTON GLASER
DESIGNER:
MILTON GLASER
DAVID FREEDMAN
ILLUSTRATOR:
MILTON GLASER
AGENCY:
MILTON GLASER INC.
CLIENT:
SIMPSON PAPER CO.
▲■ 474

■ 473 Full-page illustration from an interview with Brad Holland in *Step-by-Step Graphics*. Here he puts the question whether the commercial media allow the artist any originality. (USA)

■ 474 Double spread from an advertising brochure for Simpson paper makers. It is dedicated to the teaching profession. Professors tell about their teaching experience. The angel is a play on "Angelus Novus" – a water color by Paul Klee. (USA)

■ 473 Ganzseitige Illustration aus einem Interview mit Brad Holland in *Step-by-Step Graphics*. Er stellt hier die Frage, ob die kommerziellen Medien dem Künstler Originalität erlauben. (USA)

■ 474 Doppelseite aus einer Werbebroschüre für den Papierhersteller Simpson, die den «Lehrenden» gewidmet ist. Professoren äussern sich über ihre Erfahrungen im Unterricht. Der Engel ist eine Anspielung auf «Angelus Novus», ein Aquarell von Paul Klee. (USA)

■ 473 Illustration pleine page pour une interview de Brad Holland, parue dans *Step-by-Step Graphics*. Il s'interroge sur la création: l'originalité est-elle encore possible dans les médias? (USA)

■ 474 Double page d'une brochure publicitaire pour les papiers Simpson, ayant pour sujet «ceux qui enseignent». Des professeurs s'expriment sur leur conception et leurs expériences de l'enseignement. Ici, l'ange est une allusion à l'«Angelus Novus», une aquarelle de Paul Klee. (USA)

ART DIRECTOR:
ROBERT WARKULWIZ
DESIGNER:
WILLIAM F. SMITH
ILLUSTRATOR:
NANCY STAHL
AGENCY:
*WARKULWIZ DESIGN
ASSOCIATES*
PUBLISHER:
PROVIDENT NATIONAL BANK
■ 475

ILLUSTRATOR:
JON CONRAD
■ 476

ART DIRECTOR:
SUSAN PROSINSKI
DESIGNER:
SUSAN PROSINSKI
ILLUSTRATOR:
GARY KELLEY
PUBLISHER:
*ADAMS COMMUNICATIONS
CORP.*
►■ 477

■ 475 "Buy bonds" - full-page illustration from the customer magazine of a bank which here is giving information on fixed interest securities. (USA)

■ 476 Illustration by American artist Jon Conrad used for self promotion. (USA)

■ 477 Illustration for an article published in *Chicago Magazine* about the training of FBI agents in Chicago in the period around 1941. (USA)

■ 475 «Kauft Bonds» - ganzseitige Illustration aus der Kundenzeitschrift einer Bank, die hier über festverzinsliche Wertpapiere informiert. (USA)

■ 476 Als Eigenwerbung verwendete Illustration von Jon Conrad. (USA)

■ 477 Illustration für einen Artikel in *Chicago Magazine* über die Ausbildung von FBI-Agenten im Chicago von 1941: «Der Gabardine-Krieg». (USA)

■ 475 «Achetez des Bonds» - illustration pleine page du magazine publié par une banque pour ses clients. L'article concerne les risques des placements à revenu fixe. (USA)

■ 476 Illustration utilisée pour l'autopromotion de l'Américain Jon Conrad. (USA)

■ 477 Illustration pour un article paru dans *Chicago Magazine* sur l'entraînement des agents du FBI dans le Chicago des années 1941: «La Guerre de Gabardine.» (USA)

ART DIRECTOR:
DESIGNER:
ILLUSTRATOR:
JOHN KLEBER
CLIENT:
XEROX CORPORATION
■ 478

■ 478 Illustration for a brochure issued by Xerox Corporation. (USA)

■ 478 Illustration für eine Broschüre der Xerox Corporation. (USA)

■ 478 Illustration pour une brochure publiée par la Xerox Corporation. (USA)

CORPORATE IDENTITY

STATIONERY

LOGOTYPES

CORPORATE IDENTITY

BRIEFPAPIER

FIRMENZEICHEN

IDENTITÉ CORPORATE

PAPIER À LETTRES

EMBLÈMES

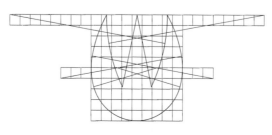

CREATIVE DIRECTOR:
Miha Takagi
ART DIRECTOR:
Hiromi Inayoshi
DESIGNER:
Hiromi Inayoshi
ILLUSTRATOR:
Hiroki Taniguchi
AGENCY:
Inayoshi Design Inc.
CLIENT:
Seiwa Corporation
■ 479-486

■ 479-486 The corporate identity of Seiwa Corp. covers architecture as well as the interior design of the firm's own restaurants – down to the smallest details such as the symbols on the toilet doors. (JPN)

■ 479-486 Das Firmenerscheinungsbild der Seiwa Corp. umfasst die Architektur sowie die Innenausstattung der firmeneigenen Restaurants bis in die kleinsten Details, wie z.B. die Symbole auf den Toilettentüren. (JPN)

■ 479-486 Le programme d'identité de Seiwa Corp. englobe la conception architecturale de l'entreprise ainsi que l'aménagement intérieur de ses restaurants. Il s'applique aux moindres détails, y compris les symboles apposés à la porte des toilettes. (JPN)

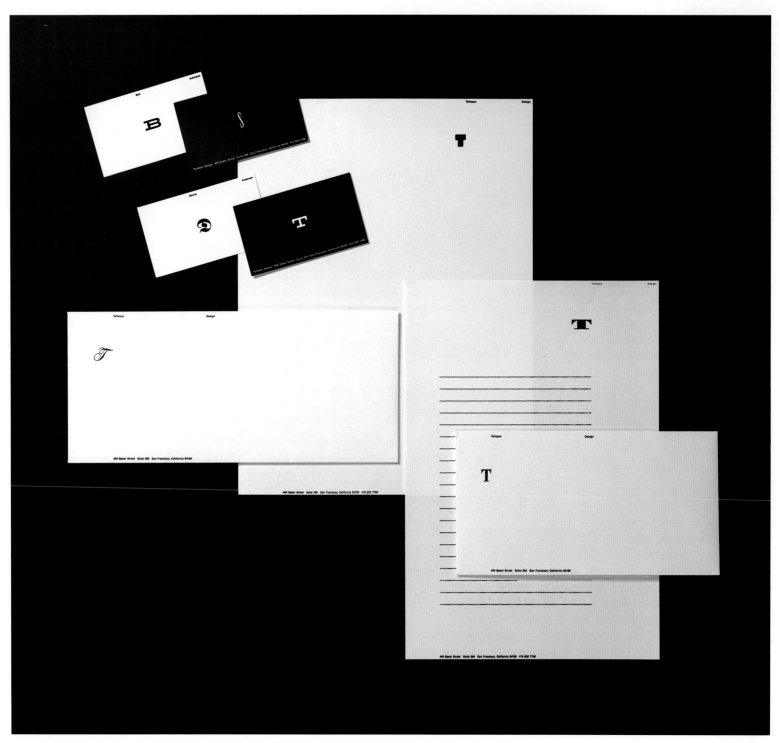

ART DIRECTOR:
STEVEN TOLLESON
DESIGNER:
STEVEN TOLLESON
AGENCY:
TOLLESON DESIGN
CLIENT:
TOLLESON DESIGN
■ 487

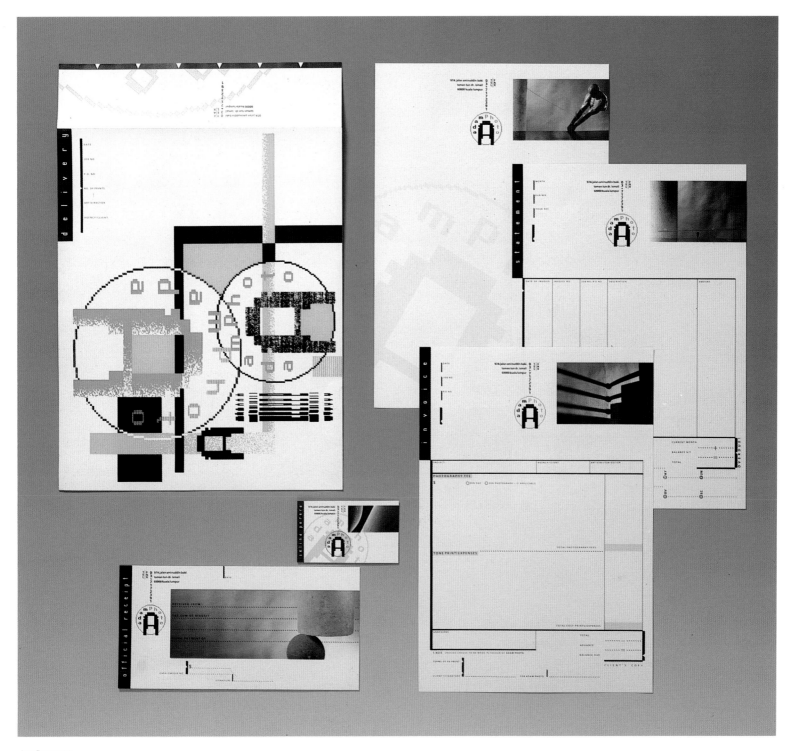

ART DIRECTOR:
WILLIAM HARALD-WONG
DESIGNER:
WILLIAM HARALD-WONG/
YEW LEONG
PHOTOGRAPHER:
ADAM
AGENCY:
WILLIAM HARALD-WONG &
ASSOCIATES
CLIENT:
ADAM PHOTO
■ 488

■ 487 Typographic variations on the letter T on the letter-heads and envelopes of Tolleson Design. The employees' visiting cards of this firm are indicated by the initial letter of their forename and surname (negative version). (USA)

■ 488 The stationery of this photo studio which specializes in black-and-white photography underscores the individuality of the photographer. (MAL)

■ 487 Typographische Variationen des Buchstabens T auf dem Briefpapier und den Umschlägen von Tolleson Design. Die Visitenkarten dieser Firma sind dagegen mit deren Initialen gekennzeichnet. (USA)

■ 488 Das Geschäftspapier dieses Photostudios, das auf Schwarzweiss-Photographie spezialisiert ist, unterstreicht die Individualität des Photographen. (MAL)

■ 487 Des variations typographiques sur le T ornent le papier à lettres et les enveloppes de Tolleson Design. La carte de visite commerciale des collaborateurs de cette entreprise est individualisée par ses initiales. (USA)

■ 488 Les cartes commerciales, le papier à lettres et les enveloppes de ce photographe, spécialisé dans le noir et blanc, mettent en valeur sa personnalité. (MAL)

ART DIRECTOR:
MARY LEWIS
DESIGNER:
JUDY VEAL
AGENCY:
LEWIS MOBERLY
CLIENT:
PEARL DOT LIMITED
■ 489

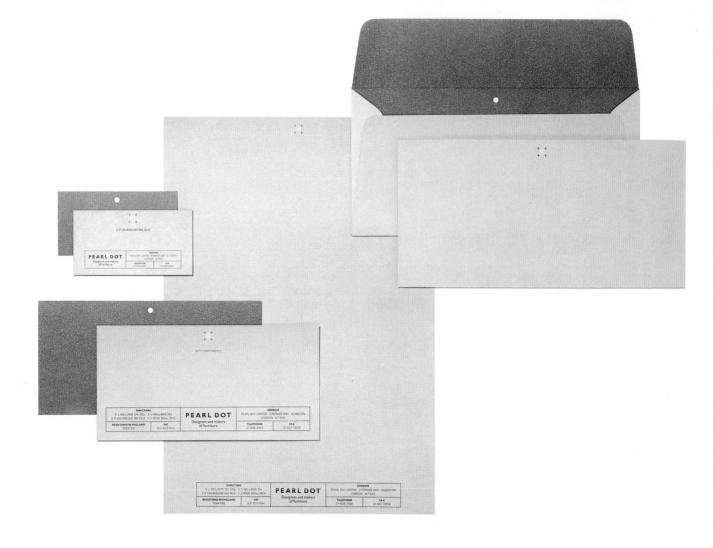

ART DIRECTOR:
JOHN C. REGER
DESIGNER:
KOBE
AGENCY:
*DESIGN CENTER
MINNETONKA*
CLIENT:
*STATION 19
ARCHITECTS INC.*
■ 490

ART DIRECTOR:
VALERY RICHARDSON
DESIGNER:
DIANE GILLELAND
ILLUSTRATOR:
REGAN DUNNICK
DIANE GILLELAND
AGENCY:
RICHARDSON OR RICHARDSON
CLIENT:
RHONDA GRAPHICS
■ 491

ART DIRECTOR:
WOODY PIRTLE
DESIGNER:
WOODY PIRTLE/JENNIFER LONG
AGENCY:
PENTAGRAM DESIGN, NEW YORK
CLIENT:
CROSSROADS FILMS
■ 492

ART DIRECTOR:
WOODY PIRTLE
DESIGNER:
WOODY PIRTLE
AGENCY:
PENTAGRAM DESIGN, NEW YORK
CLIENT:
LIBBY CARTON
■ 493

ART DIRECTOR:
SUE CROLICK
DESIGNER:
SUE CROLICK
AGENCY:
SUE CROLICK
ADVERTISING + DESIGN
CLIENT:
LAKE STREET SHIRTS
■ 494

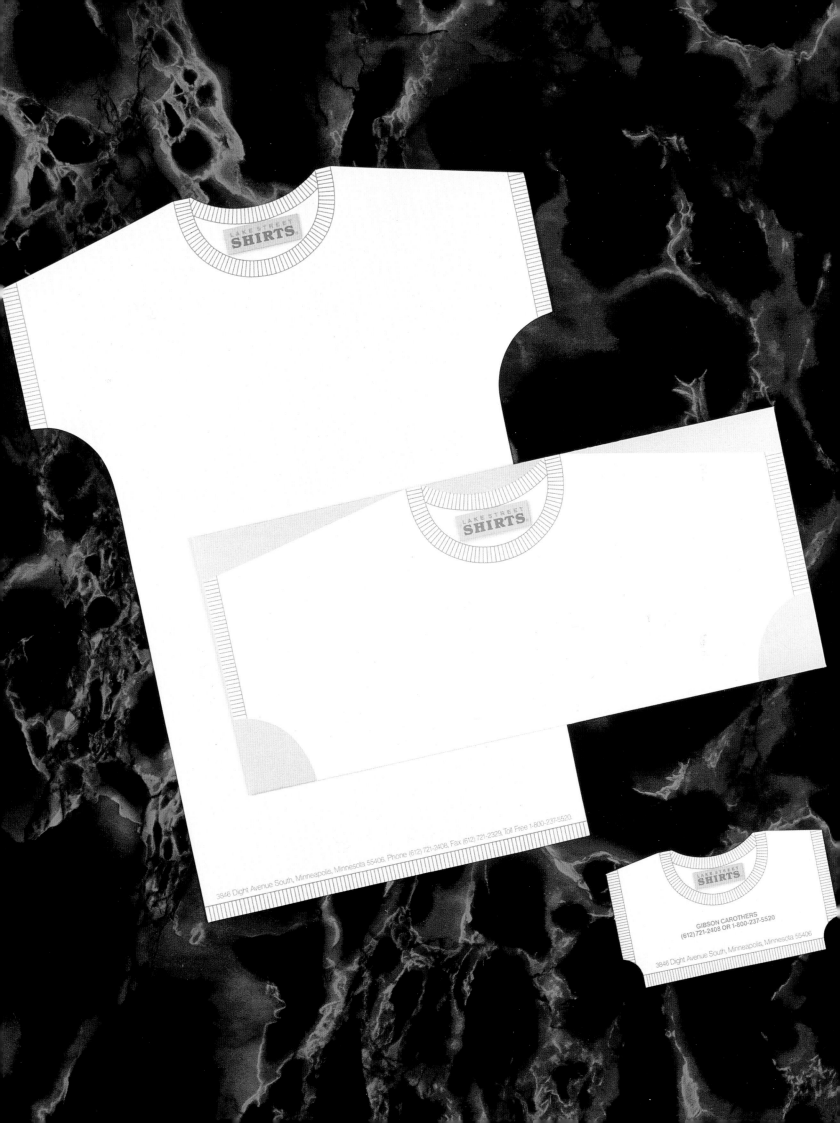

LAKE STREET
SHIRTS

LAKE STREET
SHIRTS

3846 Dight Avenue South, Minneapolis, Minnesota 55406. Phone (612) 721-2408, Fax (612) 721-2329, Toll Free 1-800-237-5520.

LAKE STREET
SHIRTS

GIBSON CAROTHERS
(612) 721-2408 OR 1-800-237-5520

3846 Dight Avenue South, Minneapolis, Minnesota 55406

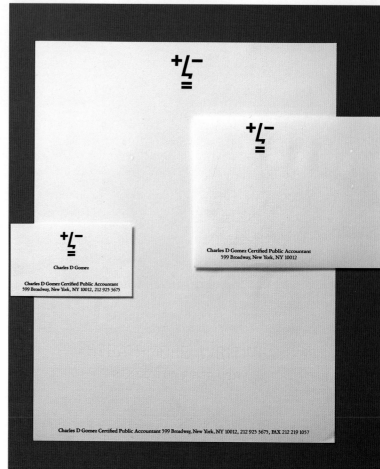

ART DIRECTOR:
Tom Meenaghan
DESIGNER:
Tom Meenaghan
ILLUSTRATOR:
Austin Carey
AGENCY:
Design Works
CLIENT:
Rourkes Bakery
■ 495

ART DIRECTOR:
Michael A. Cousins
Mark D. Landry
DESIGNER:
Mark D. Landry
AGENCY:
Cousins Design
CLIENT:
Charles D. Gomez
■ 496

■ 495 Letterheads and cards for a bakery. (IRL)

■ 496 Part of the corporate identity for an accounting firm. The logo relates to the personal care given to the customers and the mathematical nature of the profession. (USA)

■ 497 Letterheads and business card (also as sticker) for a graphic designer. (GER)

■ 498 Business stationery for a carpentry firm. (USA)

■ 495 Briefbogen und Karten für eine Bäckerei. (IRL)

■ 496 Teil des Firmenerscheinungsbildes einer Buchhaltungsfirma: das Logo deutet die persönliche Betreuung der Kunden und die mathematische Natur der Branche an. (USA)

■ 497 Briefbogen und Geschäftskarte (auch als Aufkleber) einer Graphik-Designerin. (GER)

■ 498 Geschäftspapier für eine Tischlerei. (USA)

■ 495 Papier à lettres d'une boulangerie. (IRL)

■ 496 Programme d'identité pour un comptable: le logo évoque l'attention personnelle portée au client et le côté mathématique de la profession. (USA)

■ 497 Papier à lettres, carte commerciale et autocollant d'une graphiste allemande. (GER)

■ 498 Cartes et papier à lettres pour un menuisier. (GBR)

ART DIRECTOR:
MICHAEL BUTTGEREIT
DESIGNER:
MICHAEL BUTTGEREIT
ILLUSTRATOR:
MICHAEL BUTTGEREIT
AGENCY:
DESIGNBÜRO M. BUTTGEREIT
CLIENT:
KARINA HOLBECK
■ 497

DESIGNER:
GLENN TUTSSEL
ILLUSTRATOR:
GLENN TUTSSEL-
HARRY WILLOCK
RUTH PALMER
AGENCY:
MICHAEL PETERS & PARTNERS
CLIENT:
TUTSSEL/WARNE
■ 498

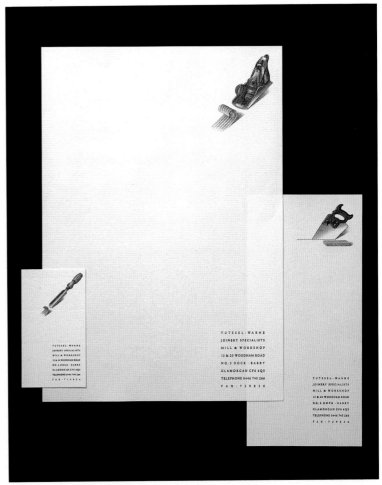

ART DIRECTOR:
PATI NUNEZ
DESIGNER:
PATI NUNEZ
ILLUSTRATOR:
PATI NUNEZ
AGENCY:
PATI NUNEZ
CLIENT:
TOKIO LINGERIE
■ 499

ART DIRECTOR:
THOMAS MCNULTY
DESIGNER:
RUSSELL BAKER
KENICHI NISHIWAKI
AGENCY:
PROFILE DESIGN
CLIENT:
APPLE COMPUTER, INC.
■ 500

ART DIRECTOR:
SCOTT RAY
DESIGNER:
SCOTT RAY
AGENCY:
PETERSON & COMPANY
CLIENT:
DALLAS REPERTORY THEATRE
■ 501

ART DIRECTOR:
JANN CHURCH
DESIGNER:
JANN CHURCH
AGENCY:
JANN CHURCH PTNRS.
ADV. & GRAPHIC DESIGN
CLIENT:
SANTA FE
INTERNATIONAL CORP.
■ 502

ART DIRECTOR:
MICHAEL VANDERBYL
DESIGNER:
MICHAEL VANDERBYL
CLIENT:
BEDFORD PROPERTIES
■ 503

DESIGNER:
MARK FOX
ILLUSTRATOR:
MARK FOX
AGENCY:
BLACKDOG
CLIENT:
EMBARKO
■ 504

ART DIRECTOR:
REX PETEET
DESIGNER:
REX PETEET
ILLUSTRATOR:
REX PETEET
AGENCY:
SIBLEY/PETEET DESIGN
CLIENT:
MESA RETAIL STORE
■ 505

ART DIRECTOR:
CHARLES S. ANDERSON
DESIGNER:
CHARLES S. ANDERSON
ILLUSTRATOR:
CHARLES S. ANDERSON
AGENCY:
DUFFY DESIGN GROUP
CLIENT:
LEE JEANS
■ 506

ART DIRECTOR:
CHARLES S. ANDERSON
DESIGNER:
CHARLES S. ANDERSON
ILLUSTRATOR:
CHARLES S. ANDERSON
LYNN SCHULTE
AGENCY:
DUFFY DESIGN GROUP
CLIENT:
ESSEX & SUSSEX
■ 507

ART DIRECTOR:
KEVIN M. LAUTERBACH
DESIGNER:
KEVIN M. LAUTERBACH
CLIENT:
SCHOOL PROJECT/
CHAMELEON CLOTHING
■ 508

ART DIRECTOR:
STEPHEN MILLER
DESIGNER:
STEPHEN MILLER
ILLUSTRATOR:
STEPHEN MILLER
AGENCY:
RICHARDS BROCK MILLER
MITCHELL & ASSOC./THE
RICHARDS GROUP
CLIENT:
ORYX ENERGY COMPANY
■ 509

ART DIRECTOR:
BERND MIRBACH
DESIGNER:
BERND MIRBACH
AGENCY:
MIRBACH DESIGN
CLIENT:
AMLING MODELLBAU
■ 510

ART DIRECTOR:
CHARLES S. ANDERSON
DESIGNER:
CHARLES S. ANDERSON
ILLUSTRATOR:
CHARLES S. ANDERSON
AGENCY:
CHARLES S. ANDERSON
CLIENT:
DOW BRANDS
■ 511

ART DIRECTOR:
STEVE GIBBS
DESIGNER:
STEVE GIBBS
ILLUSTRATOR:
STEVE GIBBS
CLIENT:
THE AMAZON CLUB
■ 513

ART DIRECTOR:
TIM GIRVIN
DESIGNER:
TIM GIRVIN
ILLUSTRATOR:
TIM GIRVIN
AGENCY:
TIM GIRVIN DESIGN, INC.
CLIENT:
WALL DATA
■ 512

DESIGNER:
KEVIN WHALEY
AGENCY:
GRAND PRE & WHALEY, LTD.
CLIENT:
JANET VIRNIG
■ 514

ART DIRECTOR:
GEPPI DE LISO
DESIGNER:
LILLI DE LISO
AGENCY:
STUDIO DE LISO
CLIENT:
NOVIELLI
■ 515

ART DIRECTOR:
MICHAEL MCGINN
TAKAAKI MATSUMOTO
DESIGNER:
MICHAEL MCGINN
ILLUSTRATOR:
JACK TOM
AGENCY:
M PLUS M INCORPORATED
CLIENT:
REBO RESEARCH, INC.
■ 516

DESIGNER:
KEVIN WHALEY
AGENCY:
GRAND PRE & WHALEY, LTD.
CLIENT:
CHARGO PRINTING/
THE ART DEPARTMENT
■ 517

ART DIRECTOR:
STEVEN TOLLESON
DESIGNER:
STEVEN TOLLESON
AGENCY:
TOLLESON DESIGN
CLIENT:
KEENAN LAND CO.
■ 518

ART DIRECTOR:
MIKE SALISBURY
DESIGNER:
MIKE SALISBURY
SCOTT BINKLEY
AGENCY:
SALISBURY COMM.
CLIENT:
GOTCHA SPORTSWEAR
■ 519

ART DIRECTOR:
CHARLES S. ANDERSON
DESIGNER:
CHARLES S. ANDERSON
ILLUSTRATOR:
CHARLES S. ANDERSON
AGENCY:
CHARLES S. ANDERSON
CLIENT:
INC., INC.
■ 520

ART DIRECTOR:
ROBERT VALENTINE
DESIGNER:
STEVEN SIKORA
ILLUSTRATOR:
STEVEN SIKORA
CLIENT:
BLOOMINGDALE'S
■ 521-536

■ 521-536 Illustrations representing the 12 Californias used in a store-wide campaign by Bloomingdale's in Spring of 1989 for the store directory, menus, department and product promotion, window and aisle displays. (USA)

■ 521-536 Zwölf Zonen Kaliforniens sind hier symbolisiert. Die Zeichen wurden von Bloomingdale's in einer Frühjahrskampagne für die Ladeninformation, Speisekarten, Werbung, Schaufenster und Gestell-Displays verwendet. (USA)

■ 512-536 Ces illustrations symbolisent les 12 provinces de la Californie. Les grands magasins Bloomingdale's les ont utilisées partout, sur les menus, les présentoires, sur les vitrines, etc. (USA)

PACKAGING

PACKUNGEN

EMBALLAGES

■ 537-540 The chemical formula for water serves as name for this line of cosmetics. The transparent flasks and tubes and the wave like shape and design of the labels support the associative impact. (USA)

■ 537-540 Die chemische Formel für Wasser dient als Name für die Kosmetiklinie. Die transparenten Behälter und die Form und Gestaltung der Etiketten sind auf diesen Namen abgestimmt. (USA)

■ 537-540 Cette ligne de cosmétiques porte le nom de la formule chimique de l'eau. Les emballages soulignent cette association: la transparence des flacons et tubes et la forme et le design des étiquettes. (USA)

ART DIRECTOR:
JIM LIENHART
DESIGNER:
JIM LIENHART
AGENCY:
MURRIE WHITE DRUMMOND &
LIENHART & ASSOC.
CLIENT:
H2O PLUS INC.
■ 537-540

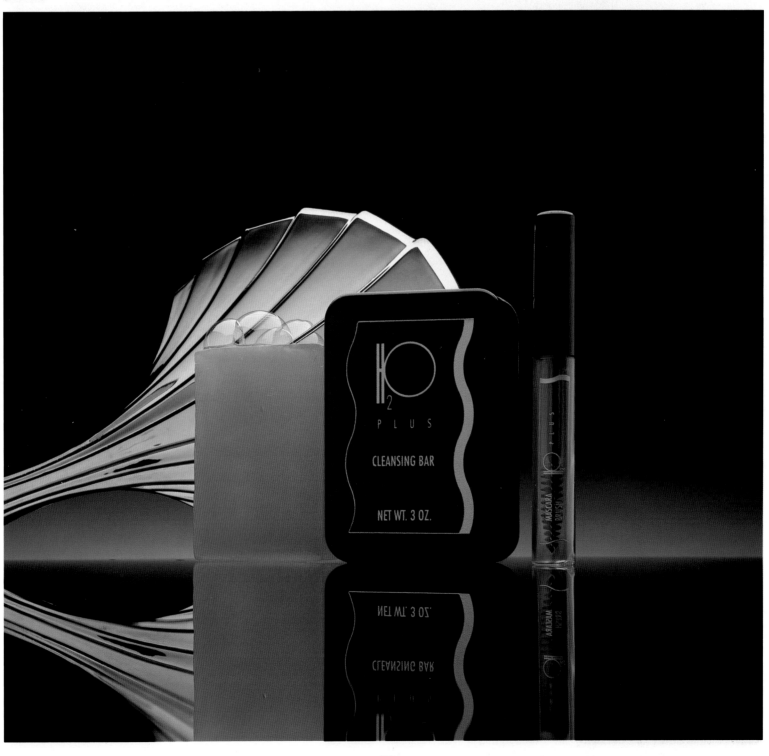

ART DIRECTOR:
TAMOTSU YAGI

DESIGNER:
SUNAO ISHII

PHOTOGRAPHER:
ROBERTO CARRA

AGENCY:
NARA SPORTS DESIGN STUDIO

CLIENT:
NARA SPORTS CO., LTD.

■ 541-543

ART DIRECTOR:
RICHARD TANINBAUM,
ROBERT LINETT

DESIGNER:
RICHARD TANINBAUM,
ROBERT LINETT,
ROBERT PIZZO

ILLUSTRATOR:
ROBERT PIZZO

CLIENT:
RHYTHM TECH INC.

►■ 544

■ 541-543 Ski equipment created for Nara Sports, Graphic variations of the logo and the different brand names serve as special design for the skis, boots and poles. (USA)

■ 544 "Rhythm Tech Percussion Bags" especially designed for the transportation of percussion instruments. The black-and-white pattern supports the theme of rhythm. (USA)

■ 541-543 Ski-Ausrüstungen für Nara Sports. Variationen des Firmenlogos und der Markennamen dienen als speziel-les Design-Element für die Skier, Stiefel und Stöcke. (USA)

■ 544 Spezielle Taschen für den Transport von Schlagin-strumenten von Rythm Tech. Die Idee des Rhythmus wird von dem Schwarzweiss-Muster aufgenommen. (USA)

■ 541-543 Equipements de skis créées pour Nara Sports. Des variations graphiques sur le logo de chaque modèle ornent les skis, les chaussures et les bâtons. (USA)

■ 544 Gamme de «sacs à percussions» conçus spécialement pour le transport des instruments à percussions de Rhythm Tech. Le dessin en noir et blanc évoque le rythme. (USA)

ART DIRECTORS:
Ann Gildea
Matthew Napoleon
DESIGNERS:
Kun-Tee Chang
Ann Gildea
Kate Murphy
Fred Weaver
AGENCY:
Fitch Richardson Smith Inc.
CLIENT:
Converse Inc.
■ 545-547

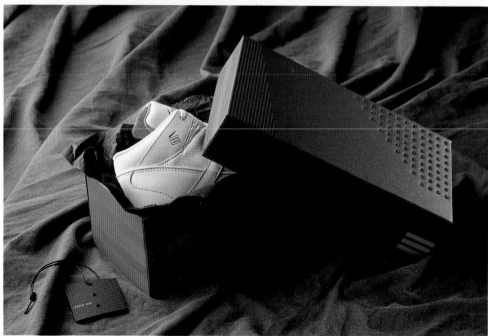

■ 545-547 Series of boxes and hang-tags for *Converse* sports shoes. A clearly differentiated positioning was to be created for each "brand" within the *Converse* family. (USA)

■ 548 Cordless headphone set marketed under the *Ross* label, in a twin box. (GBR)

■ 545-547 Schachteln und Anhänger für Sportschuhe der Marke *Converse*. Es galt, eine klare Identität für jede «Sorte» dieser Marke zu etablieren. (USA)

■ 548 Kabellose Kopfhörer der Marke *Ross* mit dazugehöriger Metallschachtel. (GBR)

■ 545-547 Série de boîtes et étiquettes pour les chaussures de sports *Converse*. Il s'agissait de donner une identité propre à chaque produit. (USA)

■ 548 Cette boîte rigide a été spécialement conçue pour un walkman sans fil de la marque *Ross*. (GBR)

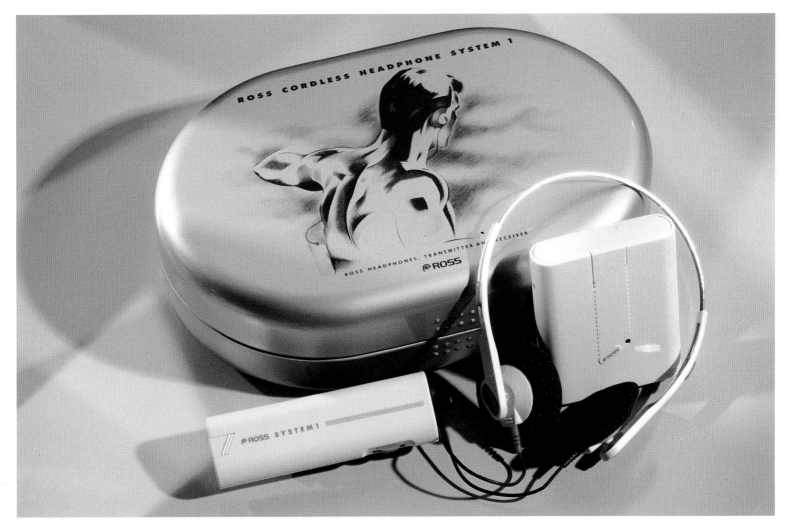

ART DIRECTOR:
MICHAEL PETERS
DESIGNER:
MICHAEL PETERS
ILLUSTRATOR:
KAREN WELMAN,
ROSEMARY HARRISON
AGENCY:
MICHAEL PETERS & PARTNERS
CLIENT:
ROSS CONSUMER ELECTRONICS
■ 548

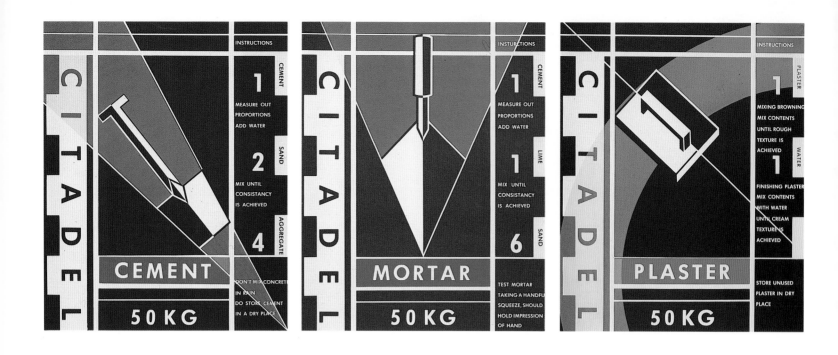

DESIGNER:
MARK BERGMAN
ILLUSTRATOR:
STEVE CALARCO
AGENCY:
SBG PARTNERS
CLIENT:
FENWICK, INC.
▲■ 550

ART DIRECTOR:
ANDREW GREETHAM
DESIGNER:
ANDREW GREETHAM
ILLUSTRATOR:
ANDREW GREETHAM
CLIENT:
APG ASSOCIATES
▲
▲■ 549

■ 549 Design for a series of industrial bags for the building industry. (GBR)

■ 550 Design for a new line of ultra-premium fishing line products. (USA)

■ 551 Carton packages for latex medical examination gloves. The goal was to humanize the otherwise typically generical packaging for medical supplies. (USA)

■ 549 Gestaltung für Industriepackungen mit Zement, Mörtel und Gips. (GBR)

■ 550 Kartonschachteln mit Anglerzubehör der gehobenen Preis- und Qualitätsklasse. (USA)

■ 551 Kartonschachteln für Wegwerfhandschuhe im medizinischen Anwendungsbereich. Ziel war es, keine typisch medizinische Packung zu entwerfen. (USA)

■ 549 Trois exemples de sacs pour le ciment, le mortier et le plâtre *Citadel*. (GBR)

■ 550 Trois emballages de lignes de cannes à pêche de qualité supérieure. (USA)

■ 551 Boîtes contenant des gants de latex à usage médical. L'objectif était de donner à l'emballage de ce produit une touche plus humaine. (USA)

ART DIRECTOR:
GERALD REIS
DESIGNER:
GERALD REIS
ALBERT TRESKIN
ILLUSTRATOR:
GERALD REIS
AGENCY:
GERALD REIS & COMPANY
CLIENT:
VAILWOOD PRODUCTS
■ 551

ART DIRECTORS:
CHARLES S. ANDERSON
DAN OLSON
DESIGNERS:
CHARLES S. ANDERSON
DAN OLSON
ILLUSTRATORS:
CHARLES S. ANDERSON
DAN OLSON
JAMES WILLIAMS
AGENCY:
CHARLES S. ANDERSON DESIGN
CLIENT:
ARAVIS DISTILLERIES
■ 552

ART DIRECTOR:
HALEY JOHNSON
DESIGNER:
HALEY JOHNSON
SHARON WERNER
AGENCY:
THE DUFFY DESIGN GROUP
CLIENT:
HALEY JOHNSON/DUFFY GROUP
■ 553

DESIGNER:
URS SCHWERZMANN
ILLUSTRATOR:
URS SCHWERZMANN
CLIENT:
GEHE AG
►■ 555

■ 552 Label design for the Aravis Distillery of France for one of their unique liqueurs. (USA)

■ 553 Photo album and a matching jewelry box made from different types of wood. (USA)

■ 554 The nostalgic illustration of the bottle label and of the wooden shipping box for orange juice evoke the old wrapping papers for oranges. (GBR)

■ 555 Study of package design for magnesium and calcium tablets. (GER)

■ 552 Etikettgestaltung für einen Birnenlikör der Aravis Brennerei in Frankreich. (USA)

■ 553 Photo-Album und passende Schmuckkassette aus verschiedenen Hölzern. (USA)

■ 554 Die nostalgische Illustration der Flaschenetiketten und der hölzernen Versand-Box für einen Orangensaft erinnern an Einwickelpapier für Orangen. (GBR)

■ 555 Nicht verwendete Verpackungsentwürfe für Magnesium- und Calcium-Tabletten. (GER)

■ 552 Etiquette pour la bouteille d'une eau-de-vie de poire de la maison Aravis en France. (USA)

■ 553 Petit coffret à bijoux et album de photos réalisés avec différents bois. (USA)

■ 554 Le sujet rétro des étiquettes ornant les bouteilles et les caisses d'emballages de ce jus d'orange rappelle les motifs des papiers qui enveloppent les oranges. (GBR)

■ 555 Projets de boîtes pour des comprimés au calcium et au magnésium. (GER)

ART DIRECTOR:
GLENN TUTSSEL
DESIGNER:
DAVID BEARD
ILLUSTRATOR:
ANDREW ALOOF
AGENCY:
MICHAEL PETERS & PARTNERS
CLIENT:
CARLETON FOODS LIMITED
■ 554

■ 556 Range of bottles for an Austrian beer. (AUT)

■ 557, 558 Bottle livery for a Pilsener sold by the British Asta Stores. The illustration refers to the industrial city of Dortmund. (GBR)

■ 556 Flaschenausstattung für österreichisches Bier. (AUT)

■ 557, 558 Flaschengestaltung für ein Dortmunder Pilsener, das von einer britischen Lebensmittelkette angeboten wird. Die Illustration bezieht sich auf diese Industriestadt. (GBR)

■ 556 Série de bouteilles pour une bière autrichienne. (AUT)

■ 557, 558 Etiquette d'une bouteille de bière Pilsener vendue par une chaine alimentaire anglaise. L'image évoque la grande ville industrielle de Dortmund. (GBR)

234

ART DIRECTOR:
ERWIN SCHMÖLZER
DESIGNER:
KRISTIN KONIAREK
ILLUSTRATOR:
MARIO KATZMAYR
CLIENT:
BRAUEREI MAYR
■ 556

ART DIRECTORS:
DAVID WOMBELL
BERNARD GORMLEY
DESIGNER:
PAUL DAVIES
ILLUSTRATOR:
PAUL DAVIES
AGENCY:
ZIGGURAT DESIGN
CONSULTANTS LIMITED
CLIENT:
ASDA STORES PLC
■ 557, 558

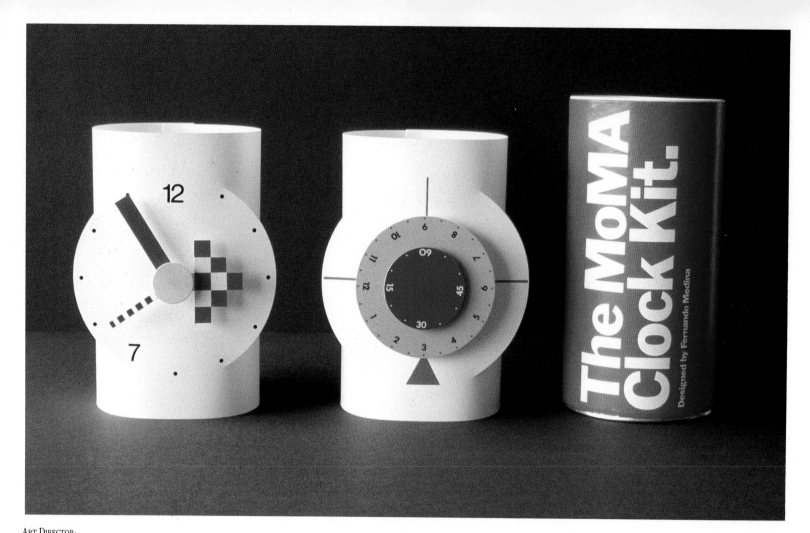

ART DIRECTOR:
FERNANDO MEDINA
DESIGNER:
FERNANDO MEDINA
AGENCY:
TRIOM DESIGN
CLIENT:
THE MUSEUM OF MODERN ART
NEW YORK
■ 559

■ 559 Clock kit and the tube in which it is packaged. The kit was designed for the Museum of Modern Art in New York. (USA)

■ 559 Zwei Uhren zum Selbermachen und die Verpackung. Sie wurden für das New Yorker Museum of Modern Art entworfen. (USA)

■ 559 Deux horloges à monter soi-même et leur emballage. Ces modèles ont été produits pour le Musée d'Art Moderne de New York. (USA)

BOOKS

CALENDARS

BÜCHER

KALENDER

LIVRES

CALENDRIERS

MARCEL IMSAND

VAUD VISIONS DE RÊVE

ÉDITIONS 24 HEURES

ART DIRECTOR:
Rita Marshall

DESIGNER:
Rita Marshall

PHOTOGRAPHER:
Marcel Imsand

AGENCY:
Marshall/Delessert

PUBLISHER:
Éditions 24 Heures

■ 560

ART DIRECTOR:
Henrik Barends

DESIGNER:
Henrik Barends

PHOTOGRAPHER:
Michel S. Krzyzanowski

PUBLISHER:
Joh. Enschede & Zonen

◄■ 561

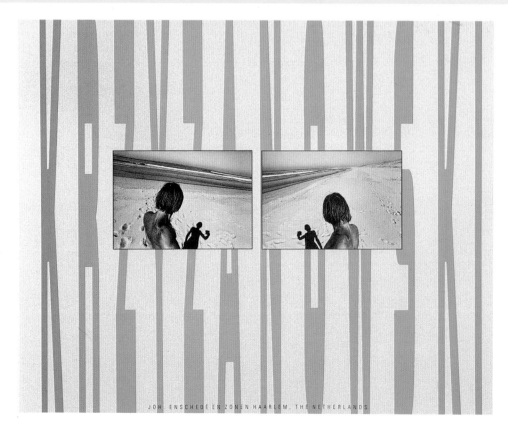

JOH. ENSCHEDÉ EN ZONEN HAARLEM, THE NETHERLANDS

■ 560 Protective cover for a book with photos by Marcel Imsand taken in the Swiss canton of Vaud. (SWI)

■ 561 "Carcans Beach", September 22 (1978) – cover of a book entitled *The First Twenty Years* showing sequences, portraits and projects by photographer Michel S. Krzyzanowski. (NLD)

■ 562 *Bad Behaviour* – for the German translation of a series of stories by American author Mary Gaitskill. (GER)

■ 563 "The Other Sides" – cover for a paperback on love, death and a lady named Rosa. (GER)

■ 560 Umschlag eines Bildbandes des Photographen Marcel Imsand über den Schweizer Kanton Waadt. (SWI)

■ 561 «Carcans Strand, 22. September (1978)» – Umschlag eines Buches mit dem Titel «Die ersten zwanzig Jahre» mit Sequenzen, Porträts und Projekten des Photographen Michel S. Krzyzanowski. (NLD)

■ 562 Umschlag eines Taschenbuchs mit Kurzgeschichten der amerikanischen Autorin Mary Gaitskill. (GER)

■ 563 Umschlag für ein bei *rororo* erschienenes Taschenbuch des deutschen Autors Frank Nicolaus. (GER)

■ 560 Jaquette d'un livre de photos de Marcel Imsand consacré aux paysages du canton de Vaud. (SWI)

■ 561 «Carcans Plage September 22 (1978)»: couverture du livre «Les vingt premières années» de Michel S. Krzyzanowski qui regroupe les séquences, les portraits et les projets de ce photographe. (NLD)

■ 562 Pour le livre de poche «Mauvaise fréquentation», un recueil de nouvelles de l'Américaine Mary Gaitskill. (GER)

■ 563 Couverture de «Revers», un recueil de nouvelles parlant d'amour, de mort et d'une femme nommée Rosa. (GER)

ART DIRECTOR:
WALTER HELLMANN
DESIGNER:
NINA ROTHFOS
PHOTOGRAPHER:
HENK MEYER
PUBLISHER:
ROWOHLT VERLAG
■ 562

ART DIRECTOR:
WALTER HELLMANN
DESIGNER:
BARBARA HANKE
PHOTOGRAPHER:
JAN COBB
PUBLISHER:
ROWOHLT VERLAG
■ 563

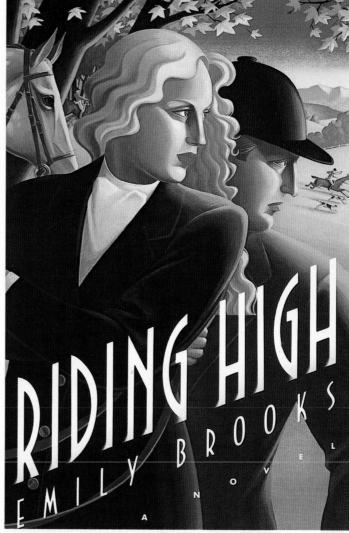

ART DIRECTOR:
Paul Browning
Paul Campbell
DESIGNER:
Paul Campbell
PHOTOGRAPHER:
Ron Baxter Smith
AGENCY:
Taylor & Browning
Design Associates
PUBLISHER:
Indecs Publishing
■ 564

ART DIRECTOR:
Frank Metz
DESIGNER:
Jackie Seow-Pracher
ILLUSTRATOR:
Cathleen Toelke
PUBLISHER:
Simon & Schuster
■ 565

ART DIRECTOR:
Stephen Doyle
DESIGNER:
Rosemarie Turk
PHOTOGRAPHER:
Herb Ritts
AGENCY:
Drenttel Doyle Partners
PUBLISHER:
American Photography, Inc.
►■ 566

■ 564 Protective cover for a book presenting a selection of the "Best in Canadian Interior Design". (CAN)

■ 565 Cover for a book with a romantic story set in a swank, fox-hunting town. (USA)

■ 566 Cover for the fifth annual volume highlighting the work of the winners of the past year's American Photography Five competition. (USA)

■ 564 Schutzumschlag für ein Buch mit einer Auswahl der besten Beispiele kanadischer Innenarchitektur. (CAN)

■ 565 Umschlag für ein Buch, in dem es um die gehobene Gesellschaft und ihren Zeitvertreib geht. (USA)

■ 566 Umschlag für ein Jahrbuch, in dem die Arbeiten der Gewinner des Photowettbewerbs «American Photography Five» vorgestellt werden. (USA)

■ 564 Jaquette d'un livre présentant un choix des meilleures créations des designers canadiens. (CAN)

■ 565 Jaquette d'un livre évoquant l'histoire qui se déroule sur fond de chasse à courre. (USA)

■ 566 Jaquette du cinquième volume annuel de American Photography. On y présente les photos des gagnants du concours de l'année précédente. (USA)

American Photography Five

■ 567 Cover of the catalog for the Annual Report Show organized by Mead paper makers. (USA)

■ 568 Book jacket for a young people's book club. It is a love story between two Jewish youths in Norway in World-war II. (NOR)

■ 569 Complete cover for a book presenting the work of seven illustrators. (ARG)

■ 570 For a book with poems by Jari Tervo. (FIN)

■ 567 Für den Katalog mit den Arbeiten der Gewinner des Jahresbericht-Wettbewerbs des Papierherstellers Mead. (USA)

■ 568 Schutzumschlag für ein bei einem Buchclub herausgegebenes Buch: eine Liebesgeschichte zwischen zwei jungen Juden in Norwegen während des 2. Weltkriegs. (NOR)

■ 569 Vollständiger Umschlag für ein Buch, in dem die Arbeiten von sieben Illustratoren vorgestellt werden. (ARG)

■ 570 Für einen Band mit Gedichten von Jari Tervo. (FIN)

■ 567 Couverture du catalogue de l'exposition des rapports annuels organisée par le fabricant de papiers Mead. (USA)

■ 568 Jaquette d'un livre pour la jeunesse racontant une histoire d'amour entre deux jeunes juifs en Norvège pendant la deuxième Guerre mondiale. (NOR)

■ 569 Jaquette dépliée du livre présentant les travaux de sept illustrateurs en noir et blanc. (ARG)

■ 570 Pour une anthologie de poésies de Jari Tervo. (FIN)

ART DIRECTOR:
ROGER COOK
DON SHANOSKY
DESIGNER:
ROGER COOK
DON SHANOSKY
PHOTOGRAPHER:
COOK AND SHANOSKY
ASSOCIATES
AGENCY:
COOK AND SHANOSKY
ASSOCIATES
■ 567

ART DIRECTOR:
ELSE HAAVIG
DESIGNER:
ELSE HAAVIG
ILLUSTRATOR:
SARAH ROSENBAUM
PUBLISHER:
DE NORSKE BOKKLUBBEN
■ 568

SERIE·SEVEN

SERIE·SEVEN

ART DIRECTOR:
OSWALDO MIRANDA
(MIRAN)
DESIGNER:
OSWALDO MIRANDA
(MIRAN)
AGENCY:
CASA DE IDEIAS
PUBLISHER:
CASA DE IDEIAS
■ 569

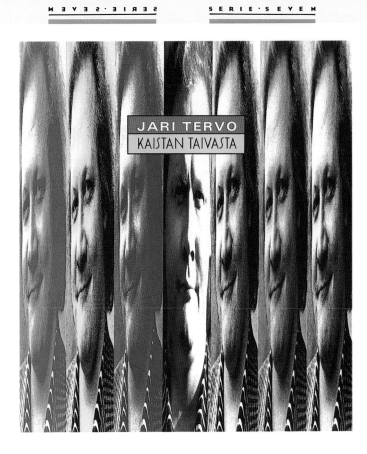

ART DIRECTOR:
ILKKA KÄRKKÄINEN
DESIGNER:
ILKKA KÄRKKÄINEN
ILLUSTRATOR:
ILKKA KÄRKKÄINEN
PUBLISHER:
WSPY
◄■ 570

ART DIRECTOR:
Victoria Birta
DESIGNER:
Victoria Birta
PHOTOGRAPHER:
Zoltan Birta
AGENCY:
Michael Peters Group
PUBLISHER:
Oxford
■ 571, 572

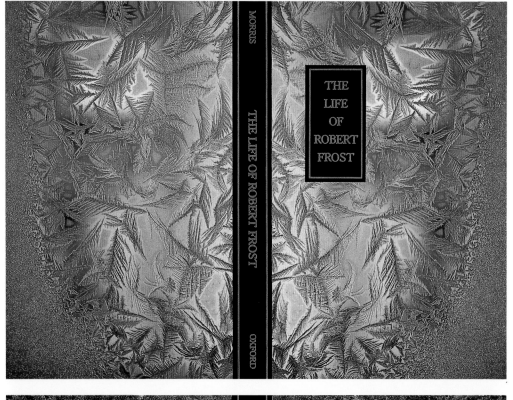

■ 571, 572 Covers of two volumes dedicated to the life and work of poet Robert Frost. (CAN)

■ 573 Cover for a large-format book showing the Trylon and Perisphere, futuristic architectural visions of Wallace K. Harrison. They became the landmarks of this "World of Tomorrow". (USA)

■ 571, 572 Umschläge von zwei Bänden über Leben und Werk des Dichters Robert Frost. (CAN)

■ 573 Umschlag eines Buches über die Weltausstellung 1939 in New York mit Trylon und Perisphere, den architektonischen Visionen von Wallace K. Harrison. Sie wurden zu Symbolen dieser «Welt der Zukunft». (USA)

■ 571, 572 Couvertures de deux volumes consacrés à la vie et à l'œuvre du poète Robert Frost. (CAN)

■ 573 La couverture du livre consacré à l'Exposition universelle de New York de 1939 montre les deux bâtiments futuristes de Wallace K.Harrison et J.André Foulihoux, symboles de cette «foire du futur». (USA)

ART DIRECTOR:
SAMUEL N. ANTUPIT
DESIGNER:
SEYMOUR CHWAST
ILLUSTRATOR:
SEYMOUR CHWAST
AGENCY:
THE PUSHPIN GROUP
PUBLISHER:
HARRY N. ABRAMS, INC.
■ 573

THE 1939 NEW YORK WORLD'S FAIR

TRYLON AND PERISPHERE

BARBARA COHEN
STEVEN HELLER
SEYMOUR CHWAST

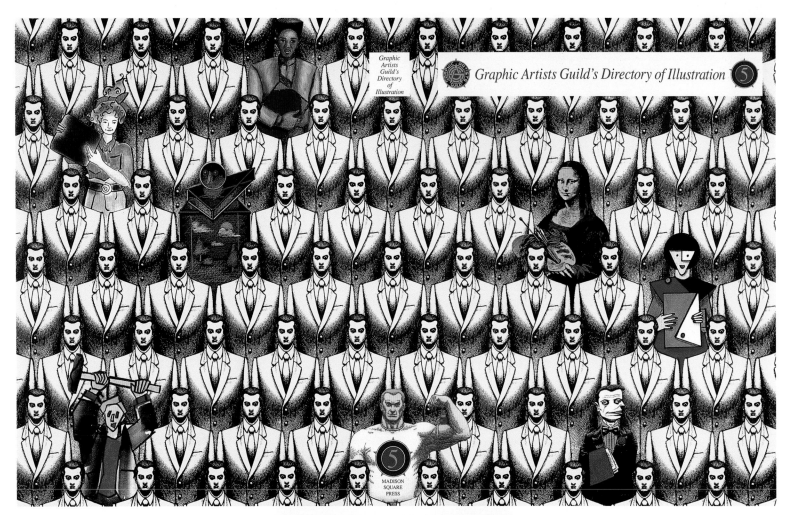

ART DIRECTOR:
WALTER BERNARD
MILTON GLASER
DESIGNER:
SHELLY FISHER
ILLUSTRATOR:
MIRKO ILIC
NICKY LINDEMAN
AGENCY:
WBMG, INC.
PUBLISHER:
MADISON SQUARE PRESS
■ 574

ART DIRECTOR:
DAVID HILLMAN
DESIGNER:
DAVID HILLMAN
AMANDA BENNETT
AGENCY:
PENTAGRAM DESIGN, LONDON
PUBLISHER:
BARRIE & JENKINS
◄■ 575

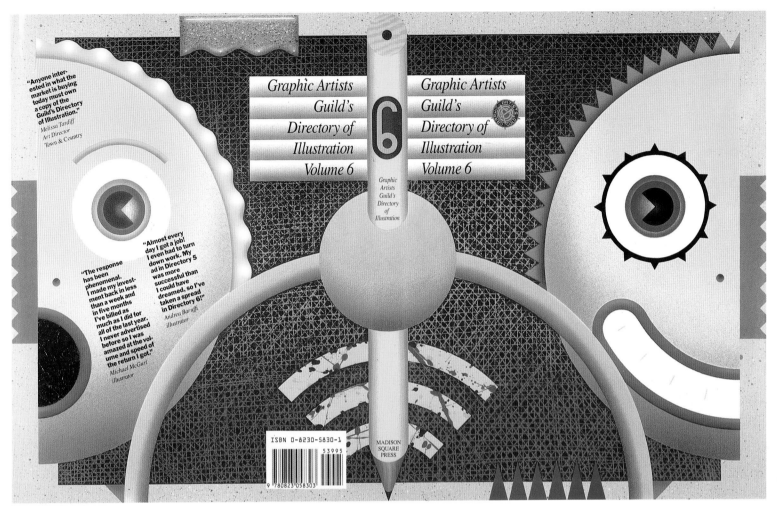

ART DIRECTOR:
SHELLEY FISHER
DESIGNER:
SHELLEY FISHER
ILLUSTRATOR:
JOSE CRUZ
AGENCY:
WBMG, INC.
PUBLISHER:
MADISON SQUARE PRESS
■ 576

DESIGNER:
UWE LOHRER
DETLEF GEHRKE
AGENCY:
ATELIER LOHRER
PUBLISHER:
LANDESGEWERBEAMT
BADEN-WÜRTTEMBERG/
DESIGN CENTER STUTTGART
◀■ 577

■ 574, 576 Complete covers of two volumes of the *Graphic Artists Guild's Directory of Illustration*. (USA)

■ 575 For a book on classic puzzles designed by Pentagram. (GBR)

■ 577 The cover of this catalog for a design exhibition plays with the visual effects of complementary colors. The same motif is repeated on the back cover in a reversed color combination. (GER)

■ 574, 576 Vollständige Umschläge von zwei Ausgaben des Illustrations-Handbuches der Graphic Artists Guild. (USA)

■ 575 Für ein von Pentagram gestaltetes Buch mit klassischen Rätseln. (GBR)

■ 577 Der Umschlag dieses Katalogs für eine Design-Ausstellung spielt mit dem visuellen Effekt von Komplementärfarben. Das gleiche Motiv wird in umgekehrter Farbkombination auf dem Rücken wiederholt. (GER)

■ 574, 576 Jaquettes dépliées de deux volumes de la Graphic Artists Guild consacrées à l'illustration. (USA)

■ 575 Couverture d'un livre de Pentagram sur les devinettes classiques. (GBR)

■ 577 Cette couverture du catalogue d'une exposition de design joue sur les effets visuels des couleurs complémentaires. Le même motif se répète au verso, mais les couleurs sont inversées. (GER)

■ 578 Protective jacket for a book on home and office interiors. (USA)

■ 579 Cover for a book presenting seven documentary photographers and their work done in regions close to their childhood homes. (USA)

■ 580 Cover for a volume with photos taken by Irving Penn presenting the work of Japanese fashion designer Issey Miyake. (JPN)

■ 581 For a book on classical American comic strips and their creators. (USA)

■ 582 Cover for a book on beer, its history, the brewing traditions and the various traditions on different regions where beer is drunk. (USA)

■ 578 Umschlag für ein Buch über Inneneinrichtungen von Wohnungen und Büros. (USA)

■ 579 Umschlag für ein Buch, in dem Aufnahmen von sieben Photographen gezeigt werden, die sie in der vertrauten Umgebung ihrer Kindheit machten. (USA)

■ 580 Umschlag für einen Photoband über die Arbeit des Modeschöpfers Issey Miyake, aufgenommen von Irving Penn. (JPN)

■ 581 Für ein Buch über grosse amerikanische Zeichentrick-Künstler. (USA)

■ 582 Umschlag für ein Buch über Bier: die Geschichte, die Braukunst und verschiedene Traditionen der Menschen in Regionen, in denen Bier getrunken wird. (USA)

■ 578 Jaquette d'un répertoire international du design intérieur. (USA)

■ 579 Couverture d'un catalogue de photographie documentaire: sept photographes présentent des images de l'environnement familier de leur enfance. (USA)

■ 580 Couverture d'un livre consacré aux créations du styliste Issey Miyake, photographiées par le célèbre Irving Penn. (JPN)

■ 581 Couverture d'un livre sur les grands artistes américains de la bande dessinée. (USA)

■ 582 Couverture d'un livre sur la bière: il y est question de son histoire, de sa fabrication et des diverses traditions des pays consommateurs. (USA)

DESIGNER:
RENEE KHATAMI
PHOTOGRAPHER:
BOREK SIPEK
PUBLISHER:
ABBEVILLE PRESS
■ 578

DESIGNER:
MICHAEL MABRY
AGENCY:
MICHAEL MABRY DESIGN
PUBLISHER:
FRIENDS OF PHOTOGRAPHY
■ 579

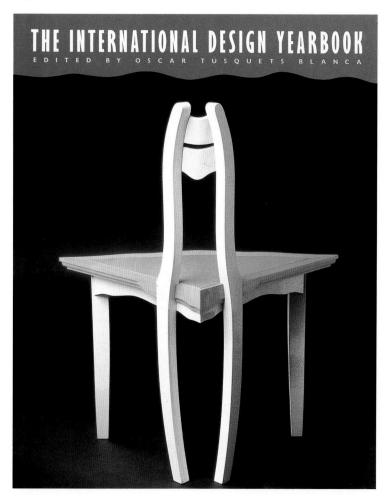

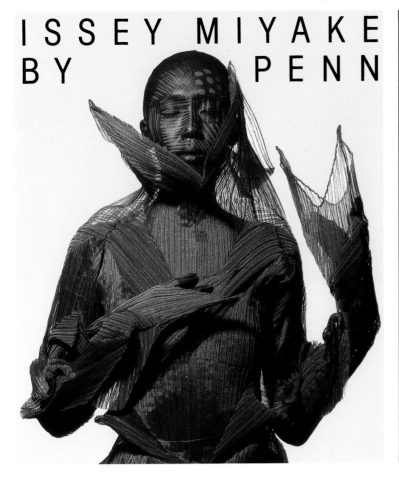

ART DIRECTOR:
Ikko Tanaka
DESIGNER:
Ikko Tanaka
PHOTOGRAPHER:
Irving Penn
AGENCY:
Ikko Tanaka Design Studio
CLIENT:
Issey Miyake International
■ 580

DESIGNER:
Renee Khatami
PUBLISHER:
Abbeville Press
■ 581

DESIGNER:
James Wageman
PHOTOGRAPHER:
John Pamell
PUBLISHER:
Abbeville Press
■ 582

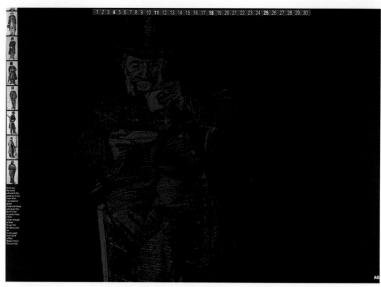

ART DIRECTOR:
WERNER VANDEVELDE
DESIGNER:
PAUL VERLEYSEN
AGENCY:
PUBLISHER:
AGFA-GEVAERT N.V.
■ 583-587

■ 583-587 Cover and monthly sheets from a calendar published by Agfa and dedicated to Van Gogh (one hundred years after his death). *583:* Cover with cut-out and self portrait. *587:* the self portraits in the size of postage stamps. (BEL)

■ 583-587 Deckblatt und einige Monatsblätter eines von Agfa herausgegebenen Kalenders zum hundertsten Todestag von Van Gogh. *583:* Der Umschlag mit Ausstanzung und Porträt Van Goghs. *587:* Selbstporträts des Künstlers in der Grösse von Briefmarken. (BEL)

■ 583-587 Couverture et pages du calendrier d'Agfa consacré à Van Gogh, réalisé à l'occasion du centième anniversaire de sa mort. *583:* couverture en découpe avec autoportrait. *587:* les autoportraits sont présentés ici à la manière d'une collection de timbres. (BEL)

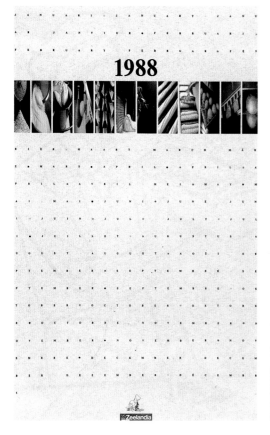

1988

januari

februari

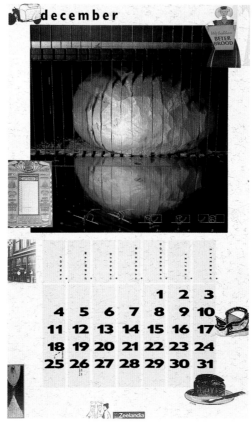

december

ART DIRECTOR:
MARIANNE VOS
DESIGNER:
MARIANNE VOS
TYPOGRAPHER:
MARIANNE VOS
SASKIA FRANKEN
PHOTOGRAPHER:
PHILIP MECHANICUS
AGENCY:
SAMENWERKENDE ONTWERPERS
CLIENT:
PIETER VAN DEN BUSKEN
ADVERTISING / ZEELANDIA
H.J. DOELEMAN BV
■ 588-591

ART DIRECTOR:
MARY H. REILLY
DESIGNER:
MARY H. REILLY
PHOTOGRAPHER:
DOUG DECKER
JOE BOONE
CLARA LUCKETT
PAUL SCHLESINGER
AGENCY:
PRICE WEBER MARKETING
COMM., INC.
CLIENT:
BROWN-FORMAN BEVERAGE CO.
►■ 592-594

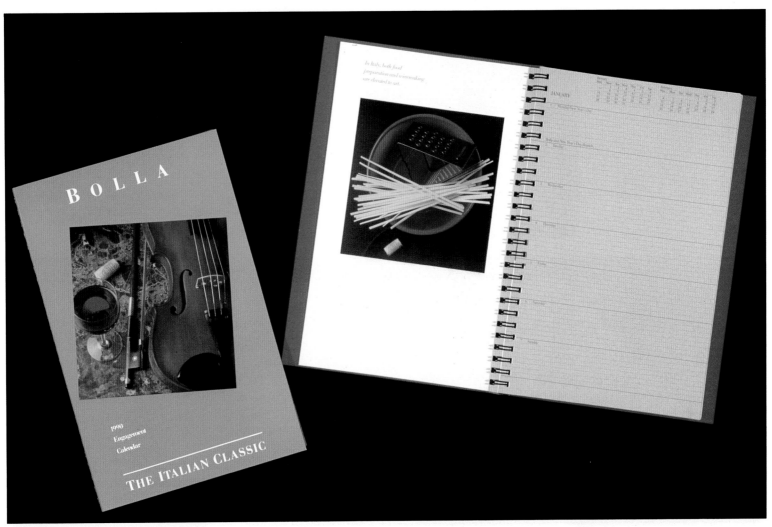

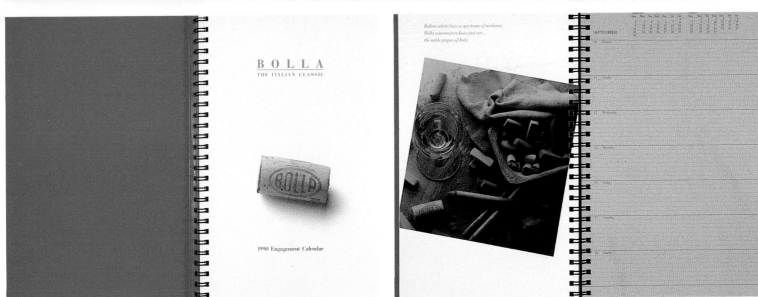

■ 588-591 Cover and three sheets from a calendar of a flour producer. The photos document the making of bread, from the grain to the finished product. (NLD)

■ 592-594 Cover and pages from a spiral-bound diary for Bolla. In order to present a selection of wines, the illustrations are based on the Italian way of living: music, noodles and fine art. (USA)

■ 588-591 Umschlag und einige Blätter aus einem Kalender für einen Mehl-Hersteller. Die Photos zeigen den vollständigen Herstellungsprozess des Brotes. (NLD)

■ 592-594 Umschlag und einige Seiten aus einer spiralgebundenen Tisch-Agenda für Bolla. Eine Auswahl von Weinen wird mit Hilfe von Bildern illustriert, die bezeichnend für Italien sind: Musik, Teigwaren, Malerei. (USA)

■ 588-591 Couverture et pages du calendrier d'une minoterie. Les photos illustrent les étapes successives de la fabrication du pain, du grain de blé à la coupe en tranches. (NLD)

■ 592-594 Couverture et quelques pages intérieures d'un agenda à reliure spirale pour Bolla. Afin de présenter une sélection de vins, l'image s'appuie sur les classiques du savoirvivre italien: la musique, les pâtes, la peinture. (USA)

ART DIRECTOR:
IVY SARRASSAT
DESIGNER:
PAUL SARRASSAT
ILLUSTRATOR:
PAUL SARRASSAT
AGENCY:
ARIES
PUBLISHER:
ARIES
■ 595, 596

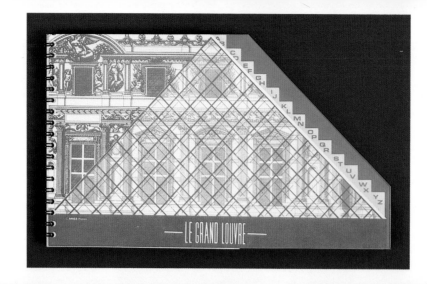

■ 595, 596 Directory designed for the Louvre. The plastified transparent cover and the special shape of this spiral-bound book take up the architectural motif of the pyramid of Pei. (FRA)

■ 595, 596 Für den Louvre entworfenes Adressbuch. Der transparente Plastikumschlag und die spezielle Form dieses spiralgebundenen Katalogs nehmen das architektonische Motiv der Pyramide von Pei auf. (FRA)

■ 595, 596 Répertoire d'adresses conçu pour le Musée du Louvre. La couverture plastifiée transparente et la découpe oblique de ce carnet à reliure spirale répète visuellement le motif architectural de la pyramide de Pei. (FRA)

CALL FOR ENTRIES

GRAPHIS DESIGN

ALL ENTRIES MUST ARRIVE ON OR BEFORE NOVEMBER 30

Advertising: Newspaper and magazine
Design: Promotion brochures, catalogs, invitations, record covers, announcements, logotypes and/or entire corporate image campaigns, calendars, books, book covers, packages (single or series, labels and/or complete packages)
Editorial Design: company magazines, newspapers, consumer magazines, house organs
Illustration: All categories may be black and white or color

GRAPHIS ANNUAL REPORTS

ALL ENTRIES MUST ARRIVE ON OR BEFORE APRIL 30

All material printed and published in connection with the annual report of a company or other organization.
Design, illustration, photography, typography, as well as the overall conception of the annual report are the criteria to be judged.
In order to do justice to this complex medium, we will present double-page spreads from the annual reports selected which are exemplary in their design and/or illustration.

GRAPHIS PHOTO

ALL ENTRIES MUST ARRIVE ON OR BEFORE JUNE 30

Advertising Photography: Advertisements, promotional brochures, catalogs, invitations, announcements, record covers, calendars.
Editorial Photography for press media – journalism and features – for books, corporate publications, etc. on the following subjects: fashion, cosmetics, architecture, arts, nature, science, technology, daily life, sports, current affairs, portraits, still life, etc.
Fine Art Photography: Personal studies
Unpublished Photography: Experimental and student work.

GRAPHIS POSTER

ALL ENTRIES MUST ARRIVE ON OR BEFORE APRIL 30

Culture: Posters announcing exhibitions and events of all kind, film, theater, and ballet performances, concerts etc.
Advertising: Posters for fashion, cosmetics, foods, beverages, industrial goods; image and self-promotional campaigns of companies and individuals
Society: Posters which serve primarily a social and/or political purpose; from the field of education; for conferences and meetings; as well as for political and charitable appeals.

GENERAL RULES

THESE ARE APPLICABLE TO ALL BOOKS MENTIONED.

By submitting work to GRAPHIS, the sender expressly grants permission for his publication in any GRAPHIS book, as well as in any article in GRAPHIS magazine, or any advertising brochure, etc. whose purpose is specifically to promote the sales of these publications.

Eligibility: All work produced in the 12 month period previous to the submission deadlines, as well as rejected or unpublished work from this period, by professionals and students.

A confirmation of receipt will be sent to each entrant, and all entrants will be notified at a later date whether or not their work has been accepted for publication. All the winning entries will be reproduced in a generous format and in four colors throughout.
By submitting work you qualify for a 25% discount on the purchase of the respective book.

What to send:
Please send the actual printed piece (unmounted but well protected). Do not send original art. For large, bulky or valuable pieces, please submit color photos or (duplicate) transparencies.
Please note that entries cannot be returned. Only in exceptional cases and by contacting us in advance will material be sent back.

Entry Fees:
For each single entry: North America: US$ 10.00 West Germany: DM 10,00 All other countries: SFr. 10.00
For each campaign entry of 3 or more pieces: North America: US$ 25.00 West Germany: DM 25,00 All other countries: SFr. 25.00
Please make checks payable to GRAPHIS PRESS CORP. Zurich, and include in parcel. These fees do not apply to students, if copy of student identification is included. (For entries from countries with exchange controls, please contact us.)

How and where to send:
Please tape (do not glue) the entry label provided (or photocopy) - with full information - on the back of each piece. Entries can be sent by airmail, air parcel post or surface mail. **Please do not send anything by air freight.** Declare "No Commercial Value" on packages, and label "Art for Contest". The number of transparencies and photos should be indicated on the parcel. (If sent by air courier, please mark "Documents, Commercial Value 00.00").

Thank you for your contribution. Please send all entries to the following address:
GRAPHIS PRESS CORP., DUFOURSTRASSE 107, CH-8008 ZURICH, SWITZERLAND

FÜR DIE GRAPHIS JAHRBÜCHER

GRAPHIS DESIGN

EINSENDESCHLUSS: 30. NOVEMBER

Werbung: In Zeitungen und Zeitschriften
Design: Werbeprospekte, Kataloge, Einladungen, Schallplattenhüllen, Anzeigen, Signete und/oder Imagekampagnen, Kalender, Bücher, Buchumschläge, Packungen (einzelne oder Serien, Etiketten und/oder vollständige Packungen)
Redaktionelles Design: Firmenpublikationen, Zeitungen, Zeitschriften, Jahresberichte
Illustration: Alle Kategorien, schwarzweiss oder farbig

GRAPHIS ANNUAL REPORTS

EINSENDESCHLUSS: 30. APRIL

Alle gedruckten und veröffentlichten Arbeiten, die im Zusammenhang mit dem Jahresbericht einer Firma oder Organisation stehen.
Design, Illustration, Photographie, Typographie und die Gesamtkonzeption eines Jahresberichtes sind die beurteilten Kriterien.
Um diesem komplexen Medium gerecht zu werden, werden aus den ausgewählten Jahresberichten verschiedene typische Doppelseiten gezeigt, die beispielhaft für die Gestaltung und/oder Illustration sind.

GRAPHIS PHOTO

EINSENDESCHLUSS: 30. JUNI

Werbephotographie: Anzeigen, Prospekte, Kataloge, Einladungen, Bekanntmachungen, Schallplattenhüllen, Kalender.
Redaktionelle Photographie für Presse (Reportagen und Artikel), Bücher, Firmenpublikationen usw. in den Bereichen Mode, Kosmetik, Architektur, Kunst, Natur, Wissenschaft und Technik, Alltag, Sport, Aktuelles, Porträts, Stilleben usw.
Künstlerische Photographie: Persönliche Studien
Unveröffentlichte Aufnahmen: Experimentelle Photographie und Arbeitenvon Studenten und Schülern.

GRAPHIS POSTER

EINSENDESCHLUSS: 30. APRIL

Kultur: Plakate für die Ankündigung von Ausstellungen und Veranstaltungen aller Art, Film-, Theater- und Ballettaufführungen, Musikveranstaltungen.
Werbung: Plakate für Mode, Kosmetik, Lebensmittel, Genussmittel, Industriegüter; Image- und Eigenwerbung von Firmen und Einzelpersonen
Gesellschaft: Plakate, die in erster Linie einem sozialen oder politischen Zweck dienen, auf dem Gebiet der Ausbildung und Erziehung oder für die Ankündigung von Konferenzen und Tagungen sowie für politische und soziale Appelle

TEILNAHMEBEDINGUNGEN

DIESE GELTEN FÜR ALLE AUFGEFÜHRTEN BÜCHER.

Durch Ihre Einsendung geben Sie GRAPHIS ausdrücklich die Erlaubnis zur Veröffentlichung der eingesandten Arbeiten sowohl im entsprechenden Jahrbuch als auch in der Zeitschrift GRAPHIS oder für die Wiedergabe im Zusammenhang mit Besprechungen und Werbematerial für die GRAPHIS-Publikationen.

In Frage kommen alle Arbeiten von Fachleuten und Studenten – auch nicht publizierte Arbeiten – welche in den zwölf Monaten vor Einsendeschluss entstanden sind.

Jeder Einsender erhält eine Empfangsbestätigung und wird über Erscheinen oder Nichterscheinen seiner Arbeiten zu einem späteren Zeitpunkt informiert.
Alle im Buch aufgenommenen Arbeiten werden vierfarbig, in grosszügigem Format reproduziert.
Durch Ihre Einsendung erhalten Sie 25% Rabatt auf das jeweilige Jahrbuch.

Was einsenden:
Bitte senden Sie uns das gedruckte Beispiel (unmontiert, aber gut geschützt). Senden Sie keine Originale. Bei unhandlichen, umfangreichen oder wertvollen Sendungen bitten wir um Farbphotos oder Duplikat-Dias.
Bitte beachten Sie, dass Einsendungen nicht zurückgeschickt werden können. Ausnahmen sind nur nach vorheriger Absprache mit GRAPHIS möglich.

Gebühren:
SFr. 10.00/DM 10,00 für einzelne Arbeiten
SFr. 25.00/DM 25,00 für Kampagnen oder Serien von mehr als drei Stück
Bitte senden Sie uns einen Scheck (SFr.-Schecks bitte auf eine Schweizer Bank ziehen) oder überweisen Sie den Betrag auf PC Zürich 80-23071-9 oder PSchK Frankfurt 3000 57-602.
Diese Gebühren gelten nicht für Studenten. Bitte schicken Sie uns eine Kopie des Studentenausweises.
(Für Einsendungen aus Ländern mit Devisenbeschränkungen bitten wir Sie, uns zu kontaktieren.)

Wie und wohin schicken:
Bitte befestigen Sie das vorgesehene Etikett (oder eine Kopie) – vollständig ausgefüllt – mit Klebstreifen (nicht mit Klebstoff) auf der Rückseite jeder Arbeit. Bitte per Luftpost oder auf normalem Postweg einsenden. **Keine Luftfrachtsendungen.** Deklarieren Sie «Ohne jeden Handelswert» und «Arbeitsproben für Wettbewerb». Die Anzahl der Dias und Photos sollte auf dem Paket angegeben werden. (Bei Air Courier Sendungen vermerken Sie «Dokumente, ohne jeden Handelswert»).

Herzlichen Dank für Ihre Mitarbeit. Bitte senden Sie Ihre Arbeiten an folgende Adresse:
GRAPHIS VERLAG AG, DUFOURSTRASSE 107, CH-8008 ZURICH, SCHWEIZ

APPEL D'ENVOIS

GRAPHIS DESIGN

DATE LIMITE D'ENVOI: 30 NOVEMBRE

Publicité: journaux et magazines
Design: brochures de promotion, catalogues, invitations, pochettes de disques, annonces, emblèmes, en-têtes, campagnes de prestige, calendriers, livres, jaquettes, emballages (spécimen ou série, étiquettes ou emballages complets)
Editorial Design: magazines de sociétés, journaux, revues, rapports annuels
Illustration: toutes catégories en noir et blanc ou en couleurs

GRAPHIS ANNUAL REPORTS

DATE LIMITE D'ENVOI: 30 AVRIL

Tous travaux imprimés et publiés en relation avec le rapport annuel d'une entreprise ou d'une organisation.
Les critères retenus pour l'appréciation sont le design, l'illustration, la photo, la typo et la conception d'ensemble des rapports annuels.
Afin de rendre justice à ce média complexe, nous présentons diverses doubles pages types des rapports annuels sélectionnés en veillant à ce qu'elles soient représentatives de la conception et/ou de l'illustration.

GRAPHIS PHOTO

DATE LIMITE D'ENVOI: 30 JUIN

Photographie publicitaire: annonces, brochures de promotion, catalogues, invitations, pochettes de disques, calendriers
Photographie rédactionnelle pour la presse (reportages et articles), livres, publications d'entreprises, etc. dans les domaines suivants: Mode, arts, architecture, nature, sciences et techniques, vie quotidienne, sports, l'actualité, portraits, nature morte, etc.
Photographie artistique: études personnelles
Photographie non publiée: travaux expérimentaux et projets d'étudiants

GRAPHIS POSTER

DATE LIMITE D'ENVOI: 30 AVRIL

Affiches culturelles: annonçant des expositions et manifestations de tout genre, des projections de films, des représentations de théâtre et de ballet, des concerts et festivals.
Affiches publicitaires: pour la mode, les cosmétiques, l'alimentation, les produits de consommation de luxe, les biens industriels; publicité institutionnelle et auto-promotion d'entreprises.
Affiches sociales: essentiellement au service d'une cause sociale ou politique dans les domaines de l'éducation et de la formation, ainsi que pour l'annonce de conférences et réunions et pour les appels à caractère social et politique.

MODALITÉS D'ENVOI

VALABLES POUR TOUS LES LIVRES CITÉS.

Par votre envoi, vous donnez expressément à GRAPHIS l'autorisation de reproduire les travaux reçus aussi bien dans le livre en question que dans le magazine GRAPHIS ou dans tout imprimé relatif aux comptes rendus et au matériel publicitaire concernant les publications GRAPHIS.

Sont acceptés tous les travaux de professionnels et d'étudiants – mème inédits – réalisés pendant les douze mois précédant le délai limite d'envoi.

Pour tout envoi de travaux, nous vous faisons parvenir un accusé de réception. Vous serez informé par la suite de la parution ou non-parution de vos travaux. Tous les travaux figurant dans l'ouvrage en question sont reproduits en quadrichromie dans un format généreux.
Votre envoi vous vaut une réduction de 25% sur l'annuel en question.

Que nous envoyer:
Veuillez nous envoyer un exemplaire imprimé (non monté, mais bien protégé). N'envoyez pas d'originaux. Pour les travaux de grand format, volumineux ou de valeur, veuillez nous envoyer des photos ou des diapositives (duplicata). **Veuillez noter que les travaux ne peuvent pas être retournés,** sauf dans des cas exceptionnels et si vous nous en avisez à l'avance.

Droits d'admission:
SFr. 10.00 pour les envois concernant un seul travail
SFr. 25.00 pour chaque série de 3 travaux ou davantage
Veuillez joindre à votre envoi un chèque tiré sur une banque suisse ou en verser le montant au compte chèque postal Zürich 80-23071-9.
Les étudiants sont exemptés de cette taxe. Prière de joindre une photocopie de la carte d'étudiant.
(Si vous résidez dans un pays qui connaît le contrôle des changes, veuillez nous contacter préalablement.)

Comment et où envoyer:
Veuillez scotcher (ne pas coller) au dos de chaque spécimen les étiquettes ci-jointes (ou photocopies) – dûment remplies. Envoyez les travaux de préférence par avion, ou par voie de surface. **Ne nous envoyez rien en fret aérien.** Indiquez «Sans aucune valeur commerciale» et «Echantillons de spécimens pour concours». Le nombre de diapositives et de photos doit être indiqué sur le paquet. (Pour les envois par courrier, inscrire «Documents, sans aucune valeur commercial».)

Nous vous remercions chaleureusement de votre collaboration. Veuillez faire parvenir vos travaux à l'adresse suivante:

EDITIONS GRAPHIS SA, DUFOURSTRASSE 107, CH-8008 ZURICH, SUISSE

SUBSCRIBE TO GRAPHIS: FOR USA AND CANADA

MAGAZINE	USA	CANADA
☐ GRAPHIS (One year/6 issues)	US$ 79.00	CDN$ 88.00
☐ GRAPHIS (Two years/12 issues)	US$ 149.00	CDN$ 166.00

☐ Check enclosed
☐ Please bill me
☐ Students may request a 25% discount by sending student ID.
IMPORTANT! PLEASE CHECK THE LANGUAGE VERSION DESIRED:
☐ ENGLISH   ☐ GERMAN   ☐ FRENCH

NAME _____

_____

STREET _____

CITY/STATE/PROV. _____

POSTAL CODE/COUNTRY _____

PROFESSION _____

TITLE _____

SIGNATURE/DATE _____

Please send coupon and make check payable to:
GRAPHIS US, INC., 141 LEXINGTON AVENUE, NEW YORK, NY 10016, USA.
Guarantee: You may cancel your subscription at any time and receive a full refund on all
unmailed copies. Please allow 6-8 weeks for delivery of first issue.

REQUEST FOR CALL FOR ENTRIES

Please put me on your "Call for Entries" list for the following title(s).
Please check the appropriate box(es).
☐ GRAPHIS PHOTO   ☐ GRAPHIS POSTER   ☐ GRAPHIS DESIGN
☐ GRAPHIS PACKAGING   ☐ GRAPHIS DIAGRAM   ☐ GRAPHIS ANNUAL REPORTS
By submitting material to any of the titles listed above, I will automatically qualify for a
25% discount toward the purchase of the title.   GDA 91

BOOK ORDER FORM: FOR USA AND CANADA

ORDER YOUR GRAPHIS ANNUALS NOW!

BOOKS	USA	CANADA
☐ Graphis Photo 90	US$ 69.00	CDN$ 92.00
☐ Graphis Annual Reports 2	US$ 75.00	CDN$ 113.00
☐ Graphis Poster 90	US$ 69.00	CDN$ 92.00
☐ Graphis Design 90	US$ 65.00	CDN$ 91.50
☐ Graphis Corporate Identity 1	US$ 75.00	CDN$ 113.00
☐ Graphis Photo 89	US$ 65.00	CDN$ 91.50
☐ Graphis Packaging 5	US$ 75.00	CDN$ 113.00
☐ Graphis Diagram 1	US$ 65.00	CDN$ 98.00
☐ Graphis Annual Reports 1	US$ 65.00	CDN$ 98.00

☐ Check enclosed
☐ Please bill me (Mailing costs in addition to above book price will be charged)

NAME _____

_____

STREET _____

CITY/STATE/PROV. _____

POSTAL CODE/COUNTRY _____

PROFESSION _____

TITLE _____

SIGNATURE   DATE

Please send coupon and make check payable to:
GRAPHIS US, INC., 141 LEXINGTON AVENUE, NEW YORK, NY 10016, USA.

REQUEST FOR CALL FOR ENTRIES

Please put me on your "Call for Entries" list for the following title(s).
Please check the appropriate box(es).
☐ GRAPHIS PHOTO   ☐ GRAPHIS POSTER   ☐ GRAPHIS DESIGN
☐ GRAPHIS PACKAGING   ☐ GRAPHIS DIAGRAM   ☐ GRAPHIS ANNUAL REPORTS
By submitting material to any of the titles listed above, I will automatically qualify for a
25% discount toward the purchase of the title.   GDA 91

SUBSCRIBE TO GRAPHIS: FOR EUROPE AND THE WORLD

MAGAZINE	BRD	WORLD	U.K.
☐ GRAPHIS (One year/6 issues)	DM 162,–	SFr. 140.–	£ 54.00
☐ GRAPHIS (Two years/12 issues)	DM 305,–	SFr. 262.–	£ 102.00

☐ Subscription fees include postage to any part of the world.

☐ Airmail Surcharges (one year/6 issues):	DM 70,–	SFr. 58.–	£ 22.00
☐ Registered mail	DM 15,–	SFr. 13.–	£ 5.00

☐ Check enclosed (for Europe, please make SFr.-checks payable to a Swiss bank)
☐ Please bill me
☐ Students may request a 25% discount by sending student ID.
IMPORTANT! PLEASE CHECK THE LANGUAGE VERSION DESIRED:
☐ ENGLISH   ☐ GERMAN   ☐ FRENCH

NAME _____

_____

STREET _____

POSTAL CODE/CITY _____

COUNTRY _____

PROFESSION _____

TITLE _____

SIGNATURE   DATE

Please send coupon and make check payable to:
GRAPHIS PRESS CORP., DUFOURSTRASSE 107, CH-8008 ZÜRICH, SWITZERLAND
Guarantee: You may cancel your subscription at any time and receive a full refund on all
unmailed copies. Please allow 6-8 weeks for delivery of first issue.

REQUEST FOR CALL FOR ENTRIES

Please put me on your "Call for Entries" list for the following title(s).
Please check the appropriate box(es).
☐ GRAPHIS PHOTO   ☐ GRAPHIS POSTER   ☐ GRAPHIS DESIGN
☐ GRAPHIS PACKAGING   ☐ GRAPHIS DIAGRAM   ☐ GRAPHIS ANNUAL REPORTS
By submitting material to any of the titles listed above, I will automatically qualify for a
25% discount toward the purchase of the title.   GDA 91

BOOK ORDER FORM: FOR EUROPE AND THE WORLD

BOOKS	BRD	WORLD	U.K.
☐ Graphis Photo 90	DM 149,–	SFr. 123.–	£ 49.00
☐ Graphis Annual Reports 2	DM 162,–	SFr. 137.–	£ 52.00
☐ Graphis Poster 90	DM 149,–	SFr. 123.–	£ 49.00
☐ Graphis Design 90	DM 148,–	SFr. 118.–	£ 46.50
☐ Graphis Corporate Identity	DM 160,–	SFr. 132.–	£ 48.00
☐ Graphis Photo 89	DM 148,–	SFr. 118.–	£ 46.50
☐ Graphis Packaging 5	DM 160,–	SFr. 132.–	£ 48.00
☐ Graphis Diagram 1	DM 138,–	SFr. 112.–	£ 45.00
☐ Graphis Annual Reports 1	DM 138,–	SFr. 112.–	£ 45.00

☐ Check enclosed (For Europe, please make SFr. checks payable to a Swiss Bank)
☐ Amount paid into Graphis account at the Union Bank of Switzerland, Acct No 3620063
   in Zürich.
☐ Amount paid to Postal Cheque Account Zürich 80-23071-9 (Through your local post office)
☐ Please bill me (Mailing costs in addition to above book price will be charged)

NAME _____

_____

STREET _____

POSTAL CODE/CITY _____

COUNRY _____

PROFESSION _____

TITLE _____

SIGNATURE   DATE

Please send coupon and make check payable to:
GRAPHIS PRESS CORP., DUFOURSTRASSE 107, CH-8008 ZÜRICH, SWITZERLAND

REQUEST FOR CALL FOR ENTRIES

Please put me on your "Call for Entries" list for the following title(s).
☐ GRAPHIS PHOTO   ☐ GRAPHIS POSTER   ☐ GRAPHIS DESIGN
☐ GRAPHIS PACKAGING   ☐ GRAPHIS DIAGRAM   ☐ GRAPHIS ANNUAL REPORTS
By submitting material to any of the titles listed above, I will automatically qualify for a
25% discount toward the purchase of the title.   GDA 91

GRAPHIS PRESS CORP.
DUFOURSTRASSE 107
CH-8008 ZÜRICH
SWITZERLAND

GRAPHIS U.S., INC.
141 LEXINGTON AVENUE
NEW YORK, NEW YORK 10016
U.S.A.

GRAPHIS PRESS CORP.
DUFOURSTRASSE 107
CH-8008 ZÜRICH
SWITZERLAND

GRAPHIS U.S., INC.
141 LEXINGTON AVENUE
NEW YORK, NEW YORK 10016
U.S.A.